D1631161

SHAKESPEARE AND THE RIVAL PLAYWRIGHTS 1600–1606

SHAKESPEARE
AND THE RIVAL
PLAYWRIGHTS
1600–1606

David Farley-Hills

London and New York

First published 1990
by Routledge
11 New Fetter Lane, London EC4P 4EE

Simultaneously published in the USA and Canada
by Routledge
a division of Routledge, Chapman and Hall, Inc.
29 West 35th Street, New York, NY 10001

© 1990 David Farley-Hills

Data converted to 11/12 Garamond by
Columns of Reading

Printed in Great Britain by
TJ Press (Padstow) Ltd, Padstow, Cornwall

British Library Cataloguing in Publication Data
Farley-Hills, David
Shakespeare and the rival playwrights 1600–1606.
1. Drama in English. Shakespeare, William, 1564–1616
critical studies
I. Title
822.3'3

Library of Congress Cataloging in Publication Data
Farley-Hills, David.
Shakespeare and the rival playwrights. 1600–1606 / David Farley-Hills.
p.   cm.
Includes bibliographical references.
1. Shakespeare, William, 1564–1616—Criticism and interpretation.
2. Shakespeare, William, 1564–1616—Contemporaries.
3. Theater—England—History—17th century.   I. Title
PR2976.F28   1990
822.3'3—dc20   89–49762

ISBN 0–415–04050–7

CONTENTS

ACKNOWLEDGEMENTS

I should like to thank my departmental colleague Johanna Procter for her kindness in looking over the typescript and offering generous advice.

INTRODUCTION

Modern estimates of the size of the population of London in Shakespeare's lifetime vary, but it is unlikely to have been much more than 200,000, of whom only a small fraction would be regular playgoers. It is not surprising therefore that among the eight or so playhouses open during 1600 there should have been much rivalry and much jockeying for the attentions of the minority of Londoners willing and able to pay their pennies to see a play. Over the centuries it has become harder and harder to see Shakespeare's professional career in the context of these rivalries, because his artistic eminence has led (by false logic) to the view of him as loftily unconcerned with what was going on around him. To think of the Swan of Avon competing with the other birds for the crusts thrown to him by the stinkards has almost become a blasphemy. Yet not only common sense, but hard historical fact, tells us that Shakespeare did not work in isolation from the theatrical world in which he was so spectacular a success. He was, for one thing, as much an actor as a playwright, at least until 1603 (for he was a principal actor in the first cast of Jonson's *Sejanus*) and this alone would have given him an extensive and intimate knowledge, not only of theatre, but of the work of many of his rivals. Jonson (as we know from Dekker's jibes in *Satiromastix*) liked to attend performances of his own plays,[1] and he was not the man to neglect his own work during rehearsals. As Jonson wrote extensively for the Globe he must have been frequently in contact with the man he was later to address so memorably as 'my beloved . . . Mr William Shakespeare'.

The picture of the theatrical life of London that emerges is one of constant contact between playwrights, of shifting rivalries and alliances, in which Shakespeare took his full share. Exactly what interconnections there were we shall never know: how often they attended performances at rival theatres, for instance; how often met to discuss their work, or simply to enjoy each others' company. Who else was present with Francis Beaumont and Ben Jonson at the Mermaid to hear

1

> words that have been
> So nimble, and so full of subtle flame,
> As if that everyone from whence they came
> Had meant to put his whole wit in a jest,
> And had resolv'd to live a fool the rest
> Of his dull life. . . [2]

– we shall never know. In one, not necessarily apocryphal story, we are told that Shakespeare met his death after a heavy drinking bout with fellow playwrights Ben Jonson and Michael Drayton.

There is plenty of evidence of constant communication between the playwrights and of interest in each other's work. Shakespeare was by no means the only 'beloved' playwright of Jonson's acquaintance, though none other gets so handsome a final tribute. Chapman addresses Jonson as his 'worthy and honoured friend', while Fletcher commends *Catiline* with a poem to 'his worthy friend, Master Ben Jonson', having earlier written a poem of commendation for *Volpone*. Both Jonson and Chapman, in their turn, write commendatory verses for the publication of Fletcher's *Faithful Shepherdess*. A little later we find Thomas Middleton writing commendatory verses for his fellow Londoner John Webster.[3] Marston dedicates his *Malcontent* to his 'frank and sincere friend Benjamin Jonson, the most elegant and weighty poet' (one is tempted to decode those first two epithets as 'rude and opinionated'). Relationships were not always so polite and cordial. Jonson records in his conversations with William Drummond of Hawthornden, along with gossip about other fellow-playwrights, including Shakespeare, that 'he beat Marston, and took his pistol from him' and the quarrel between the two men bubbled over (before *Malcontent*) into the most notorious of all the stage quarrels, the so-called war of the theatres, between Jonson on the one side and Marston, Dekker and (it seems) Shakespeare on the other.

Shakespeare's part in the war of the theatres is somewhat obscure, but it was the Globe as well as Paul's Boys that provided space for Dekker's bludgeonly attack on Jonson in *Satiromastix* and that is unlikely to have been without Shakespeare's knowledge and approval. That Shakespeare was at least thought to have been more directly involved is attested by the anonymous play *The Return from Parnassus* where we are told Shakespeare gave Ben Jonson 'a purge that made him betray his credit'.[4] If Shakespeare, in spite of his gentleness,[5] did get irritated from time to time by the irrepressible Jonson, we need not be surprised, for Jonson was constantly aiming squibs, and sometimes broadsides, at Shakespeare: from objections to the rambling structure of the history plays in the new prologue to *Every Man in his Humour*, to his mockery of 'those that beget *Tales*, *Tempests* and such like drolleries' in the Introduction of *Bartholomew Fair*.

The closest co-operation between playwrights can be seen in the large

2

number of plays that were written jointly by two or more of them in collaboration. The most famous of all the partnerships was between Francis Beaumont and John Fletcher, of whom we are told (by John Aubrey), 'They lived together. . .not far from the Play-house, both batchelors; lay together; had one Wench in the house between them. . .';[6] it is not entirely clear what role the wench played in the threesome. No Jacobean professional playwright disdained such collaboration and this includes Shakespeare, who collaborated with Fletcher in his last three plays (*Henry VIII*, *Two Noble Kinsmen* and the lost *Cardenio*), and who had earlier collaborated with Middleton on *Timon of Athens* (as the new Oxford Shakespeare contends), with George Wilkins on *Pericles* and perhaps with Ben Jonson on the Globe version of *Sejanus*.[7] Even the fastidious Jonson joined forces with his friend Chapman and his erstwhile enemy Marston to produce the splendidly funny *Eastward Ho*.

Eastward Ho is a particularly interesting play, not only as an example of successful co-operation between three major playwrights, but because it illustrates how complex the dialogue between playwrights and theatres had become in the early Jacobean period. For *Eastward Ho* is itself a Blackfriars 'answer' (as the Prologue indicates) to the slightly earlier collaboration between Dekker and Webster in *Westward Ho*, which in turn was followed by the two playwrights' *Northward Ho*; both for Paul's Boys. *Northward Ho* contains a comic, but good-humoured, portrait of Chapman.[8] In the Paul's plays good fun is had at the expense of the fashionable gallants, who are made fun of by the merry, but essentially virtuous, City wives (Paul's was a City theatre): Jonson and his friends reply with a London comedy that laughs at the bourgeoisie. Blackfriars, closer to the West End and the Court, would have a larger Court clientele.

Rivalry and alliances between playwrights and theatres was not gratuitous, for we are dealing here with a commercial theatre competing for a limited audience and it made as much sense to cash in on your rival's latest success with something similar (or even better if you could) as it does now to imitate the rival firm's successful detergent. In this competitive atmosphere playwrights tended to shop around between theatres, presumably for the best terms, and most of the chief playwrights wrote for more than one theatre. Shakespeare is an exception here, having the advantage of a commercial share in his company. Shakespeare took his rivals seriously enough, however, to intrude his professional concerns into one of his plays, for in the famous allusion to the 'little eyases' of Blackfriars in *Hamlet*, we catch a glimpse of the great man worrying that the boy players are enticing away the Globe's audience. As I argue later, Shakespeare is more likely to have been worried by loss of prestige than of cash in this particular instance and it is worth remembering in dealing with Jacobean society that social standing sometimes takes preference over financial profit.

It would be naïve to believe that Shakespeare's own practice as a playwright was not affected by this competitive atmosphere and these shifting alliances. Indeed certain instances where Shakespeare is responding directly to his rivals are widely acknowledged. F. P. Wilson's pioneering book on *Marlowe and the Early Shakespeare*[9] shows the two playwrights reacting to one another, and it is acknowledged as more than coincidental that Shakespeare's *Jew of Venice* appeared in the repertory of the Chamberlain's Men, while the rival firm of Henslowe's Admiral's Men were doing such successful business with the *Jew of Malta*. Similarly, Shakespeare's revival of revenge tragedy in *Hamlet* is not likely to be unrelated to Henslowe's long-running success with Kyd's *Spanish Tragedy*. This is not merely a phenomenon of Shakespeare's earlier work, for we find Shakespeare equally sensitive to the new mode of romantic tragicomedy introduced by Beaumont and Fletcher towards the end of his stage career.

These influences are widely acknowledged, but their implication for the study of Shakespeare's work as a whole has never been fully explored or adequately tested. Shakespeare's drama has been studied in a majestic isolation, as if he conjured up his splendid house in Stratford-upon-Avon with Prospero's wand. To understand Shakespeare's stature, we need to understand the theatrical world in which he earned his cakes and ale; to whom he was listening (at the Mermaid or elsewhere) and whose latest success he was bearing in mind. Jonson's fervent proselytizing for a more serious attitude to theatre and a respect for neo-classical rules left its mark on him (it would be surprising if they hadn't) as did the commercial successes of his rivals in the big popular theatres and the *succès d'estime* of the boys' theatres. It was not only money that counted, as I said, but the prestige that went with attracting the 'wiser sort', and eventually the wisest sort of all – the wisest fool in Christendom, no less.

I have confined my study of Shakespeare's plays to the years from *Hamlet* to *Lear*, that is, from roughly 1600 to 1606, because these were the most exciting years in the history of our drama, when competition was not only at its height, but also at its most rewarding in terms of the stimulus it provided. Without the extraordinary changes in theatrical taste brought about by Marston and then Middleton at Paul's (reopened in 1599), by Chapman at Blackfriars (opened in 1600) and by the gadfly Jonson, Shakespeare's work in these years would be very different and in my view considerably less impressive. The newer-come playwrights of the 1590s forced Shakespeare to re-think his methods in ways that can only be understood by studying his plays with those of his rivals and colleagues – and that has been my aim in this book. My concern throughout is not primarily to argue for specific influences and borrowing from one play to another. In many cases the dating of these plays – both by Shakespeare and his rivals – is too vague to make it at all certain which take precedence. It is unlikely that we shall ever know for certain whether Heywood's *Iron Age* preceded *Troilus and Cressida* (as I believe) or Marston's *Antonio's Revenge* preceded *Hamlet*, or *Phoenix*, *Measure for Measure*, nor for the purpose of my argument is it of fundamental importance. I have tried where possible to give reasons for a particular dating, but generally I have accepted what I take to be the scholarly consensus and I leave the reader to follow more detailed arguments for dating that can readily be found in the various scholarly editions of the plays. My central purpose has been to place Shakespeare's plays in the context of the rapidly changing tastes and fashions of Jacobean theatre, so that we can assess the theatrical milieu in which they were conceived and of which they form an integral part. Not to understand the theatrical 'field of force' within which Shakespeare worked (to borrow a phrase from Professor Cioffi)[10] is not to understand Shakespeare. By discussing Shakespeare's plays in the light of what was going on in the theatre around him, we can see more clearly how his development as a playwright took the course it did.

For the most notable aspect of Shakespeare's work from *Hamlet* to *Lear* is the extraordinary range and variety of theatre he attempted: starting with affective tragedy, then switching in *Troilus* to satirical drama outside his usual dramaturgical range. This is followed by an equally unexpected and radical change to a kind of mythic comedy in *All's Well that Ends Well* that has been much misunderstood, because it is not related to what was going on at this time in Chapman's comedies for Blackfriars. *Othello* brings us back to the tragedy that the adult players could handle, for obvious reasons, so much better than the boy players. Yet *Othello*, too, marks a change in direction, showing a much greater respect for the new classicism Jonson and Chapman were anxious to see replacing the older, gothic freedoms. After *Othello*, yet another volte-face in *Measure for Measure* where we can detect the influence of the new demand for city 'realism' that Middleton met so successfully in his comedies for Paul's Boys and Blackfriars. After 'realistic' comedy, Shakespeare makes another attempt (with Middleton) at satire in the least successful of his plays, the unfinished *Timon of Athens*. Finally, and least predictable of all, stands Shakespeare's greatest work, *King Lear*, a play that out-tops his rivals and challenges in its grandeur the greatest achievement of the ancient Greek theatre. Such extraordinary changes and re-directions cry out for explanation, more especially because in the years immediately before 1600 Shakespeare's output had been devoted with remarkable consistency to romantic comedy and the long series of English history plays – each sufficiently different from its predecessor, but forming a clear line of internal development that does not ask so insistently for an explanation in terms of outside pressures and influences.

In each of the seven Shakespeare plays I deal with, there are clear (and not so clear) signs of the influence of other playwrights in dramaturgy and in the treatment of related themes. Only in one respect is the influence minimal: Shakespeare rarely borrows verbally from his fellow playwrights.

The reasons for this are not far to seek. In many cases it would be difficult, virtually impossible, to obtain the text of a rival's play. Comparatively few plays were published during Shakespeare's working life; often those that had proved unsuccessful on the stage (*Sejanus* is a case in point). To possess the text of a successful play was to hold a trade secret too precious to part with in normal circumstances and it was clearly in the interest of the possessing company to hang on to it. Those plays that did get away were often in garbled, pirated editions. The plays you knew best were obviously those of your own company, the others you were more likely to hear than read. Verbal borrowing is therefore not very common among playwrights of this period until the Webster of *White Devil* and *Duchess of Malfi*[11] by which time a sizeable body of dramatic literature had been published. Shakespeare's verbal exuberance, in any case, must have militated against his building a play into a mosaic of other people's lines − though he was quite capable of borrowing extensively from non-dramatic sources, as he does from North's *Plutarch* for the later tragedies.

My emphasis on the competitive circumstances in which Shakespearean theatre flourished is not meant to suggest that the milieu alone explains the achievement. In any enterprise culture talent is as important a key to success as opportunity. My aim has been to let the circumstances throw light on the genius. Traditional bardolatry has emphasized the genius without sufficiently exploring the influences which helped to mould it. That Shakespeare was a man of his time makes him no less a man of ours.

In the treatment of texts I have preferred the printed over the acted word as the basis of my discussion, although I have always considered the theatrical context within which the printed word is to be interpreted. I do this primarily not because we do not know how Jacobean actors spoke their lines (though that is a good reason), but on critical grounds. Any acted performance is itself, like any other critical reading, an interpretation of the text, but with the interpretive handicap that alternative readings can less readily be entertained simultaneously. The actor's spoken text, therefore (even when we know what it is), has no special critical status. In the following pages I have assumed that what justifies any critical interpretation is its ability to realize as fully as possible the artistic integrity of the text. The plays I discuss are worth discussing above all because they have, and have long been agreed to have, artistic merit. This is not something they acquire in production, but that can be assessed by the attentive modern reader. The critic's primary duty, as I see it, is to explain something of the complex structure of words and thoughts that is the vehicle of artistic value. These words and thoughts are Jacobean words and thoughts; the structures and the artistic value that inheres in them can only become available to the twentieth century in the context which gave meaning and value to them. My aim throughout the book is to provide a sufficient context to make the original structures clearer for the modern reader.

1

HAMLET AND THE LITTLE EYASES

Two of the three early texts of *Hamlet* have curious and much discussed passages, in which Shakespeare, leaving medieval Denmark behind, gives us a brief glimpse of the state of the contemporary London theatre. The earliest text, the garbled 1603 quarto, has 'Gilderstone' explaining to Hamlet why the actors who have arrived at Elsinore are on their travels. The adult troupe, he says, has found the competition of the boy players in the capital too hot; the 'principall publike audience' has deserted the public theatres in favour of the 'private players' in the children's company. This passage, in a text that it is now widely assumed was memorially reconstructed by a small-part actor or actors for a provincial tour, would appear to be a part summary of the much longer passage that occurs in the folio text (1623) where, in the equivalent conversation between Hamlet, Rosencrantz and Guildenstern, we are told that the reason the troupe is travelling is an 'inhibition' (presumably a Government prohibition) on their playing in the capital and that a war of words has broken out between the adult and boy companies, in which the boys have got the better of the argument. To bring the matter right home, Rosencrantz tells us, in an apparent reference to the signboard of the Globe playhouse 'Hercules and his load', that Shakespeare's own company is one of the victims.

It is extremely unusual, indeed unique to these passages, for Shakespeare to use one of his plays to discuss his own affairs so openly, and we must assume that it reflects a unique concern with a threat to his professional status. Such a threat in early 1601 is understandable. When he started to write *Hamlet* in 1599 or early 1600 he found himself almost without serious rivals in the London theatre. Only one major dramatist older than himself, George Chapman, had survived into the new century, writing for the rival company, the Admiral's Men. This superiority had seemed to find official recognition in June 1600 when the Privy Council decreed there should be two professional theatre companies in London, one of which was Shakespeare's. His company, the Chamberlain's Men, had recently constructed a large and well-appointed theatre on the south bank of the Thames at Southwark, ideally situated not only for attracting city clientele over London Bridge, but also for the 'wiser' and freer spending sort from the West End of London and Westminster who had easy and comfortable access by water across the Thames. Shakespeare was continuing what proved to be his steady progress up-market. He must have felt vulnerable, therefore, when, in the autumn of 1600, Henry Evans opened the 'private' theatre of Blackfriars on the western side of the City, charging prices that reflected not only the greater comforts of an indoor theatre, but a wish to exclude *hoi polloi*. To add to Shakespeare's problems a new generation of playwrights, stimulated by the prospect of a well-educated, sophisticated audience, both for Blackfriars and the small covered theatre of the Paul's Boys' company that had reopened in the City centre (probably in 1599) was beginning to challenge a supremacy that had made him the most popular playwright of his day. It was not surprising that his professional concern bubbled over into print.

As a major theme of this book is to be Shakespeare's response to these challenges and how it affected his own writing for the theatre, it might be as well to have a closer look at the two *Hamlet* passages in question. The passage in Q1,[1] somewhat contradictorily, has Gilderstone assert both that the adult players' 'reputation holds as it was wont' and that the 'noveltie' of the children's troupe carries the day in attracting the 'principall publike audience', where 'principall' perhaps means the more eminent part of the audience, the gentry. The complaint is what we might expect from a travelling group of London actors, that it has been a victim of the vagaries of fashionable taste rather than that its decline in popularity is a result of its own deficiencies. The redactors of Shakespeare's original text would seem to be adapting the complaint to their own circumstances. The folio text, though published much later, must reflect Shakespeare's original more closely for it is much more precisely related to the theatrical situation in London in 1600 and early 1601. It clearly refers to what has come to be called the 'war of the theatres', in which Jonson, writing for the newly opened Blackfriars theatre, composes a series of plays poking fun at rivals in both the public theatre and the other 'private' theatre of Paul's Boys. In contrast to the complaining tone of Q1, the account of theatrical warfare in the folio version is humorous, though laughter and tears are never far apart in *Hamlet*. Hamlet at this moment is in a particularly volatile mood and the conversation with Rosencrantz and Guildernstern is carried on in a spirit of banter. Rosencrantz's description of the boys' troupe as an 'ayrie of Children, little Yases, that crye out on the top of question; and are most tyranically clap't for't' refers (as Reavely Gair points out)[2] to the Blackfriars theatre where the auditorium was on an upper floor. The reference to the Globe has about it the air of a private joke:

8

Hamlet: Do the Boyes carry it away?
Rosencrantz: I that they do my Lord, Hercules and his load too.
(F.II, ii, 375–6)[3]

It is usually assumed that this passage reflects Shakespeare's concern with loss of revenue,[4] for Jonson in *Poetaster* has his public theatre actor, Histrio, complain 'this winter ha's made us all poorer than so many starv'd snakes: No bodie comes at us; not a gentleman' (III, iv, 330). Jonson in *Poetaster*, however, is much more concerned with scoring points than with God's truth and there is no evidence at all that Shakespeare's company was seriously affected financially at this time. Unlike the Elsinore troupe, they seem to have been acting regularly in the capital over the period and in contrast to the Q1 references the folio passage does not seem in general appropriate to the circumstances of the actors playing it. Rosencrantz gives as the reason for the troupe's travels an 'inhibition' placed on them 'by the late innovation' – an explanation that has greatly puzzled the commentators when they try to relate it to Shakespeare's company. One explanation is that the 'innovation' (which in Shakespeare elsewhere refers to political turmoil)[5] alludes to the Essex rebellion of 1601,[6] but again there is no evidence that Shakespeare's company was 'inhibited' at this time.[7] It is much more likely that this part of the conversation between Hamlet and Rosencrantz does not refer to contemporary England at all, but to the requirements of the plot where the 'innovation' would be the political crisis caused by King Hamlet's recent death. It would clearly have been the kind of prudent move one would expect from Claudius to 'inhibit' the city players during the crisis in order to forestall unwanted comment. This would also explain why Q2, the 'authorized' version of the play published in 1604, while it omits all reference to the now *passé* war of the theatres, keeps the earlier lines referring to the 'innovation' and the reasons why the troupe has to go on its travels. Clearly Shakespeare felt that this passage was germane to the plot, whereas the jokes about the 'little eyases' had ceased to be topical by 1604 and so had lost their point. Further evidence leads us in the same direction. Dover Wilson in the new Cambridge edition of *Hamlet* argues that Rosencrantz's description of the Elsinore troupe as 'tragedians of the city' would be more suitable for the Admiral's Men than for Shakespeare's company, who had principally excelled in comedy at this date and for whom the description would be inappropriate.[8] Wilson also thinks it unlikely that Shakespeare would mock his own standing when Rosencrantz asserts the players have lost popularity,[9] but in this case it surely fits in with the bantering, self-mocking tone of the reference to the Globe. Shakespeare is not seriously concerned for his bread and butter here, but for his reputation as a playwright who can appeal to the 'wiser sort', for the Blackfriars theatre was small compared to the Globe

9

and usually only staged plays one day in the week;[10] in the event neither 'private' theatre turned out to be financially viable.[11] It is possible, to judge from the Folio passage where we are told the boy players 'are now in fashion', that the gentry are being persuaded by ridicule to avoid the 'common stages'. The reference in Q1 to the 'principall publicke' reflects the original emphasis. Shakespeare seems to have been concerned throughout his career to be regarded as a gentleman and it would have been a matter of concern if he thought there was a danger of the Globe becoming regarded as unfashionable or fit only for the stinkards. Certainly his response to the new situation shows a marked concern to be abreast of the latest theatrical fashions.

We don't know exactly when Shakespeare, thumbing over an old play (perhaps by Kyd) on the subject of Hamlet, Prince of Denmark, began to write his updated version. Harold Jenkins prefers a date sometime late in 1599 for its first performance, arguing that the passage on the war of the theatres is a later interpolation;[12] most commentators have placed the date rather later, accepting the reference to the little eyases as part of the original script and therefore dating the first performance in the spring of 1601. *Poetaster* (of 1601) was Jonson's last blast in the war of the theatres. While *Hamlet* is (as I shall explain) somewhat old-fashioned in its dramaturgical techniques, there are also signs of a reaction to Marston in the play, as we shall see. By 1602, in *Troilus and Cressida*, a play we can be certain was written after the advent of the new rivals, Shakespeare is clearly attempting to counter-attack by playing the 'private' theatres at their own satiric game, and we shall find that from *Troilus* on, Shakespeare consciously strives to keep abreast of the fashions as they are dictated by the 'elite' theatre of Paul's and Blackfriars until the advent of James causes a further adjustment to a yet more exalted clientele. In all this Shakespeare shows, as far as we can see, an acute responsiveness to the demands of his particular audiences and an increasing tendency away from the demands of a purely popular audience, which however he never completely loses sight of. One of the most interesting aspects of his writing throughout his working life is his ability to respond to change and while this ability is evinced in the first half of his professional career it becomes much more obvious and more far-reaching in his response to the revolution in theatrical fashion that accompanied the opening of the 'private' theatres.

Hamlet, by the tokens of the new theatre, is, as I said, (for all its brilliant inventiveness) a rather old-fashioned play. It follows hard upon the heels of *Julius Caesar*, to which it alludes,[13] and which was seen at the Globe by the Swiss traveller Thomas Platter on 21 September 1599. John Dover Wilson conjectures that *Julius Caesar* was the inaugurating play for the Globe.[14] This plausible suggestion would imply that Shakespeare was making a bid, in returning to tragedy after a period in which he confined himself to comedy and English history, to challenge the Admiral's Men at their own game in competing for the custom of the audience of the neighbouring Rose theatre. *Hamlet* could be explained as a continuation of this appeal combined with a concern (shared to some extent with *Julius Caesar*) to attract the fashionable from the West End. Its unmistakably more learned appeal, remarked on by Gabriel Harvey, who considered it a play with qualities to 'please the wiser sort',[15] could it is true be accounted for as an attraction to the gentry, who might be sensitive to Jonson's ridicule; but equally it could be a shrewd way of cashing in on the proximity of the new Globe to the better side of London across the water.

A further reason for supposing that Shakespeare had his old rivals, the Admiral's Men, in his sights when he decided to refurbish the old play of *Hamlet* is that the rival company had successfully revived Kyd's most popular play, the *Spanish Tragedy*, in 1597 in a revised version and so kept alive the popular interest in revenge tragedy.[16] Indeed the *Spanish Tragedy* had proved one of Henslowe's best investments,[17] for he was still cashing in on it in 1602, when he paid one 'bengemy Johnsone' in June of that year 'for new adicyons for Jeronymo'[18] (Jonson continued as usual to keep a finger in all the theatrical pies). Even more popular through the 1590s was Marlowe's *Jew of Malta*, which Shakespeare had successfully countered with his own play about a Jew, the *Merchant of Venice c.*1597. But while Shakespeare was thus engaged in responding to his rivals' successes he was also subtly changing the terms of the debate. Henslowe's most successful money-spinners – Marlowe and Kyd in tragedy, Chapman in comedy[19] – were essentially sensational, centring above all on action and intrigue. To this Shakespeare added a concern for characters as individuals that increasingly led his plays away from sensationalism towards an affective drama, where the audience were encouraged to see the characters as if they were real people, identify with them and respond emotionally towards them. In achieving this shift Shakespeare was simply responding to his own supreme talent for creating the illusion of reality in his characters. No clearer example can be seen of this than by comparing Marlowe's Barabas with Shakespeare's Shylock, in whom the bugbear figure becomes so humanized that the thematic implications of the source material become ambiguous. That this ambiguity is not fully controlled and intentional is suggested by the sudden lurch from the trial scene in Act IV, in which Shylock is distressingly tricked and humiliated, to a serenely lyrical fifth act based on the emotional assumption that Shylock's expulsion from the play eliminates the source of evil and disruption. Two dramaturgical methods are in uncomfortable juxtaposition here, the sensationalism of the Jew-baiting source material and the affective, humane presentation of the Jew as a real person. This problem continues to recur in Shakespeare's plays at this time, as he explores his own extraordinary powers of characterization; it recurs clearly in the *Henry IV* sequence in the figure of Falstaff. *Hamlet*, however, is the supreme example, and the curious ambiguity of the

11

play and its constant appeal for a critical 'solution' that is never achieved can be traced to the same source: Shakespeare's use of sensational material for the exploration of character.

We have only to compare *Hamlet* with revenge plays of the rival theatres of the same time to see how Shakespeare's search for affectiveness disturbs the expectations aroused by the sensational material. We will take three such plays, two from Henslowe's company, *Lust's Dominion* by Marston, Dekker and others (1600) and the *Tragedy of Hoffman* by Chettle (1602), and a rare example from the 'private' theatres (where such sensationalism proved not to be popular), Marston's *Antonio's Revenge* (1600). *Lust's Dominion* is an interesting play for a number of reasons, not the least of which is that its probable date of production, by the Admiral's Men sometime in 1600, makes it possible that it was providing a rival attraction at the new Fortune theatre to the new *Hamlet* playing at the Globe. If we accept Professor Hoy's very plausible conjectures that the play was a revamping of an old play whose revision was begun by Marston and then handed over for completion to Dekker with the aid of Day and Haughton,[20] it illustrates (like *Hamlet*) that tendency in the popular theatre to bring up to date old material that had presumably proved viable on the stage earlier. Certainly *Lust's Dominion* is notably derivative, being stuffed with Marlovian echoes. It also owes a considerable debt to the rival playwright's *Titus Andronicus*, the play that as late as 1614 still had its appeal to some (with the *Spanish Tragedy*) as together 'the best playes yet'.[21] Shakespeare's earlier plays are much closer in their dramatic methods to Dekker here than to his own dramaturgy later. *Lust's Dominion* is a highly professional play, as we might expect of the product of a team of experienced professional playwrights. It is all the more convincing, therefore, as an indicator of what met the expectations of the popular audiences at this time. The conservatism of the play is not confined to its use of earlier dramatic material: its characters are unashamedly stereotyped to fit an immediately recognizable framework of dramatic reference. The central character, the revenging Moor, Eleazar, is labelled by his blackness as a manifestation of evil. As such his behaviour is only made other than totally predictable by the conventional requirement that evil involves prevarication and double dealing. Associated with this embodiment of evil (another convention involved here is that evil is primarily, as with the devil, of the male sex) is the 'lascivious queen' of the subtitle, Queen Eugenia, whose lustful perversity is expressed through her infatuation with the black man – a symbolism echoed from Tamora's relation to Aaron in *Titus Andronicus*. The dominion of lust (meaning greed as well as its more specialized meaning) is illustrated in a series of examples of sexual infatuation and its evil consequences. The playwrights have no interest in explaining their characters' attitudes in plausible psychological terms. Eleazar's desire for revenge against the Spanish hierarchy is touched on fleetingly as the result of his father's death in battle at Spanish hands;

but as he has married into the Spanish nobility and has a prominent place in Spanish society (eventually becoming king) his hatred of the Spaniards is a matter of stance rather than genuine grievance. His desire to be evil far outweighs his political interests as, for instance, when he keeps his enemies alive in order to enjoy tormenting them in prison (V, ii). Vengeance is not a problem for Eleazar, but a definition of his status as the evil genius of the play. The playwrights' use of soliloquy – as in *Hamlet* confined principally to the central figure – in marked contrast to *Hamlet* demonstrates their concern with stereotype. Such soliloquies are manifestos defining the hero's course of action, expressing his mind as revenge villain, not revealing its inner processes. Like all the other characters, Eleazar is essentially a symbol of a state of mind; accordingly characters do not change and develop, but rebound off one another in feverish action and counteraction. His soliloquy as he rests from battle is typical. He is commenting on the dead body of one of his soldiers:

> Oh for more work, more souls to send to hell;
> That I might pile up *Charons* boat so full,
> Untill it topple o're, Oh 'twould be sport
> To see them sprawl through the black slimy lake.
> Ha, ha; there's one going thither, sirrah, you,
> You slave, who kill'd thee? how he grins! this breast,
> Had it been tempered, and made proof like mine,
> It never would have been a mark for fools
> To hit afar off with their dastard bullets.
>
> (IV, ii.57–65)[22]

There is nothing crude in the language here, indeed dramatically it shows considerable sophistication in its switch of tone from the excitement of the opening lines, reflecting the exhilaration of the battle, to the sardonic meditation on the corpse, and the soliloquy ends on a note of seriousness as Eleazar promises the body a dignified burial. There is also sophistication in the way in which Eleazar's evil nature expresses itself in a materialism that sees the difference between life and death on the battlefield in terms of the quality of one's armour. Indeed a certain amount of individuality is imparted. Failure to supply psychological depth is not due to a lack of the appropriate medium for doing so, but to the whole concept of character as moral symbol.

The action of the play is grounded on a simple moral pattern in which evil characters like Eleazar and the Queen are in conflict with such symbols of righteousness as Prince Philip and his sister Isabella; between these opposing forces are those characters like the Cardinal Mendoza who are pulled in contradictory directions. This moral patterning (a familiar one deriving from the old morality plays) is not the subject of the play but provides the familiar ground rules by which the action of the play is governed. It is, in contrast, the absence of such clear ground rules in *Hamlet* that explains the curious disorientating effect the play has on its readers though (for reasons that will become clear) not so obviously on its audiences. Shakespeare is willing to subordinate both moral clarity and plot to the exploration of character, whereas *Lust's Dominion* is concerned above all with action. The clarity with which the opposing forces are distinguished has the function of heightening the dramatic impact of their clash. The play is primarily about the shock that is engendered, and the very predictability of the stereotypes frees the audience from concerns with individuality that would weaken the impact. Essentially the two dramaturgical methods are in opposition. The playwrights pile horror on horror, including the ultimate Elizabethan horror of regicide, when Eleazar stabs to death the new king Ferdinand in full sight of the audience (weakening, one would have thought, arguments that Hamlet's failure to kill Claudius is to be explained in terms of royal inaccessibility). Because the playwrights can take for granted a moral seriousness in their audience the play avoids absurdity, but it is interesting that where Marston's hand is most noticeable (in Act V) absurdity is deliberately courted in the increasingly sardonic tone that Eleazar adopts, reflecting Marston's characteristic association of comedy with moral chaos. It was in the 'private' theatres that this association was to be more fully explored, notably by Marston and, later, Middleton.

Lust's Dominion does not seem to have been outstandingly popular and its survival and printing in 1657 by Francis Kirkman would seem to have been largely fortuitous. Henry Chettle's *Tragedy of Hoffman* on the other hand, for which Henslowe (seemingly) recorded a part payment of 5 shillings in December 1602, must have had a marked success on the Jacobean stage. Although it was not published until 1631, the title page of the quarto of that year records that the play was 'divers times acted with great applause at the Phoenix in Drury Lane'; as it must have been originally written for the Admiral's Men playing at the Fortune this implies a successful revival or series of revivals from 1617 onwards, the year that Christopher Beeston opened the Phoenix (or Cockpit) theatre in the fashionable area of Drury Lane. Like *Lust's Dominion* it is a moralistic play illustrating the evil of vengefulness and like the earlier play it uses a familiar and orthodox moral patterning as the groundwork of a display of sensational events. Like *Lust's Dominion* it uses character to symbolize the moral forces whose clash is the substance of the drama. The hero, Hoffman, like Eleazar, is perfunctorily motivated in his desire for revenge – we hear that his father was condemned to death for piracy – but Chettle is clearly much more interested in the consequences of the hero's stance than in his motivation. The desire for revenge is made the excuse for a series of sensational (and mostly incredible) killings that punctuate the action at frequent intervals. It is particularly interesting that two or three years after the first presentation of *Hamlet* Chettle reproduces the conventional picture of the wicked revenge hero driven by the sin of vengefulness to a series of brutal acts until he is brought low in his turn by the 'fickle dame', Fortune.[23] That he descends from a long line of vice figures is made clear (as with Eleazar) by the sardonic humour with which he expresses an inhuman delight in the misery of others and by his open defiance of God's ordinance:

> Had I Briareus' hands, I'd strive with heaven
> For executing wrath before the hour. . .
> (lines 1519–20)

Hoffman too, like Eleazar, expresses his evil nature not merely through his violence, but in his unlicensed sexuality, as, for instance, in the plan he develops with his henchman Lorrique to rape the Duchess of Luningberg, mother of his first victim Charles, who is killed by having a burning crown placed on his head. To ensure Lorrique's silence he murders him as soon as the plan is made (V, i). Ranged against the demonic Hoffman are a series of rather colourless characters representing the normality that is duly restored at the end. This normality includes the suggestion (by Mathias, the brother of one of Hoffman's victims) that vengeance against Hoffman is justified and should be in a manner befitting the crimes (lines 2004–10). Hoffman is eventually killed in the manner of his first victim. The moral distinction involved here is that between private revenge (which is condemned as wicked) and the public extermination of an enemy of society – a distinction relevant to *Hamlet*, but characteristically left unstated and ambiguous in that play. That Mathias's vindictiveness is endorsed by the playwright (and, we must assume, by the admiring audiences) is made clear by the explicit approval given to it by the saintly Rodorick, the hermit brother of the Duke of Saxony, whose dramatic function it is to remind us of the eternal Christian truths that the play embodies.

Although *Hoffman* is a cruder play than *Lust's Dominion*, its popularity must be accounted for by the purposeful and single minded way in which sensationalism is pursued, reinforced by a gothic setting in German forests and castles which generates a wild and lawless feeling very different from the over-ripe decadence of the Italy of the Jacobean stage and perhaps owing something here to *Hamlet*. Its popularity needs to be remembered if we are to understand the theatrical context of *Hamlet*. It certainly helps to explain what Marston was about in his unaided adventure into revenge tragedy, *Antonio's Revenge*, another revenge play almost exactly contemporaneous with *Hamlet*, to which it bears some striking similarities. Indeed G. K. Hunter, in his edition of Marston's play, remarks that these resemblances 'are greater than those between either play and any other surviving Elizabethan drama'.[24] Both plays exhibit a rather different revenge pattern from that of the two plays we have been considering. In

Lust's Dominion and *Hoffman* the revenger is the embodiment of evil and the plays plot the destructive effects of this evil until, at the end, the forces of virtue triumph, the revenger is killed and the evil is extirpated. The origin of this revenge pattern would seem to owe more to the old morality play, via Marlowe's *Jew of Malta*, than to Seneca. In *Antonio's Revenge* and *Hamlet* on the other hand, the revenger is presented as essentially a good man whose virtue is tempted by the need to avenge a palpable wrong. *Hamlet*, however, as we shall see, is fraught with ambiguities that complicate the picture. Shakespeare had already adopted the pattern of the sympathetic revenge hero in *Titus Andronicus* and it is found earlier in Kyd's *Spanish Tragedy*; its origins are in Seneca and Renaissance imitations of Seneca. It has been frequently pointed out that *Hamlet* exhibits a pattern of revenge remarkably close in many ways to that of Kyd's play.[25] One explanation of the relationship between *Hamlet* and *Antonio's Revenge*, put forward by (among others) Reavely Gair in his edition of Marston's play, suggests that both plays were directly influenced by the Kydian so-called ur-*Hamlet*, a lost play which it is assumed adopted a plot patterning similar to that of *Spanish Tragedy*.[26] *Antonio's Revenge* dates from 1600 (its first performance seems to have been at the end of 1600) and the lack of clearly recognizable verbal echoes in plays that are otherwise so closely allied may imply that they were being written at the same time from a common source. Jenkins, on the other hand, argues that there are clear verbal echoes of Shakespeare in Marston's play, but the few convincing examples he cites could as readily be explained by a common source as by the borrowing of one from the other. At least as important as the marked similarity in the plots of the two plays is the very different treatment of these plots, showing not only the completely different dramaturgical principles upon which the two playwrights were writing, but also demonstrating the wide gap between what the public theatre audiences would support at the Globe compared to the new select audience of Paul's. Marston's plays were highly innovatory in their sophisticated use of 'alienating' techniques; yet in other ways Marston's dramaturgical technique is the more conservative of the two, for he shares with the two popular revenge dramas we have already discussed the delight in the sensational and he relates that sensationalism to a clear and explicit moral framework. We have seen that there is good evidence that he had a hand in fashioning one of these plays. At this period Shakespeare had developed, out of a theatre of characters, a theatre of personalities. His remarkable emphasis on particularity, on the phenomenal, in a religious age that cultivated the noumenal, is made explicit in the play by Hamlet's definition of theatre as 'the abstract and brief chronicles of the time' (II, ii, 520). Few, if any, Elizabethan or Jacobean plays fit this definition, but in *Hamlet* Denmark is firmly established as a space in Elizabethan time, while Marston's Venice is another name for Middle-earth, and its inhabitants as likely to have allegorical as personal

16

names. In *Hamlet* Shakespeare takes his innovatory affectiveness further than in any of his other plays in presenting his *dramatis personae* with great realism and Hamlet in particular with great psychological subtlety, not so much analytically as to encourage an intense identification between audience and character. We even watch Hamlet's mind changing and developing under the pressure of events, an extremely difficult feat to achieve in a three hour play. There is no doubt that Shakespeare is the innovator here, even allowing for the potential for psychological realism in the old morality play's focus on the spiritual development (or decline) of the everyman hero; but Shakespeare had evolved his techniques over the years pragmatically for an audience that responded by demanding more. If the Queen's reputed reaction was typical,[27] audiences could not have enough of Falstaff and it may have been for the sake of his own artistic conscience that Shakespeare finally decided to kill him off so publicly in *Henry V*.

The theatrical revolution initiated by Marston and quickly followed by Jonson was to some extent a return to older ways of looking at character as part of the religious and moral patterning, rather than something to be cultivated for itself. Marston differs from his sensationalist contemporaries on the popular stage in making the sensationalism self-conscious to the point of parody in order to give priority to the moral theme. In *Antonio's Revenge* sensationalism is a function of the morality, with Chettle it is the other way round. It is for this reason that the moral patterning of *Antonio's Revenge* is so much clearer than it is in *Hamlet* where Shakespeare sacrifices moral clarity for psychological subtlety. The future turned out to be with Shakespeare — acceleratingly so, as the modern world increasingly saw as a main function of literature the exploration of personality in a secular world.

Antonio's Revenge is certainly a strange play. Like *Hamlet* it presents the story of a son whose father is poisoned, as in *Hamlet* the ghost of the father visits the son to demand revenge on his killer, as in *Hamlet* the poisoner seduces the dead man's wife and persuades her to become his bride, like Hamlet, the hero (Antonio) affects madness as part of the stratagem leading up to the revenge killing, in both plays the hero's preoccupation with revenge involves him in the death of the woman he loves, in both plays the political significance of what is happening is touched on from time to time, but remains of secondary importance. The contrast in the treatment of these remarkably similar plots, however, could hardly be greater. Whereas Shakespeare does everything he can to encourage us to identify with the revenge hero, including an extensive use of soliloquy to reveal the inner thoughts of the character quite unprecedented both in its extent and in its appeal for audience sympathy, Marston uses dramatic techniques — including the soliloquy — to exclude audience feeling. The purpose of this exclusion is not unlike that of Brecht's *Verfremdungseffekt*, to keep the intellectual sight-lines clear of emotional clutter. For Marston's is a sophisticated dramatic technique designed to remind the audience constantly that they are in a theatre watching a group of actors on a stage, not participating vicariously in exotic adventures. Harold Jenkins, in his discussion of the two plays, complains that Marston arbitrarily drags in from Hamlet's response to the players a comparison that Pandulpho makes between his grief and that of a stage player (I, v, 76–80).[28] *Antonio's Revenge*, however, is full of explicit allusions to the theatre and to the theatrical, all with the purpose of reminding the audience of the illusory nature of the theatrical experience and, by analogy, with the experience of life itself. This is particularly appropriate in the case of Pandulpho, who represents the stoical position that man should be master of his passion, a philosophical stance that is itself exposed as illusory when Pandulpho fails to overcome his grief on being presented with his son's corpse and throws in his lot with the active avengers. The most extreme example of Marston's deflationary techniques is when the play's fool, Balurdo, is made to come on stage with 'a beard half off' (II, i, 20, s.d.) and gives the explanation 'the tiring man hath not glued on my beard half fast enough' (II, i, 31). The dislocatory nature of this device becomes all the clearer when we remember that this play was written for boy actors. A particularly macabre use of the acting metaphor is when Strotzo is persuaded by Piero to pantomime his own death in a kind of dress rehearsal of the 'real' event later (II, v, 19–36). This is the most complex of Marston's uses of the metaphor of life as a theatre as Strotzo 'rehearses' for a death that is itself a 'rehearsal' of the reality of final judgement. The episode tremors with ironic reverberation, showing man's absurd vulnerability in life and death. Strotzo's evil credulity is rewarded by Piero's brutality, but the ultimate irony is that we, the audience, are watching a paradigm of the vanity of human hopefulness.

The central theme of the play is the Christian notion that life on earth is itself illusory – that we see life through a glass darkly – and the theatrical metaphors are thus given philosophical import. Because this life is illusory it is also essentially absurd, incoherent and meaningless without reference to a supernatural authority. Marston's grim and uncompromising view of life is made clear in the Prologue to the play where he proclaims his intention of showing the bitter reality of 'what men were, and are/. . .what men must be'. The very setting of this Kydian play in decadent Italy, in contrast to *Hamlet's* romantic setting, promises that the play will be an exposition of human wickedness. The use of theatrical metaphors is only one way in which Marston represents his philosophy in his dramatic technique. The fragmentary nature of experience is also represented by the constant resort to literary allusion. This works in a number of ways. At its simplest it is represented in the sudden intrusion of long passages of Latin, usually derived from Senecan material. In earlier Senecan plays like *Spanish Tragedy* and *Titus Andronicus* quotations from Seneca were primarily devices of authentication; here they act as disruptive elements, shattering the consistency of the linguistic medium. There is a good example of this in the scene in church where Maria finds Antonio just after he has been visited by his father's ghost (III, ii). When she asks him why he is not in bed he breaks into a long (and relevant) quotation from *Thyestes* in Latin, to which his mother responds 'Alas my son's distraught'. Comic dislocation here becomes a symbol of human isolation. Marston uses variations in style to similar effect throughout the play. Sometimes indeed words begin to take on a macabre life of their own divorced from meaning, as when Balurdo takes up the more exotic utterances of others to relish them without knowing what they mean.[29] Two of the examples I have cited of the uses of theatrical allusion (Pandulpho's stoical refusal to lament and Balurdo's accusation against the tiring man) have literary echoes, for both (as Gair notes) refer us back to moments in the *Spanish Tragedy*. The inadequate beard for instance, reminds us of the preparation of the masque in Act IV of *Spanish Tragedy* when Hieronimo asks Balthazar to prepare himself for his performance by getting his beard fixed on (IV, iii, 18–19): in Kyd the device is entirely contained within the realistic conventions, in Marston it has the opposite effect, its arbitrary introduction breaks through the 'realism' and exposes it as convention. It seems reasonable to assume that the ur-*Hamlet* text was also made use of in this way and this might explain why Marston's play is so concerned with the *Hamlet* material. Other recurring devices for shattering realistic illusion include the frequent use of song – sometimes at inappropriate moments – and the use of mime at the beginning of scenes.

None of these stylistic and dramaturgical devices is entirely new to the sensationalist tradition of Senecal tragedy, Marston simply presses the logic of sensationalism towards absurd conclusions and does so deliberately to further his dramatic ends. The same is true with his characterization. We have already seen how character in popular revenge plays is subordinated to the search for sensation and this is as true of the tradition of more learned Senecanism with which Marston associates himself in this play. Some semblance of psychological realism is, however, usually maintained. Again Marston strains the conventions almost to breaking point. Piero, the play's villain, is typical of the sensationalist tradition in being arbitrarily devoted to evil ways, for his wickedness is largely unmotivated. His reason for killing Andrugio, Antonio's father, is merely that they were once rivals for the love of Andrugio's wife, Maria. Other acts are even less plausibly motivated; he kills Pandulpho's son, Feliche, simply to 'hale on mischief' and (seemingly) to enable him to perpetrate the macabre joke of having Feliche's body propped up at the window where Maria and her son, Antonio, expect to find Antonio's loved-one, Mellida. Nothing could be more theatrical and less likely than the opening of the curtain to reveal the body as Antonio eulogizes the vision of his bride-to-be (I, iii, 128–9).

Piero accuses his own daughter of unchastity as an excuse for having her imprisoned. Piero's reaction to his daughter's death illustrates the arbitrariness of his responses:

> And so she died! I do not use to weep;
> But by thy [Maria's] love (out of whose fertile sweet
> I hope for as fair fruit) I am deep sad.
> I will not stay my marriage for all this!
> Castilio, Forobosco, all
> Strain all your wits, wind up invention
> Unto his highest bent; to sweet this night,
> Make us drink Lethe by your quaint conceits,
> That for two days oblivion smother grief;
> But when my daughter's exequies approach,
> Let's all turn sighers.
>
> (IV, iii, 187–97)

Emotion here is treated as a form of acting, there is no expectation that it will correspond to anything in the mind of the character. Piero is only unusual here in the extreme to which he takes such attitudes, but the inner motivation of the other characters is equally obscure. We are shown Maria accepting Piero's offer of marriage in dumb show at the beginning of Act III and though she expresses regrets over the death of her former husband it does not prevent her acquiescing in the marriage arrangements. Even the ghost, in contrast to King Hamlet's frenzy, merely remarks 'Thy sex is weak'. Antonio, the revenge hero, is also a stereotype taken to the point of caricature. We must assume that the ur-*Hamlet* had its revenge hero pass through a period of simulated madness, for both Shakespeare's Hamlet and Antonio adopt an antic disposition. In *Hamlet* (characteristically) the motive for this is not clear, for Shakespeare is interested much less in the logic of the plot than in the opportunity it gives him for a fascinating exploration of the borderline between sanity and madness in Hamlet's behaviour. The motivation for Antonio's antic disposition, however, is clear; it enables him to take on the disguise of a Fool, a disguise which Piero fails to penetrate. This allows Antonio to plot his revenge without fear of retaliation. Marston is careful to comply with the logic of his plot, but he also uses Antonio's disguise as an opportunity to distance him from the audience's sympathies. Antonio is made to appear blowing bubbles and Marston actually draws the audience's attention to this absurdity by having other characters point to its inappropriateness, when, for instance, Alberto remarks: 'Fie, 'tis unsuiting to your elate spirit' (IV, i, 2). Marston has Antonio specifically repudiate all decorum of character at this point:

Antonio: He is not wise that strives not to seem fool. . .
Maria: Ay, but such feigning, known, disgraceth much.

20

Antonio: Pish! Most things that morally adhere to souls
  Wholly exist in drunk opinion,
  Whose reeling censure, if I value not,
  It values naught.

(IV, i, 25, 29–33)

Here Antonio is appealing to those eternal truths which we can only perceive fleetingly in a world in which we are all fools. He goes on to praise the fortunate lot of those born fools whose folly protects them from the more absurd idiocies of the wise:

  Whilst studious contemplation sucks the juice
  From wizards' cheeks, who, making curious search
  For nature's secrets, the first innating cause
  Laughs them to scorn as man doth busy apes
  When they will zany men.

(IV, i, 44–8)

The whole of this important speech, indeed, could be read as a commentary on Hamlet's vanity in puzzling over the nature of divine wisdom, for Antonio's picture of the foolish wise (in which he is reluctantly forced to include himself) has a remarkable likeness to Shakespeare's hero:

  Had heaven been kind,
  Creating me an honest, senseless dolt,
  A good, poor fool, I should want sense to feel
  The stings of anguish shoot through every vein;
  I should not know what 'twere to lose a father;
  I should be dead of sense to view defame
  Blur my bright love; I could not thus run mad
  As one confounded in a maze of mischief
  Staggered, stark felled with bruising stroke of chance;
  I should not shoot mine eyes into the earth,
  Poring for mischief that might counterpoise
  Mischief. . .

(IV, i, 48–59)

Being one of the foolish wise, dazzled by earthly wisdom, and being fully aware of his wrongs, Antonio is forced (like Hamlet) to take up arms against a sea of troubles, hence his acceptance of his role of revenger, by which he becomes an instrument of God's justice.

It is interesting (at the risk of breaking the strict sequence of my argument) to contrast Marston's central preoccupation with the theme of *vanitas* in *Antonio's Revenge*, with Shakespeare's use of the theme in *Hamlet*, for it shows both the opposed dramaturgy of the two playwrights and the reasons underlying that opposition. The Gravedigger's scene at the

21

beginning of the fifth act of *Hamlet* gives the hero, newly arrived from his
escape from death in England, the opportunity to meditate on the perennial
Christian theme. Here Hamlet is in a place of skulls, that chief emblem on
which such meditation centred in Elizabethan churches and in gentlemen's
studies. But for Hamlet the emphasis is not on the 'putrefacted slime' (as
Antonio is later to call it) of man's ephemerality – the traditional focus of
such meditation – but on the sadness of the lost world of life and
enjoyment that these relics conjure up. Whereas Antonio's meditations,
and indeed the thrust of Marston's play as a whole, is to reject the things of
this world as corrupt and vicious, Hamlet's assumptions are the very
opposite. Hamlet is the humanitarian whose delight in the world's richness
and strangeness makes the knowledge of death the occasion of infinite
sadness. It is this feeling, not the metaphysical implications, that
dominates the scene. The meditation upon the skulls, far from prompting
Hamlet to a rejection of the world (as Eleanor Prosser, following Marz,
would have it)[30] stimulates his imagination to recreate the delights of the
past. It is a daring departure in its secularism from habitual meditations on
the skull:

> *Hamlet*: That skull had a tongue in it, and could sing once. How the
> knave [the gravedigger] jowls it to th' ground, as if 'twere Cain's
> jawbone, that did the first murder. This might be the pate of a
> politician which this ass now o'er-offices, one that would circumvent
> God, might it not?
>
> *Horatio*: It might, my lord.
>
> *Hamlet*: Or of a courtier, which could say, 'Good morrow, sweet lord.
> How dost thou, sweet lord?' This might be my Lord Such-a-one, that
> praised my Lord Such-a-one's horse when a meant to beg it, might it
> not?
>
> *Horatio*: Ay, my lord.
>
> *Hamlet*: Why, e'en so, and now my Lady Worm's, chopless, and
> knocked about the mazard with a sexton's spade. Here's fine
> revolution and we had the trick to see't. Did these bones cost no more
> the breeding but to play at loggets with'em? Mine ache to think on't.
>
> (V, i, 74–91)

There is, of course a macabre side to this re-creation of the past, but
Hamlet's rich imagination, his sensitivity to the complexities of man's
nature – 'infinite in faculties, in form and moving how express and
admirable' (II, ii, 304–5) – leads him to create a picture of this living
complexity, from singing lady to insensitive gravedigger in the present (no
wish here for Antonio's praise of the insensitive-foolish), the Machiavellian
politician, the flattering courtier, the confidence man and men of business
and later too a long disquisition on lawyers. Cain is evoked, not to remind
us of man's ineradicable wickedness (as in orthodox meditation) but to add

to the variety of examples of human potential, for ill as well as good. Moreover the focus of all this imaginative meditation is on Hamlet's feeling – the sadness is in Hamlet's sense 'of the world he's lost and he characteristically brings the meditation down to a feeling in himself: 'mine [bones] ache to think on't'. The usual purpose of Elizabethan religious meditation is the opposite of this, to lift the thoughts above the narrow confines of the self towards the eternal.[31] But Shakespeare's drama is a drama of particular experience which would 'jump the life to come', if only man could free himself from the aching thoughts of his own destiny. Nowhere is it clearer how much Shakespeare centres his drama, at this moment in his career as dramatist, on personality, and on his extraordinary gift for conveying a character's feeling to an audience. It is this intense concentration on feeling that pushes the moral significance of the events to the margins of the audience's interest and so creates that sense of confused immediacy that is a characteristic of living in the real world.

Marston's characterization does the opposite of this. It is not in the least concerned with the feelings of particular individuals, but in the general significance that particularity can be forced to yield. Marston's tragic methods consequently often court laughter in their search for emotional detachment. This is well illustrated by the scene that is the philosophical climax of *Antonio's Revenge*, the scene where Antonio laments the death of his beloved Mellida (IV, iv). Antonio's soliloquy at the beginning of the scene, far from being used (like Hamlet's) to express the intense feelings of the hero at this new calamity, is made the opportunity for Antonio to express the central philosophical theme of the play: the need to submit one's self to God's will:

> Ay, Heaven, thou mayst; thou mayst, Omnipotence.
> What vermin bred of putrefacted slime
> Shall dare to expostulate with thy decrees?
> O heaven, thou mayst indeed: she was all thine,
> All heavenly, I did but humbly beg
> To borrow her of thee a little time.
>
> (IV, iv, 1–6)

In place of Hamlet's delight in differentiation, in particularity, we have here a reductive language in which the whole of humanity is characterized (as so frequently in Christian meditation at this time) as 'vermin', 'putrefacted slime'. Antonio is of course expressing deeply felt emotion at this point, but the emotion is merely part of that illustration of human frailty that can only be overcome in death. At the end of the soliloquy Antonio envisages the death of his affections through his sufferings: 'My breast is Golgotha, grave for the dead.' Individual suffering is to be dedicated to the service of God by a single-minded determination to extirpate the tyrant Piero. That Marston is concerned not to allow this scene to arouse audience sympathy for his hero is clear from the progress of the action. At the end of the soliloquy Pandulpho and others enter carrying the dead body of Pandulpho's son Feliche. Antonio has lain down on his back during the course of his soliloquy and Pandulpho places his son's corpse to rest on Antonio's breast. This emblematic gesture is then explained at length by Pandulpho as a mark of their unity in suffering, he for his dead son, Antonio for his dead beloved. In this curious and totally unrealistic and ludicrous situation a philosophical conversation now ensues between Pandulpho and Antonio which turns on the distinction between the stoic (Pandulpho) who maintains that suffering can be transcended and the orthodox Christian view (of Antonio and the play) that mankind in its frailty is bound to suffer in this life as part of our imperfection. That Pandulpho's position is to be repudiated becomes clear in one of the extraordinary reversals that Marston delights in and which illustrate the dislocations in our understanding of reality, when Pandulpho's stoical resolve suddenly breaks down and he admits to the same weakness as Antonio:

> Man will break out, despite philosophy.
> Why, all this while I ha' but played a part,
> Like to some boy that acts a tragedy. . .
>   . . .I spake more than a god,
> Yet am less than a man.
> (IV, v, 46–8, 51–2)

Again the acting metaphor (reminding the audience characteristically of the boy player) illustrates the illusory nature of man's search for certainty in this world. The emblematic nature of this scene, its total and uncompromising rejection of realism, is then further illustrated when 'They strike the stage with their daggers and the grave openeth' (there is none of *Hamlet's* realistic digging here) and by the formal dirge that Pandulpho speaks over the dead body as he now admits (in orthodox Christian fashion) 'there's no music in the breast of man' (IV, v, 70). The dramaturgy throughout this scene has been deliberately sensational. Realism and emotional involvement have been kept at arm's length so that the full intellectual significance of the action can be made clear.

In spite of this, many commentators have felt the ending of *Antonio's Revenge* to be ambiguous. Pandulpho and Antonio devise a gruesome end for Piero whereby he is first deprived of his tongue and then fed with the chopped body of his son, before being ritually murdered. This deliberately recalls the ending of Seneca's *Thyestes*, and its function is again to alienate us from any sympathy with the characters on stage. Antonio's murder of Piero's innocent son, Julio (III, iii) is perhaps the most sensational horror of the play, more especially because the scene in which it happens shows that Antonio and Julio have been particular friends (Julio is Mellida's brother).

Farley Hills

The murder is made particularly shocking and surprising to the audience because at one point in the scene we are led to believe the plan to murder the boy has been given up. The ghost of Andrugio appears, however, to whet Antonio's 'almost blunted purpose' and the murder is carried out in full view of the audience. The inevitable alienation of the audience from the hero that results is the main purpose of the killing and the intervention of the ghost is to make it clear that we are meant to see the event as part of God's mysterious purpose. Again there is no ambiguity here as there is in *Hamlet*. Marston follows the conventions of Italian Senecanism where the ghosts function as divine messengers,[32] in spite of the ghost's sounding on one occasion in *Antonio's Revenge* beneath the stage. Piero's brutal and tormented death is the one appropriate to so evil a ruler – as Antonio points out when (like Hamlet on a similar occasion) he has the opportunity of killing him (III, ii), but stays his hand so that the punishment can more adequately fit the crime: 'blood cries for blood, and murder murder craves' (III, iii, 71). Piero's death is presented, as it most frequently is in the Italianate Senecan tradition that Marston is following, as the appropriate death for a tyrant. It is a death, for instance, like that of Giraldi's villain Sulmone in *Orbecche*,[33] which is explicitly justified in Christian terms:

> Ma non é stato mal a uccider lui;
> ch'a Dio non s'offre vittima più grata
> d'un malvaggio tiran, com'era questo.

('But it was not wrong to kill him; for no more acceptable victim is offered to God than a wicked tyrant, as this man was.') However 'un-Christian' this attitude appears to the twentieth century, the brutality of Christian against Christian in the sixteenth and seventeenth centuries is far too extensively documented to need recalling in detail here. The Spanish Inquisition was only one of the many institutions that openly expressed itself duty-bound to adopt a policy of killing and maiming fellow-Christians. There is no ambiguity, then, in the ending of *Antonio's Revenge*. Antonio triumphs over the vicious Piero, who is duly made to eat the seed of his own evil nature; God's providence is asserted. Antonio's triumph, however, is not a vindication of human nature, for we are all 'vermin bred of putrefacted slime' (IV, iv, 2) as theologians from St Augustine to Luther and Calvin have repeatedly reminded us. We achieve God's purposes in spite of the evil nature we all share.

Arriving in Shakespeare's Denmark from the lands of *Lust's Dominion*, *Hoffman*, and – even more – *Antonio's Revenge*, is at first an extraordinary experience of arriving back into the familiar world of ordinary people going about recognizably ordinary business, and this in spite of the mystery of the play's opening and the appearance of the Ghost. Look how much of the first two acts of *Hamlet* Shakespeare spends recreating the experiences of the normal everyday world. Polonius, immediately established as a 'character'

25

and not just a character, sends his young son Laertes, as any Elizabethan courtier might, to sow a few (but not too many) wild oats in Paris before coming back to settle down to make a living in the politics of Court life. To keep a discreet eye on his son and heir, he dispatches Reynaldo to oversee Laertes at a distance and report back. How prudent, how worldly wise, how ordinary. Claudius and Gertrude settle into their new reign in businesslike fashion. As always for a ruler there are foreign entanglements and the hot-headed Fortinbras has to be headed off from his aggressive intentions against Denmark (another aggrieved son of another father) and persuaded to plunder Poland instead. Shakespeare gives valuable stage time to a scene only tangential to the revenge plot, in which Norwegian ambassadors are received at the Danish Court to report on the success of Claudius's diplomacy. The players arrive at Court and Hamlet, fond of theatre, joins them in a rehearsal of lines from a tragedy on the Trojan war. Of course all this air of normality has a relevance to the revenge theme, for within this world of normal comings and goings Hamlet appears as an element of disruption. Clothed in black (Eleazar's colour) he seems to defy the logic of events and, like Hoffman, in his wildness refuses to conform to common expectations. Here we are immediately plunged into ambiguity. The Ghost protests that this too, too solid world is fraudulent, a world of seeming, while at the same time we have already become part of it, judged the pleasantly tedious Polonius for what he is, sympathized intensely with Hamlet's intense difficulties and the dilemmas they pose for Gertrude and Ophelia, admired the efficiency of Claudius. Shakespeare has successfully asked us to enter a world which has all the reality and substance of our own world, even while that substantiality is being questioned and undermined. The play takes as one of its themes the way evil undermines this sense of reality; but this theme is presented not as statement but as experience. We are taken on a journey of disorientation with Hamlet until the actual no longer seems real.

Ambiguity is at the very heart of the play. Shakespeare's method takes us through the experience of doubt and uncertainty in association with his hero. The usual Elizabethan and Jacobean method that we have seen in the other revenge plays is to create a thematic framework in which each character can be placed and judged as part of the total pattern of a meaning that is clear and unequivocal. In *Hamlet* Shakespeare inverts this process and uses the events of the play to convey the hero's state of mind, with which the audience is asked to identify, to share his experience. This experiential focus, whether consciously intended by Shakespeare or simply the result of the furthest development of a tendency already evinced to make characterization the central concern of his drama, is not unknown elsewhere in Elizabethan art. When Milton praises the *Faerie Queene* for showing us Guyon in the Cave of Mammon 'that he might see and know, and yet abstain'[34] he is expressing a view of art as vicarious experience that is not uncommon at this period; yet even here Spenser's (and Milton's) ultimate purpose is doctrinal, to relate the experiences we share in the ordinary world to the eternal truths that the work as a whole displays. *Hamlet*, unusually, would make the vicarious experience itself a central truth of the play.

One way Shakespeare achieves this (whether intentionally or not) is by playing off one set of revenge expectations against another. I have just been arguing that our entry into the *Hamlet* world seems to be setting Hamlet up not as the revenge hero, but as the revenge villain, although overall it is clear that the play essentially follows the Kydian pattern that requires sympathy for the revenger. We are never, however, allowed to settle into any comfortable pattern of expectations in this play. In *Antonio's Revenge* and in the *Spanish Tragedy* (and in later plays that follow a similar pattern, like Middleton's *Revenger's Tragedy*) we not only have no doubts which is the aggrieved party, but this certainty is reinforced by the manifest villainy of the hero's main opponent or opponents. Shakespeare's play, on the other hand, presents Claudius more in the manner of Prince Philip in *Lust's Dominion* or the Duke of Saxony and Mathias in *Hoffman's Tragedy*, the revenger's opponents who, while to some extent implicated in the action that begins the revenge process, are presented as triumphant opponents of the revenger's evil nature. Claudius is presented in the beginning of the play as an eminently reasonable man and as an efficient ruler. He shows considerable patience with the eccentric behaviour of his wife's son, and his advice on the inevitability of death (I, ii, 87–106) is a passage of orthodox 'consolation' deliberately couched in Christian terms.[35] The fact that it turns out to be spoken by the murderer of Hamlet's father is an irony we can retrospectively savour, although the villainy of the messenger does not (as any Elizabethan audience would know) invalidate the message. There are other signs, even in this speech, that, in a sense, Shakespeare is pulling the wool over our eyes. For the 'machiavel' of the play Claudius is extraordinarily naïve in (apparently) not connecting Hamlet's eccentric behaviour with a 'prophetic' suspicion that his father was murdered. Why, for instance, is Claudius so insistent on Hamlet's remaining in Elsinore when the Prince is anxious to return to the University of Wittenberg (I, ii, 113)? In the eyes of a true 'machiavel' Hamlet would be better out of the way (as Claudius much later decides) where his popularity with the multitude (IV, iii, 4) would go for less. But Shakespeare prefers to give substance to Claudius's protestations of love and affection for his stepson (I, ii, 107–12) by making it appear he wants Hamlet's company. Like so many 'facts' in this play Hamlet's popularity is of uncertain status, for within a short stage time we hear that it is Laertes the people want to be king (IV, v, 106). The play abounds in such uncertainties. Hamlet, for instance, complains that the King engages in the Danish vice of excessive drinking (I, iv, 8–12), though whenever we see the King he is a model of sober self-control, indeed the very language of the King exhibits a sense of control and ceremony that belies the accusations of insobriety. Hamlet's assertion that drinking 'is a custom/More honour'd in the breach than in the observance' (I, iv, 15–16) does not, either, seem to square with his own invitation, (not necessarily ironic) to Horatio: 'We'll teach you to drink deep ere you depart' (I, ii, 175). These are minor matters, but they are important in indicating Shakespeare's preferences. Hamlet is the disaffected melancholic and a contrast is to be set up between his way of thinking and that of the Court. Yet Hamlet is no stereotype melancholic, he has a hearty appreciation of good fellowship and the normal appetites of a young man, including, to judge from his conversation with Ophelia during the play scene, a healthy, or perhaps unhealthy, preoccupation with sex (III, ii, 110–20, 240–6). Ambiguities arise because we can never establish to what extent Hamlet's views are justified – and the more emotionally involved we become with Hamlet the more difficult this becomes. Indeed Shakespeare plays on the difficulties that these ambiguities give rise to in order to create in his audience the kind of mental uncertainties that characterize the hero. Ambiguity is made a device of the characterization whereby we are inducted into the hero's world.

Aspects of Claudius's role are also deliberately kept ambiguous. The justification of the revenge hero (as is made very clear in *Orbecche*)[36] is that he (or she) is doing God's will in extirpating a tyrant. Marston's Piero is obviously such, for his decisions are arbitrary and cruel. Claudius, on the other hand, is not only shown to be a judicious and efficient ruler, but he also seems to be accepted as the legitimate ruler of Denmark. It is true that Hamlet progressively throws doubt on the legitimacy of Claudius's accession, accusing him of 'stealing' the kingdom (III, iv, 99–101) and of interfering in some way with the succession (V, ii, 65), but this is highly partial evidence and does not seem to be supported from more dispassionate sources. As Jenkins notes, 'the play does not question the legality of his [Claudius's] title'.[37] Again the effect is one of considerable ambiguity; the clear-cut opposition between villain and revenger is made more a matter of personal antagonism than of political principle.

As the murderer of his brother, Claudius evokes the audience's condemnation, but unlike the villains of other revenge plays, Claudius is presented as a man of conscience whom we see suffering for his transgression. Again Shakespeare's predilection for humanizing his characters transforms the stereotype and he provides Claudius with a soliloquy (III, iii, 36) whose function is to reveal his character's state of mind. Elsewhere in Elizabethan drama soliloquy provides the villain with the opportunity for displaying his villainy and defining it more precisely. Typically it announces a programme of action for the destruction of the good. Claudius's soliloquy on the other hand has the opposite function: to demonstrate the essential humanity behind the stereotype, the essential goodness even in a murderer. It is this humanizing of the villain more than Hamlet's curious vindictiveness in abstaining from killing Claudius while he is at prayer lest his soul go to heaven, that drastically alters and confuses the audience's response to the scene. That the revenger is tainted by the very process of revenge he is committed to is a commonplace of revenge tragedy and it is well illustrated in Antonio's killing of Julio. At the end of the *Revenger's Tragedy* the condemnation of the revenge hero Vindice makes the point with unusual clarity, but in those instances there is no question of shifting sympathies towards the villain. In *Hamlet* on the other hand Hamlet's outburst comes immediately after Claudius is presented at his most vulnerable and sympathetic. It is not really surprising that generations of critics have agreed with Dr Johnson that 'this speech, in which Hamlet, represented as a virtuous character, is not content with taking blood for blood, but contrives damnation for the man that he would punish, is too horrible to be read or to be uttered'.[38] As a result it came to be argued that Hamlet could not mean what he says and must be making this an excuse for an inability to act.[39] Johnson is surely right to detect an irresolvable tension between our feeling that Hamlet is essentially a virtuous character, with whom we readily identify, and the intrinsically evil nature of his vindictiveness. Here again the play leaves us with an unsolvable dilemma: are we after all to see Hamlet as the revenge villain at this point and repudiate those feelings of sympathy Shakespeare has so successfully cultivated, or are we to revise our ethical assumptions about the appropriateness of eternal damnation for a regicide, in accordance with the traditions of neo-Senecan revenge drama and the vindictiveness of so much Renaissance Christianity? The play, characteristically, rests in its ambiguity.

Hamlet's relationship with his mother is even more fraught with uncertainties than his relationship with Claudius. At least we know that Claudius did commit the crime of which he is accused. In Gertrude's case we cannot be certain what her crime is or, indeed, whether she can be regarded as having committed one. Like Claudius she is presented as a sensible, if insensitive, person, fulfilling her role as consort in the Court scenes with dignity and decorum. She never speaks to us as directly as Claudius and this in itself causes uncertainty about her complicity in Claudius's crime and about her own view of the adultery she is accused of having committed. Nevertheless she is presented as a personality in her own right whom we can relate to and sympathize with. Her response to Hamlet's revelation of Claudius's crime is simply to repeat Hamlet's words 'As kill a king', which is only a clear manifestation of innocence if we accept the Folio's question mark.[40] More ambiguous still is her innocent-seeming response, after the accusation of adultery as her 'husband's brother's wife' (III, iv, 14) – a clear accusation if we accept the relevance of the Book of Common Prayer's injunction (quoted by Jenkins): 'a woman

29

may not marry with her. . .husband's brother.' The Queen's response 'What have I done, that thou dar'st wag thy tongue/In noise so rude against me?' would seem, in the light of this, to be impudent in the extreme. But that is not, in fact, how it appears in performance; rather Gertrude seems genuinely puzzled by her son's behaviour and seems to believe him truly mad when he purports to see the ghost that she cannot see. Again Shakespeare chooses ambiguity by having us question the ghost's reality at this point. Both Claudius and Gertrude adopt a similar air of innocence to each other when, immediately after, they discuss Hamlet's behaviour and Gertrude tells her husband of Hamlet's killing of Polonius (IV, i). It is almost as if we are intended to interpret the two scenes from two different ethical standpoints simultaneously: Hamlet's Elizabethan view that Gertrude has committed adultery and Gertrude's apparent pagan view that she has done nothing wrong (a view that many social systems would endorse).[41] In the bedroom scene Shakespeare has preferred a drama of personality, in which the Queen is presented as wife and mother, to the obscuring of her allegorical role as accomplice to the devil's disciple. Once again the signposts point in contrary directions and we are left in a perplexity that is as disorienting as (though not identical with) Hamlet's own.

Such enigmas abound throughout the text, so that small discrepancies, like Horatio's both appearing to be familiar with Danish customs and ignorant of them,[42] and the radical change that comes over Fortinbras's character in the course of the play, that could be dismissed as a working dramatist's minor aberrations elsewhere, here contribute to the disorientation that afflicts the reader whenever he attempts to take his bearings. Hamlet's treatment of Ophelia needs special mention as part of this process. Here again Hamlet's role would seem to relate him more obviously to the revenge villain. Admittedly Hamlet's abuse of Ophelia is a more refined abuse of womanhood than Hoffman's attempted rape or Eleazar's lustfulness, but its brutality is not the less striking on that account.

In *What Happens in Hamlet* Dover Wilson describes Hamlet's attitude to Ophelia as 'without doubt the greatest of all the puzzles in the play'[43] and similar views have been expressed by such other distinguished Shakespeareans as Bradley[44] and Geoffrey Bullough[45] – indeed articles have been written on the impossibility of solving the problem.[46] Harold Jenkins, on the other hand, argues that there really is no Ophelia problem.[47] Bullough presents a succinct account of where he feels the problems lie and we cannot do better than quote him:

> Hamlet's relations with Ophelia are left mysterious. What would almost certainly have been a scene of farewell in the ur-*Hamlet* is narrated in *Hamlet*, so that we hear only Ophelia's side of it (II, i, 75–100). We are left wondering whether (some weeks after the

Ghost's revelation) this is a sign of his self-dedication to vengeance, or whether he sees her as inevitably bound to prove that 'Frailty, thy name is woman', as a potential ally of the other side, or just as a pawn in his game of pretended madness. His love-letter is that of a potential wooer, yet real pity struggles with his revulsion and disgust in the nunnery-scene, and his protest at her graveside rings true, 'I loved Ophelia', though mingled with the rhodomontade of pretended madness (V, i, 261–91). Since the plot did not allow the dramatist to show the two together in a happier time, we are left with an unsolved puzzle.[48]

Jenkins dismisses all these doubts by arguing firmly for one of these alternatives: that Hamlet had genuinely loved Ophelia, but now sees her through the eyes of his disillusionment with his mother, and indeed – following what he regards as his mother's betrayal – with life itself. Jenkins's argument is persuasive, but so is Dover Wilson's totally contradictory argument in defence of a sane and rational Hamlet who suspects Ophelia's willingness, (or at least agreement) to act as Claudius's spy. Jenkins's reduction of the problem simply turns it into the problem of Hamlet's real or supposed madness – for to allow one's disillusionment with the world at large to turn into such a ferocious assault on the woman you love must surely be neurosis of a very high order. There have been (inevitably) critics who interpret Hamlet's disorder in such strongly pathological terms, but there are too many contradictory signs that Hamlet sees clearly a hawk from a handsaw to make this view entirely convincing, quite apart from the difficulty of explaining why Hamlet shares his sexual neurosis, apparently newly acquired, with the Ghost.[49] Jenkins has invoked one mystery in trying to solve another. All I am concerned with here, however, is to illustrate yet again my theme of the treacherous uncertainty of the *Hamlet* landscape. Ophelia, like the hero himself, appears out of the mists of an insufficient past, a 'real' and highly sympathetic girl whose love is mysteriously sacrificed to unknown gods. The dramatic effectiveness of Shakespeare's method is no more vividly illustrated than in the scene where the rejected girl sings in her madness of a sexual fulfilment that has been denied her for ever: there is no scene more full of pathos in the whole body of dramatic literature. But of course at the heart of the play's mystery is the hero himself.

One consequence of Shakespeare's decision to centre his play on the personality of the hero and to ask his audience to share his hero's thoughts and feelings is that it is difficult to separate critical from psychological judgements. The disagreement between Dover Wilson and Jenkins involves such a crossing of wires. Dover Wilson's explanation of Hamlet's treatment of Ophelia appeals to literary criteria: the logic of the plot requires Ophelia to act treacherously towards Hamlet in obedience to her father, and

Hamlet's outrage towards her follows logically from his suspicion of this treachery. Jenkins, on the other hand, evolves his interpretation in terms of Hamlet's state of mind and appeals to our experience of the way human minds work to explain how the hero comes to behave so illogically at this point. Jenkins's response is eloquent witness to Shakespeare's success in making Hamlet come alive, as indeed are all those attempts to psychoanalyse the Prince, culminating in Ernest Jones's Freudian analysis in *Hamlet and Oedipus* (1949). But just as these psychological analyses founder on the simple fact that Hamlet is not a person but a dramatic character,[50] so equally, but for a different reason, do those attempts that appeal to purely literary criteria. These fail to convince because of the text's ambiguities. Dover Wilson's case, for instance, rests on the doubtful assumption that Hamlet overhears Polonius and Claudius instructing Ophelia to spy on him. The text gives no warrant for that assumption and an emendation of the stage directions of both Q2 and F is needed to allow it. Eleanor Prosser, in her stimulating book, *Hamlet and Revenge* (2nd edn, 1971), appeals to Senecan convention to explain Hamlet's conduct in the 'nunnery' scene. Hamlet is tempted into irrational rage by the Ghost's demand for revenge, his treatment of Ophelia illustrates the well-attested Elizabethan theme that revenge is a form of madness. Again this is a persuasive argument, especially when presented with such impressive documentation as Prosser musters, but it presupposes an objective standpoint which Shakespeare steadfastly refuses to give us.

It is crucial to Prosser's argument that the Ghost is seen as evil. Hamlet himself considers this possibility in his soliloquy at the end of Act 2:

> The spirit that I have seen
> May be a devil, and the devil hath power
> T'assume a pleasing shape, yea, and perhaps,
> Out of my weakness and my melancholy,
> As he is very potent with such spirits,
> Abuses me to damn me.

> (II, ii, 594–9)

Hamlet's test of the Ghost's truthfulness, however, is usually taken to dispel that doubt, and the proof that 'it is an honest ghost' (I, v, 144) is usually assumed to mean both that Hamlet accepts the justice of the demand for revenge and that we too, in the audience, are expected to accept the justice of Hamlet's cause. There is, however, as Prosser points out, no necessary connection between the Ghost's honesty in telling the truth and the rightness of the revenge. Every member of Shakespeare's audience would know that 'the devil can cite Scripture for his purpose'[51] and that 'oftentimes, to win us to our harm,/The instruments of Darkness tell us truths'.[52] Prosser produces a considerable amount of evidence to show that the Ghost would be considered evil by an Elizabethan audience. Its fading with the crowing of the cock, for instance, explicitly identifies it with the world of the evil and un-Christian:

> Some say that ever 'gainst that season comes
> Wherein our Saviour's birth is celebrated,
> This bird of dawning singeth all night long;
> And then, they say, no spirit dare stir abroad,
> The nights are wholesome, then no planets strike,
> No fairy takes, nor witch hath power to charm,
> So hallow'd and so gracious is that time.
>
> (I, i, 163–9)

It is not only that here Marcellus clearly implies that the Ghost is evil but that Shakespeare introduces to the language of the play a rare glimpse of that benign lyricism which the action and the hero's torment generally precludes, until it is briefly heard again at the end of the play in Horatio's few words over the body of his friend. If the signs are so clear then, why do we resist them and agree readily enough with Bradley that 'Hamlet. . . habitually assumes, without any questioning that he aught to avenge his father'?[53] The reason seems to be that Shakespeare asks us to interpret the Ghost's instructions not objectively, not as data to be measured against Hamlet's state of mind, but through Hamlet's eyes. For Hamlet never comes to the conclusion that the Ghost is evil, even though he scouts the possibility that it might be. The soliloquy 'O what a rogue and peasant slave am I' (II, ii, 544ff) seems rather to imply a connection between the Ghost's veracity and the justice of the revenge (594–600). The signs are not clear to Hamlet; the Ghost 'may be' the devil, the call to revenge may come from heaven or hell, or both. Hamlet is never allowed to decide, nor is the play; a word from Horatio on the illogicality of Hamlet's assumption would have saved much agonizing (as Prosser ruefully notes),[54] but Shakespeare is careful to see that such clarification never comes. Even towards the end of the play Hamlet can consider, in conversation with his philosophical friend, that he has a moral right to avenge his father:

> is't not perfect conscience
> To quit him with this arm? And is't not to be damn'd
> To let this canker of our nature come
> In further evil?
>
> (V, ii, 67–70)

It is interesting that the two texts (Q2 and F) differ markedly at this point, the speech in Q2 ending with the question 'is't not perfect conscience?' The effect in the quarto is to suggest greater uncertainty and incoherence, as if Hamlet is trying to persuade himself, whereas the folio text, by spelling out what his conscience requires him to do, makes it seem as if Hamlet is bringing an internal debate to a conclusion. The addition perhaps shows that the experience of performance surprised Shakespeare into seeing that he had created a more sympathetic hero than he had originally intended. It is always Hamlet's version that we are inclined to accept, with all its doubts and uncertainties, and to the scholarly Hamlet there is no certainty about the Ghost's status, only an impulse to obey it. Shakespeare leaves the matter open so that we can share the hero's moral confusion. The appeal to revenge convention only compounds the ambiguity, for we have seen in *Antonio's Revenge* the Senecan convention of the virtuous ghost. Once again Shakespeare uses the conventional expectations to puzzle rather than to enlighten. To what extent we tend to share Hamlet's viewpoint can be seen in Jenkins's discussion of the revenge motif. 'Those who maintain that the prompting is wholly diabolical and so to be resisted are confuted by the text', he argues.[55] On the contrary, the text (or rather texts), looked at closely, seem to justify Prosser's case that the Ghost is evil: it is Hamlet who resists this and he carries us with him, for the best evidence that the Ghost is not evil, apart from the negative evidence of Horatio's silence, stems from Hamlet's doubts.

It is because we cannot settle in our minds the reality of Hamlet's world that we cannot decide on the validity of his response to it. This gives rise to yet another uncertainty in the play, the question of Hamlet's 'madness'. Here again a literary and a psychological explanation confront each other. Senecan revenge tragedy frequently shows the hero afflicted by madness. Sometimes (as in the *Spanish Tragedy*) the madness is real enough, in other cases (as in *Antonio's Revenge*) the madness is assumed to protect the hero and deceive his enemies. It seems likely that the ur-*Hamlet* presented feigned madness, for the chronicle sources of the Hamlet story, Saxo-Grammaticus' *Historiae Danicae* and its French translation in Belleforest both show Amleth/Hamblet pretending to be mad. Shakespeare does something far more interesting, he blurs the distinction between reality and pretence so that we cannot decide exactly how much Hamlet is in control of his actions. We cannot, that is, make a critical judgement at all in terms of a precise character and the actor and producer are forced to create an arbitrary psychology from the text that might account for Hamlet's actions and opinions. It is characteristic of the play that Shakespeare gives us no clear indication of why Hamlet adopts his 'antic disposition'. In *Antonio's Revenge* it is a disguise to protect Antonio and it proves successful, for Piero fails to see through it. Its purpose of protecting the hero from the villain would seem to derive from the source material. Hamlet's feigned madness, on the other hand, simply draws attention to himself and arouses Claudius's suspicion. Failing to find any objective reason for his behaviour we are again forced to look inwards to Hamlet's state of mind.

Shakespeare's principal device for turning the action of the play inwards is the soliloquy. There are few Elizabethan tragedies that do not use the soliloquy, but the soliloquies given to Hamlet are of a different order, not only from that found generally in Elizabethan drama, but from those found in other Shakespeare plays. The usual function of Shakespearean soliloquy – which it shares with those of other Elizabethan dramatists – is to identify the place of the character speaking in the dramaturgical pattern. This pattern may be predominantly moral, as when Richard III identifies himself in his opening soliloquy as the evil genius of the play, or may be more directly related to the action of the play, as it is, for instance, in *Julius Caesar*, when Brutus meditates on the need to assassinate Caesar (II, i, 10–34), or it may be both equally, as when Macbeth debates the likely consequence of killing Duncan (I, vii, 1–28). From Macbeth's soliloquy we learn a lot about his state of mind, but even so, like the other examples I have cited, the primary function of the speech is to strengthen and clarify the framework of reference by which we learn to judge the nature of the action, the theme and the character. They are primarily interpretative devices. This is also true of the soliloquies of *Hamlet* other than those of Hamlet himself. Claudius's confession clarifies the issue of his guilt and his role as the villain in the revenge scheme, while Ophelia's soliloquy in the 'nunnery' scene is largely on Hamlet (though characteristically the information we obtain from it further confuses our response to the hero by presenting a picture of him that is difficult to reconcile with what we see of him).

Hamlet's major soliloquies not only occupy more stage time than those of any other Shakespearean hero, they singularly fail to clarify the issues that they touch upon. Without them (as Q1 witnesses in several instances) the action of the play is not greatly affected and though they reveal, in bewildering variety, Hamlet's rapid changes of mood and thought, they reveal little of his function as character within the dramatic framework of the play. Instead they take us into the very turmoil and confusion of his responses, which we are asked to share and re-enact to the point where (as we have seen) it is no longer possible to distinguish between the 'facts' of the play and Hamlet's view of them. In the first of these soliloquies 'O that this too too sullied flesh would melt' (I, ii, 129) it is true that Hamlet articulates the chief charge against his mother: her marriage to Claudius 'within a month' of his father's death and the incestuous nature of her relationship to her new husband. The speech does therefore have some informative function in establishing part of the motive for revenge, but its informative function is overridden by the strength of the emotion with which it is presented. Hamlet begins the speech, not with the facts, but by expressing a desire for suicide that is only checked by his consciousness that it is forbidden by Christian law. The feeling of overwhelming despair and of disgust with life dominates over the speech's functional purpose, as the language itself illustrates. For this is no coherent presentation of a dilemma, but the expression of the emotions created by that dilemma expressed in broken syntax, in sudden changes in direction, that suggest the mind in turmoil:

> That it should come to this!
> But two months dead – nay, not so much, not two –
> So excellent a king, that was to this
> Hyperion to a satyr. . .

(lines 137–40)

Other playwrights were capable of this kind of dramatic immediacy – we saw a contemporary example in Eleazar's soliloquy over the dead soldier, for Dekker had learnt more than a thing or two from Shakespeare. But in *Lust's Dominion* Eleazar's speech can be readily placed and interpreted within the thematic pattern of the play. Here, in *Hamlet*, this outburst of intense emotion takes place in a world where no clear pattern emerges. Even here, where some cogent reasons are given for the emotion expressed, there is (on critical contemplation) some unease at a disparity between the problem and the response (as T. S. Eliot noted of the play in general)[56] and so uncontrolled an outburst is even harder to square with such later evidence as Ophelia's description of the Prince as 'The glass of fashion and the mould of form' (III, i, 156). In the theatre we do not contemplate, we are caught up in the passion and made accomplices of it; it is only in retrospect that we find it difficult to explain precisely how the feeling arose.

The discrepancy between the apparent problem and the response is even more evident in the second long soliloquy: 'O, what a rogue and peasant slave am I' (II, ii, 553ff). Here again the speech serves some functional purpose, for it spells out Hamlet's intention of using the players to test the Ghost's veracity. But this functional purpose is strongly overlain by the emotional intensity with which Hamlet expresses his state of mind, and in particular his disgust at his own inaction. The players provide him first with a contrasting image of detachment, through which he can emphasize the intensity of his emotional involvement; the use of the players to further the plot appears very much like an afterthought. As in the first soliloquy the viewpoint is introspective, relating the outside world to the inner landscape of Hamlet's mind. It is hard to gauge the truth of his self-accusation that he has unreasonably delayed the revenge, an accusation that is first broached in this speech, though repeated later and urged by the Ghost, who in this, as in the sexual nausea, seems to function as Hamlet's *alter ego*. The whole debate about delay and whether in fact there is any[57] is yet further evidence of the uncertainty with which we account for Hamlet's feelings in terms of the play's action.

The third soliloquy: 'To be or not to be', the most famous of all the examples of this dramaturgical device, comes rapidly on the heels of the one just discussed. This speech, more than any other in the play, is almost wholly concerned with Hamlet's mental anguish. It has no bearing at all on

36

the action (or on the inaction come to that) and far from adding to our understanding of the hero's role in the scheme of things is itself extremely difficult to unravel. Yet even Q1, for all its concern with speed of action, retains much of the soliloquy, if in garbled form. For in the theatre, however we interpret what Hamlet says, the speech comes across with the utmost force as an expression of the agony of soul that afflicts him. It is also clear that this agony of soul originates not merely from the circumstances in which he finds himself, but from a philosophical consideration of the nature of being in relation both to this world and the next (if there is one). The exact nature of the metaphysical problem Hamlet confronts has been much debated; clearly Shakespeare is much more concerned to create a mood than to define philosophical problems. The mood is cogently defined earlier in the play during Hamlet's conversation with Guildernstern and Rosencrantz as one of disillusionment with the world:

> I have of late, but wherefore I know not, lost all my mirth, foregone all custom of exercises; and indeed it goes so heavily with my disposition that this goodly frame the earth seems to me a sterile promontory, this most excellent canopy the air, look you, this brave o'erhanging firmament, this majestical roof fretted with golden fire, why, it appeareth nothing to me but a foul and pestilent congregation of vapours. . .
>
> (II, ii, 295–303)

This (as we saw) is very much the mood out of which Marston was creating his new plays for his City audience. But where Marston relates his theme of the vanity of the world to a traditional Christian viewpoint, Shakespeare accounts for his hero's melancholy in terms of a psychological malaise. Characteristically Hamlet cannot explain his feelings in terms of his view of the world ('wherefore I know not'); instead he explains his viewpoint in terms of his feelings. The gravitational pull of feeling is so strong that fact is unable to escape from its field. This same emphasis dominates the soliloquy. In 'To be or not to be', the metaphysical speculation is not there to interpret the mood, the mood generates the intellectual speculation. Hence the soliloquy presents a series of alternatives between which it is impossible to decide: whether man's true identity exists in suffering or in action, whether death pre-empts this problem or transforms it, and if it transforms it, whether the transformation is for good or ill. Shakespeare is presenting Hamlet with Marston's premises about the vanity of the world as a psychological rather than a metaphysical problem. It is Hamlet's mood that exposes for a moment a philosophical void that converts the play's secularism into metaphysical statement. Because such speculation is the result of Hamlet's shifting feelings, neither the hero nor the play rest at this point. Hamlet ultimately comes to reject this vision of metaphysical uncertainty in favour of a trust in Providence, and Horatio finally accords the hero Christian consolation. Shakespeare was later to explore a metaphysic of emptiness both more objectively and more profoundly in the greatest of his plays, *King Lear*. In *Hamlet* such metaphysical speculation disturbs still further that confidence in an outer presence against which the inner world of Hamlet's mind can be measured and judged. It is interesting, however, that Hamlet's remark to Horatio: 'there are more things in heaven and earth than are dreamt of in your philosophy' (I, v, 175) is usually taken as a stricture on Horatio's limitations, rather than on Hamlet's.

The fourth, and last, of the major soliloquies: 'How all occasions do inform against me' is rather different in tone from the other three. It is more coherent and orderly in presentation and less introspective, although it rehearses again the earlier theme of his inability to act. The effect is rather that Hamlet is now trying to objectify the problem of his inaction:

> Now whether it be
> Bestial oblivion, or some craven scruple
> Of thinking too precisely on th'event –
> A thought which, quarter'd, hath but one part wisdom
> And ever three parts coward – I do not know
> Why yet I live to say this thing's to do,
> Sith I have cause, and will, and strength, and means
> To do't.
>
> (IV, iv, 39–46)

The puzzlement that exercises us too is still there, but some of the passion, the despair has gone out of it; compared to the frenzied, hysterical outbursts of the closet scene (III, iv) Hamlet's language is restrained, almost calm:

> How stand I then,
> That have a father kill'd, a mother stain'd,
> Excitements of my reason and my blood,
> And let all sleep. . .
>
> (IV, iv, 56–9)

The self-accusation is the same, but reason seems to be reclaiming the language from blood. 'That capability and godlike reason' Hamlet speaks of is now once again asserting itself, though it squares oddly with the thoughts of revenge to which Hamlet still feels himself wedded and the irrationality of the aims he praises in Fortinbras. The Marstonian nightmare of sin's dominion is receding. The folio discards this speech, but it serves the very useful function of preparing us for the marked change that will appear in the Prince when he returns after his long sea voyage, a return that will no longer require soliloquy to mediate between the inner world of Hamlet's mind and the mysterious, uncertain world with which it attempts to grapple.

When Hamlet returns to Denmark and the play at the beginning of Act V after a considerable gap in stage, as well as narrative, time, the dislocated man Hamlet has been so far now appears to be at one with himself, as Hamlet explains to Laertes:

> If Hamlet from himself be ta'en away,
> And when he's not himself does wrong Laertes,
> Then Hamlet does it not, Hamlet denies it.
> Who does it then? His madness.
>
> (V, ii, 230–3)

As soon as we see Hamlet again, in the graveyard scene, that same feeling of the everyday world that we had experienced intermittently in the first two acts, returns. The gap between Hamlet's inner life and the world in which he acts disappears, there are no more soliloquies because the imagination of the audience is no longer to be stretched intolerably and painfully between inner and outer worlds that do not match. The fifth act might almost be regarded as an 'answer' to Marston's Calvinism: the obsession with man's evil nature is itelf a blight that destroys man's trust in God's creation. It is only when trust in God's providence is reasserted that the sense of reality returns. Shakespeare is reasserting his habitual Christian optimism. But even at the end of the play, where a certain distancing between hero and audience is achieved, we find it impossible to review our shared experience dispassionately. We do not at the end simply see Hamlet as a young man (though even our estimate of his age introduces an uncertainty between our feelings about it and the apparent facts)[58] who has come to his senses, but rather as a man with whom we have shared a profoundly disturbing journey; some sort of 'bonding' has taken place between audience and hero that prevents the detachment required in learning from his example. The history of *Hamlet* criticism illustrates over and over again the difficulty (which Dr Johnson expresses) in reconciling a virtuous Prince with the viciousness of his actions. The variety of critical responses is largely the record of the varying ability of critics to escape the bond.

In *Hamlet* Shakespeare had pursued the drama of personality as far as his contemporaries would allow. The new dramaturgy fostered by Marston and rapidly followed by Jonson and others, pointed in the opposite direction. We are soon to hear of Jonson's complaints (only thinly disguising their Shakespearean targets) that the popular theatre lacks moral purpose; the framework of judgement is to be reconstructed, if in more sophisticated forms than in the past. Jacobean society could not provide the social democracy required for the flourishing of such individual liberties and it was inevitable that the Shakespearean experiment should be checked by the pervasive conformity. But Shakespeare had also, in *Hamlet*, run into dramaturgical problems in trying to develop the drama of personality from

39

conventions designed for other purposes: the assertion of moral precept by sensational means. As Chapman was later to put it: 'materiall instruction, elegant and sententious excitation to Vertue, and deflection from her contrary; [are] the soule, lims, and limits of an authenticall Tragedie'.[59] After *Hamlet* Shakespeare notably retreats from his exploration of personality and begins a series of experiments in response to the new directions the theatre was now taking. To some extent this was for Shakespeare a return to earlier ways, for his early work had evinced a central concern for action as the expression of moral pattern. There were times when the new fashions led him too far from his natural bent, and we shall see an example of this in the next play he wrote, *Troilus and Cressida*. But the effect of the new stimuli was largely beneficial, producing works where his supreme genius for characterization was to be subordinated to a pattern of complex moral or aesthetic statement.

2

PORTRAITS OF THE IRON AGE:
TROILUS AND CRESSIDA

Hamlet was probably followed in the same year by *Troilus and Cressida*. As for most of the Shakespeare canon the play cannot be precisely dated, but modern scholarly opinion is all but united in placing it as the next play after *Hamlet*. There are no clear echoes of the earlier play of the kind we find of *Julius Caesar* in *Hamlet* and of *Troilus and Cressida* in *All's Well that Ends Well*, though the Trojan war was running in Shakespeare's mind as he wrote Hamlet's first scene with the players (II, ii). The lack of clear echoes is not surprising, for *Troilus* shows a radical departure in dramaturgy that marks a distinct break between it and its predecessor. Nor is Shakespeare's choice of subject surprising for his purpose. There had been a small flurry of plays on the matter of Troy by the turn of the century. Henslowe's *Diary* records a new play of Troy in 1596 and then payment in April 1599 to Dekker and Chettle for the quaint-sounding *Troyeles and Creasse daye* and in May the same prolific authors were paid for a play entitled *Agamemnon*[1] (probably a sequel to the former). These plays do not survive, but Dekker's probably reflect a renewed interest in the story of the Trojan wars sparked off by the publication of George Chapman's *Seven Bookes of the Iliades* in 1598. This is certainly true of the only other Trojan play of the period to survive, Thomas Heywood's two-part play the *Iron Age*, which uses Chapman's translation as a source. The date of Heywood's play is a matter of some controversy, but its most recent editor, Arlene Weiner, gives cogent reasons for dating the first part of the *Iron Age* around 1600[2] and comes to the firm opinion that it was written before Shakespeare's *Troilus and Cressida*:

> I cannot say how much time elapsed between the writing of *Iron Age* and *The Second Part of the Iron Age*, but I believe in that time Heywood came to know Shakespeare's *Troilus and Cressida*.[3]

Weiner goes further in showing that several scenes of *Troilus* reveal the influence of Heywood's play.[4] Certainly the case for regarding the first part as of the same period as the *Age* plays with which it shares part of a title (*The Golden Age, The Silver Age, The Bronze Age*) looks very weak. *Iron Age,*

41

Part 1 is a chronicle history play, a genre characteristic of the 1590s and very popular through that decade, and its relationship to the early play *The Four Apprentices of London* is considerably closer than to those later mythological dramas. Even if it were as late as 1610 (that is, after the publication of Shakespeare's play, as is sometimes maintained) it would serve as a good example of the style of epic chronicle play Shakespeare himself wrote in the 1590s and can usefully illustrate the immense gap there is between Heywood's sober treatment of his material as history (Heywood asserts the 'gravity of the subject' in his address to Mr Thomas Hammon) and the quasi-parodic, satirical treatment we find in *Troilus and Cressida*. An earlier date for Part 1 of *Iron Age* would appear much more likely. Heywood's two plays would seem to fit into the pattern of reply and counter-reply so characteristic of the Elizabethan theatre. Both parts look like a reply to the Dekker and Chettle play for the Admiral's Men in 1600. The Rose, on the South Bank, had been going since 1587, and the somewhat old-fashioned epic, chronicle play might have been felt an appropriate reply to Dekker's presumably more sentimental play on Troilus and Cressida for the Admiral's Men a little earlier.[5] As Part 2 of Heywood's play shows not only the influence of *Troilus and Cressida*,[6] but even more clearly of *Hamlet* in a 'closet' scene between Clitemnestra and Orestes (V, iii) which reveals unmistakable echoes of *Hamlet* III, iv, it would seem reasonable to suppose that Part 2 followed soon after *Troilus,* but when *Hamlet* was still very much in playgoers' minds.

A further piece of evidence which Weiner adduces to support her view may be found in Shakespeare's own prologue to *Troilus*. It has often been remarked that the Prologue seems to be alluding to the 'war of the theatres' and in particular to the armed prologue of Jonson's *Poetaster*.[7] The topicality of the Prologue might explain why it does not appear in the 1609 quarto, by which time the allusions would be forgotten (the folio presumably resurrects it from the playhouse manuscript in preserving all the Shakespearean material). The reference to *Poetaster* is not the only topical allusion, for Shakespeare goes on to explain his own treatment of his material in terms that seem to imply a contrast with what his audience might expect. His prologue comes, he says:

> To tell you, fair beholders, that our play
> Leaps o'er the vaunt and firstlings of those broils,
> Beginning in the middle, starting thence away
> To what may be digested in a play.

This concern for classical structural decorum (the idea derives from Horace's *De Arte Poetica*)[8] is in marked contrast to the gothic freedom of the Prologue to *Henry V* written only three or four years before. Shakespeare is now allying himself with the neo-classical sentiments of the kind found (a little later) in the new Prologue Jonson wrote for *Everyman in his Humour* and touched on in the Prologue to *Volpone,* the address to the readers of *Sejanus* and elsewhere. Shakespeare's lines also imply a contrast with others' treatment of similar material, for he is not primarily concerned to draw attention to a change in his own dramaturgical allegiances. The only play that fits the bill is Heywood's. The Dekker and Chettle play on Troilus and Cressida and its sequel *Agamemnon* seem to be (from their titles) plays centring on particular episodes of the Trojan war, and this impression is confirmed if the plot summary that survives in manuscript is of the first part of Dekker's play.[9] Heywood's play, on the other hand, exactly fits Shakespeare's anti-type. It is a chronicle play that covers the whole history of the fall of Troy from the initial capture of Hesione by the Greeks to the deaths of Hector, Troilus and Achilles in the first part, promising in the epilogue a second part which, in the event, sweeps on to depict the fall of Troy, the return to Greece, the assassination of Agamemnon, the revenge of Orestes and the deaths of almost everyone.

Shakespeare's prologue, then, makes a break, not only with his own former practice, but with the erstwhile practice of the public theatres. This impression is equally justified in terms of the style and tone of the new play, which mark a considerable change from the humanistic realism of *Hamlet.* For there is a marked difference between the affective methods of the popular revenge tragedy and the 'alienating' techniques of *Troilus.* But before we seek to explain and account for this difference, we need to look at Heywood's *Iron Age* more closely to see there an example of the kind of play we might have expected a popular playwright to make out of the matter of Troy round about 1600. This is all the more interesting because Heywood's drama seems to have been outstandingly popular. Heywood is not usually given to boasting of his successes, but he is unequivocal in the address to the reader he wrote for the publication of the two parts in 1632, in claiming exceptional popularity for his plays:

> these were the Playes often (and not with the least applause,) Publickely Acted by two Companies, uppon one Stage at once, and have at sundry times thronged three severall Theaters, with numerous and mighty Auditories. . .[10]

This suggests not only popularity over a considerable number of years, but in both the large public and the 'private' theatres.[11] Such popularity makes Shakespeare's use of and reference to the play all the more plausible.

It is not difficult to appreciate why Heywood's two plays should have been so roaring a success. Both parts concentrate above all on action; plot dominates over both character and language, and that this was the intention is made clear in the Epilogue to Part 2 where Heywood makes Ulysses his spokesman:

> Accept me for the Authors Epilogue.
> If hee have beene too bloody, 'tis the Story;

Truth claimes excuse, and seekes no further glory,
Or if you thinke he hath done your patience wrong
(In teadious Sceanes) by keeping you so long,
Much matter in few words, hee bad me say
Are hard to expresse – that lengthned out his Play.[12].

Certainly Heywood does not exaggerate in claiming to be including 'much matter' in this second part, for it would be difficult to imagine cramming more action into the two hours' traffic of the stage. Equally justified is the claim to be conveying unvarnished truth for, as Weiner points out,[13] Heywood shows greater fidelity to his 'historical' sources than Shakespeare, as well as a greater preference for the classical versions of the events.

Part 1 of the *Iron Age* is a considerably better play than Part 2, though I do not agree that the two parts differ as markedly in kind as Weiner argues.[14] Both are essentially 'epic' theatre in their concentration on action above all else; but in Part 1 the handling of the plot is better paced and Heywood gives greater rhythmic variety to the plotting by inserting scenes where issues are debated. Heywood is less concerned than Shakespeare to debate the philosophical issues prompted by the action, and more concerned that what is debated should relate directly and immediately to the action. The play indeed opens with a scene in which the Trojans debate whether to resume hostilities with the Greeks, who have carried off Priam's sister, Hesione, as their captive. As in the Trojan debate scene in *Troilus and Cressida* (II, ii), Hector is against continuing a war for so slender a reason; but whereas Shakespeare has Hector arbitrarily change his mind in the middle of the debate (*T & C*, II, ii, 190–2) – an example of the dislocational moments that characterize the play – Heywood is careful to motivate Hector's change of heart in terms of the action. In the middle of the Trojan debate in *Iron Age* Antenor arrives from Greece to report further insults and Hector is understandably swayed into agreeing to an expedition to bring Hesione back. It is surely likely that Heywood's logical handling of the action should have preceded Shakespeare's illogicality, because the unexpectedness of Shakespeare's treatment gets part of its effect from an expectation of consequentiality: it is Heywood who asserts the convention that gives Shakespeare's unconventional treatment point. There is nothing equivalent to Shakespeare's subtleties and complexities of language in Heywood's play, where language is generally pared down to allow the action to be presented with the maximum of clarity. There are, however, moments where (as Weiner notes)[15] Heywood adopts a quasi-Marlovian grandeur for such special occasions as when Ajax declares his determination to see Troy destroyed (II, iii, 42ff).

There are many scenes of the *Iron Age* where the plot dictates the action, as for instance in the splendid scene where Ajax and Hector meet in single combat (II, v), a scene that seems to have been particularly successful with its audiences to judge from its being used to illustrate the title-page of the

1632 edition. Here, however, Heywood's concern to motivate his characters adequately is again in contrast with Shakespeare's treatment of the same incident. Ajax, in Heywood's play, has won the right to appear for the Greeks after they have all drawn lots. It is Achilles' failure to draw the right lot that accounts for his chagrin and consequent sulky withdrawal into his tent. In *Troilus and Cressida* on the other hand Achilles' behaviour is far less rationally accounted for, so that Thersites' railing seems to find justification in the irrationality of his target. We hear from Ulysses that Achilles is moping in his tent before Ulysses hits on the idea of rigging the ballot to ensure that Ajax becomes the Greek champion:

> with him Patroclus
> Upon a lazy bed the livelong day
> Breaks scurril jests,
> And with ridiculous and awkward action,
> Which, slanderer, he imitation calls,
> He pageants us.
>
> (*T & C* I, iii, 146–51)

Not only is the emphasis on arbitrariness and irrationality (the hint of an illicit relationship with Patroclus, gloated on by Thersites, is neither confirmed nor denied here), but Ulysses' own proposals for shaming Achilles out of his sulkiness smack equally of the squalid and illicit. We are in a world of uncertain and shifting values in which grown men behave like spoilt children, but with unchildlike capacities for doing mischief.

Heywood, on the other hand, accounts for the identical behaviour of Achilles in terms that keep his dignity essentially intact. We merely hear from Ajax, as he explains to Hector, why he, rather than Achilles, is representing the Greeks:

> Hee keepes his Tent
> In mournful passion that he mist the combate. . .
>
> (II, v, 37–8)

As Achilles and Ajax have quarrelled for the privilege of fighting Hector, Achilles' deep disappointment is perfectly understandable. In the next scene Achilles reappears to take his part in the festivities between the Greeks and Trojans after a truce has been agreed, Heywood, with admirable economy, giving Achilles one sour aside (III, i, 45–8) before he joins in the spirit of the festive occasion. In such circumstances the bitter comments of Thersites seem much more like the ravings of a knave than the expression of a general malaise, as those of Shakespeare's Thersites appear to be. Heywood is much readier to allow his characters to speak for themselves in their actions as well as in their words. Shakespeare manipulates his sources so that the events are presented through a distorting medium.

45

The feast that follows the encounter of Ajax and Hector in Heywood's play is a splendid example of how brilliantly Heywood achieves variety of pace and mood in his plays. Here words take over from the violent action of the combat. In place of the field of battle, in which all eyes (on stage as well as in the audience) are focused on the two combatants, we move to a scene of music and relaxation where the attention constantly shifts from one group to another. There is subtlety in the contrast too: on the field of battle, through all the violence of the physical action, Hector and Ajax have behaved with courtesy to one another – the heroic nature of their civilization vindicated. Now in the atmosphere of enjoyment and relaxation intrigues and rivalries blossom. Agamemnon grandly accepts Priam's welcome at the start of the feast as Hector arranges that Greek and Trojan shall alternate round the table, but the feeling of well-being is soon undercut. Achilles, struck by Hector's character, but still smarting from his unsuccessful drawing of lots, cannot forbear an aside: 'till hee set/Wee cannot rise'. Allusions are made to past controversies which Menelaus has difficulty in resisting:

> but that these our tongues
> Should be as well truce bound as our sharpe weapons,
> We could be bitter Paris: but have done.
>
> (III, i, 51–2)

In this way Heywood keeps before us the tensions that underlie the festivities. Achilles is suddenly drawn by the attractions of Priam's daughter, Polixina – an infatuation mentioned but not dramatically presented in *Troilus and Cressida*, but which in Heywood's play further helps to explain Achilles' reluctance to engage in battle later. Immediately Heywood switches our attention to a quite different matter: we hear Calchas, convinced by the prophecies of Troy's destruction, successfully attempting to persuade his daughter, Cressida, to leave Troy and Troilus, whose love affair has been briefly presented in a single earlier scene. Each of these sub-scenes is handled with both admirable clarity and admirable brevity and the juxtaposition can often produce brilliant dramatic effects. No sooner (for instance) has Cressida agreed to abandon Troilus, than we are taken into the middle of an argument in which Troilus' voice is heard quarrelling with Diomed, though ironically on a subject other than their real cause for rivalry in their relationship with Cressida. The quarrelling spreads from this centre until the whole table erupts in recrimination and anger, only quietened by the introduction of 'a lofty dance of sixteene Princes, halfe Troians, halfe Grecians' (III, i, 145, s.d.). The scene ends with a quarrel between the husband and lover of Helen, which is brought to a hostile end and a declaration of further enmity when Helen is asked to declare her preference and chooses Paris. There is little in the language of this scene to excite the reader, but its dramatic quality could hardly be bettered and makes the play's popularity on stage fully understandable. Nor does Heywood seem especially concerned to direct us towards a judgement of these events. Neither the outstanding and unfailing courtesy of Hector, nor Thersites' scurrility provides a springboard for a general interpretation of events; instead 'truth claims excuse'. Behind the drama we sense the professional reporter giving us as close a reflection of what might be supposed to have happened as his sources will allow.

Shakespeare's play is less concerned with what happened than with what to make of what happened. Against Shakespeare's habitual practice the author is intrusive in insisting, in the manner of Marston, on presenting his material with a jaundiced slant. Shakespeare adds to Heywood's epic material a detailed account of the love affair between Troilus and Cressida which he probably obtained from a source unused by Heywood, Chaucer's *Troilus and Criseyde*. The equal attention to be paid to the two great subjects of Renaissance poetry, love and war, has of itself dramaturgical implications: the boudoir is to be given equal importance to the battlefield. Oddly, the prologue to the play, found only in the folio version, does not mention Troilus and Cressida at all: it rehearses the subject of the play in epic terms, though brief mention is made of Paris' adulterous affair with Helen as the cause of the martial dispute between Greek and Trojan. This again suggests (as I argued earlier) that Shakespeare is inviting specific comparison with Heywood's play as covering similar material. The quarto version of the play, on the other hand (published in 1609), not only drops the prologue, but is given a title-page that (in its second version) highlights the love story: 'Excellently expressing the beginning of their loves, with the conceited wooing of Pandarus Prince of Licia' — as if the printer is concerned now to emphasize the differences between Shakespeare's play and its more popular rival. This version of the quarto also adds an epistle to the reader which is particularly concerned to emphasize the appeal of the play to a select audience:

> It deserves such a labour, as well as the best Commedy in Terence or Plautus. . .nor like this the lesse, for not being sullied, with the smoaky breath of the multitude.

This epistle is often interpreted as evidence that the play was never presented on the 'public' stage (i.e. at the Globe) at all. The writer of the epistle begins by telling us that we are being presented with 'a new play, never stal'd with the Stage, never clapper-clawd with the palmes of the vulgar, and yet passing full of the palme comicall'. These statements, however, are highly ambiguous. The expression 'breath of the multitude' might mean 'approval of the multitude' as it does elsewhere in Shakespeare.[16] Equally the highly obscure phrase 'never clapper-clawd with the palmes of the vulgar', which is often taken to mean 'that the play had never been performed publicly'[17] could as well mean: never approved by

47

public applause (where a pun on 'clapper-clawd' to suggest the play was never clapped on stage[18] would make more sense of the use of 'palmes' than can be made of the literal meaning of clapper-claw as 'to exchange blows, thrash, maul').[19] Again the assertion of the epistle that the play was 'never stal'd with the Stage' could as readily mean it was never on the stage long enough to become stale, as that it never appeared there. If (as I believe) the epistle is telling us that the play was unsuccessful when it was presented to the public (hence the epistle's stress on the play as caviare to the general) this would accord with other important evidence that the play was intended initially as a Globe play. First, the Stationers' Registry entry of February 1603 tells us that the play 'is acted by my lord Chamberlens Men', which strongly suggests a more-or-less current public presentation; second, the first version of the quarto title page of 1609 presents the play 'As it was acted by the Kings Majesties Servants at the Globe'. Finally, the play itself shows unmistakable signs of two different endings, which strongly suggest two different audiences. In the folio version Pandarus is given what looks like his curtain line at the end of Act V, scene iii, where Troilus sends him packing with the words 'Hence brother lackie; ignomie and shame/Pursue thy life, and live aye with thy name.' These words are then repeated at the end of Act V, scene x just before Pandarus speaks his epilogue. In the quarto version the lines appear only once, in the final scene. Almost all commentators are agreed that in one version the play was presented without the epilogue and that Troilus' lines in that version appeared only at the end of V, iii. This suggests a version in which Pandarus was less prominent and would therefore be closer to the prologue's 'argument' than to the quarto second title-page.

One explanation of the two versions of the ending is that they represent the difference between a 'public' and a 'private' showing of the play. Pandarus' epilogue, as was originally pointed out by Peter Alexander, would be peculiarly appropriate if addressed to a law-school audience. In particular Pandarus' reference to making his will 'some two months hence. . .here' is taken by Kenneth Palmer to suggest Pandarus is addressing a law-school audience at the Christmas festivities, when plays were often performed.[20] The unlikelihood of any Inns of Court being able to afford to commission the wealthy Chamberlain's Men and London's wealthiest playwright has been pointed out both by Alfred Harbage and T. W. Baldwin and strongly supported by Robert Kimbrough.[21] It is much more likely, on the evidence we have, that the play was written for the Globe in the normal run of events to add a Troy play to their repertoire, shrewdly combining Dekker's romantic with Heywood's martial interest, in answer to the rival companies the Admiral's Men and Worcester's, the latter of which had achieved an outstanding success with *Iron Age*. The adaptation of Shakespeare's play for a 'private' audience would make more sense as a salvaging operation after a 'public' flop. The most likely venue for this revival, in view of Shakespeare's relationship with Marston at this time, would be Paul's playhouse, which seems always to have had a sizeable number of law students in its audience, and whose plays (especially Middleton's) are often characterized by their legal allusions. One might, however, have expected some reference to a Paul's performance on the second title-page of the quarto, as the epistle claims highbrow status for the play and this omission may imply that it was transferred in its alternative form to a genuinely private stage such as that of a law school. The first title-page of the quarto would imply a further attempt to put the play on at the Globe after Shakespeare's company had become the King's Men in May 1603. The reason usually conjectured for the change of the quarto title-page is that the printer was correcting an error, but it is just as likely that it was thought wise, at the last minute and with parts of a sheet to spare,[22] not to remind the reader too conspicuously of the Globe failure.

Gary Taylor has recently argued that the 'private' version preceded the 'public' with the implication that the adaptation was for the Globe, not the other way round.[23] He bases his argument on a highly plausible claim that while the quarto derives from Shakespeare's 'foul papers', the folio text shows clear evidence of deriving from the quarto 'corrected' by reference to a prompt-book version. One can accept Taylor's general bibliographical argument without accepting all his conclusions. The dismissal of Pandarus at the end of V, iii, when Troilus is preoccupied with the battle, is far more in keeping with the action than having Pandarus appear without cause on the battlefield at the end and remain after Troilus has dismissed him – Troilus' 'hence', after all, suggests he's sending Pandarus away, not making his own final exit. It looks therefore as if the 'private' version, containing the epilogue, is an adaptation. There is no reason, however, why that revision should not have been made to the 'foul papers' that were used in setting up type for the quarto, indeed Shakespeare is more likely to have made his adaptations for another theatre from his own papers rather than from the Globe copy. Further, if the play had first been acted in 1602 at the Globe, there would by then have been a prompt-book version that reflected Shakespeare's original intention and that came to be used as copy for the folio text. Taylor argues that the epistle found in the quarto version must have been written soon after the first ('private') performance of the play because it refers to the play as 'new', but as we know from Henslowe's *Diary*[24] 'new' can mean revised, or it may mean simply (as Palmer hints)[25] newly 'escaped' (as the epistle has it) into print. Palmer provides some evidence for supposing that the epistle was added at the last minute by the printer to use up (with the new title page) a half sheet (sheet M) left over from a miscalculation in casting off.[26]

Perhaps we could conjecture an early history of the play something like this: Shakespeare wrote the play for his own company, the Chamberlain's

Men, to be played at the Globe in 1602, in a manner in part deriving from the satirical comedies of Marston at Paul's. As in *Hamlet*, Shakespeare attempts to combine popular and more sophisticated elements to attract as wide an audience as possible. The Globe audience, not being attuned to satire, reject the play and it is transferred after a while and with modifications made by Shakespeare to his original draft, to Paul's, or alternatively for a private performance of some kind. The modifications increase the satirical content. They include the abandoning of the Globe prologue that challenges comparison with Heywood's popular *Iron Age* at the Rose, both because it is beginning to lose its topical interest and because it is no longer an account of the revised play appropriate for an audience (and a boy cast) more attracted to the satire than to the heroics. The modifications also include a new, comic ending in which Pandarus speaks his mocking epilogue aimed directly at the strong lawyer contingent in the audience. The play was probably successful with this small, elite audience, because a further attempt, again unsuccessful, is made to revive the play at the Globe after March 1604 when the theatre is allowed to reopen under the new style of its company as 'the King's Men'. The revised version becomes the basis of the quarto edition of 1609, which contains an epistle to the reader describing the play as a comedy, appealing to a sophisticated readership and boasting of its failure to attract the vulgar. The initial title-page of the quarto, which describes the play as history, is changed in a second title page to emphasize the unheroic element of Pandarus' 'conceited wooing' to bring it into line with the epistle, also newly added, and to avoid too obvious a reference to the play's failure with the Globe audience. The epistle explicitly refers to the play as a comedy, and that is how it would have been presented to the Paul's audience by Paul's Boys' company, who specialized in comedy. When, in 1623, the folio version is published, the original Globe prompt-book is used as copy, but including the quarto revisions, and the play is placed among the tragedies, a reflection of how it was played at the Globe. In the folio version the original prologue is restored, as are the lines of the original ending at V, iii in spite of the retention of the comic epilogue. Presumably the folio editors, Heminges and Condell, were concerned, like most modern editors, to preserve all the Shakespearean material.

We know that during the squabble between Marston and Jonson that has now come to be dignified with the title 'war of the theatres', Shakespeare came to be associated with Marston's side of the argument, because in the university play the *Return from Parnassus*, Part 2, we are told that Shakespeare has become involved in the controversy over *Poetaster*:

> O that Ben Jonson is a pestilent fellow, he brought up Horace giving the Poets a pill, but our fellow Shakespeare hath given him a purge that made him beray his credit.[27].

As these lines are spoken by 'Will Kemp' we can assume the comment is intended to be highly partial, but it makes it clear that Shakespeare joined in, or was thought to have joined in, the controversy. I have already mentioned the reference to *Poetaster* in the Prologue to *Troilus and Cressida*, but there is nothing in the play itself that explains the reference to a Shakespearean purge of Jonson. It seems more likely that 'Kemp' here is referring to Shakespeare not as playwright, but as player (unless the anti-Puritan Sir Toby Belch is an affectionate take-off of the rare Ben Jonson), for around this time the Chamberlain's Men were staging Dekker's contribution to the quarrel, *Satiromastix*. Presumably Shakespeare was in the cast of this play and might well either have impersonated Jonson in the part of Horace or played the part of Tucca, who is the chief 'purger' of Horace in the play. *Satiromastix*, as we are told on the 1602 title-page, was 'presented publikely, by the Right Honourable, the Lord Chamberlaine his Servants; and privately, by the Children of Paules'. This suggests the two companies were working closely together at this time. If Dekker's play could make the transition one way, there is no reason why Shakespeare's could not have followed the same route in reverse. We actually have the two versions of Marston's *Malcontent* that similarly switched between Blackfriars and the Globe a year or two later. Paul's theatre was run by Marston in 1602. He was not only its chief playwright, but seems to have been responsible for its productions. The plays staged at Paul's were mostly comic satires, at which the boys were particularly adept and the satiric tone of *Troilus and Cressida*, especially with the addition of its epilogue, would make the play suitable for the Paul's repertoire. *Troilus* is the one play of Shakespeare that shows the unmistakable influence of Marston. Both playwrights, at the time of its writing, were under attack from Ben Jonson as comedians who do not 'put the snaffle in their mouths who crie we never punish vice in our interludes' (as Jonson was later to put it) and therefore had considerable identity of purpose, but no doubt Shakespeare also felt that to hold at least the fashionable part of his audience he needed to take account of Marston's current popularity.

Shakespeare's choice of subject is not in itself remarkable, not only because other public companies had staged plays about Troy, but because *Troilus and Cressida* reflects concerns that are central to Shakespeare's interest in history. The epic trilogy of the *Henry VI* plays has as its central theme the breakdown of order in a society where individualism is rife. The central theme of *Troilus and Cressida* both looks back at the social disintegration recorded in the *Henry VI* plays, and forward to *King Lear* in depicting a society in terminal decline. The general feeling that the world was in its dotage and would shortly be ended is common among Shakespeare's contemporaries. That the King himself shared the view is evident from the concluding lines of his dialogue *Daemonologie* of 1597:

Philomathes: . . . I pray God to purge this Cuntrie of these divellishe practises [of witchcraft]: for they were never so rife in these partes, as they are now.

Epistemon: I pray God that so be to. But the causes ar over manifest, that makes them to be so rife. For the greate wickednesse of the people on the one parte, procures this horrible defection, whereby God justlie punisheth sinne, by a greater iniquitie. And on the other part, the consummation of the worlde, and our deliverance drawing neare, makes Sathan to rage the more in his instruments, knowing his kingdome to be so neare an ende.

The robust Ben Jonson can be equally lugubrious when he contemplates the world in its dotage:

. . .and no wonder if the world, growing old, begin to be infirme: Old age it selfe is a disease.It is long since the sick world began to doate, and talke idly: Would she had but doated still; but her dotage is now broke forth into a madnesse, and become a meere phrency.

(*Discoveries*, lines 301–5)

Even Heywood, in spite of the greater respect for the heroic in his play, still describes the world of Homer as an age of iron, the last, degenerate age before the final dissolution of the world. It is characteristic of Shakespeare's humanism, however, that he associates such a collapse into disorder more readily with the pagan worlds of *Troilus* and *Lear* than with Christendom. The War of the Roses is brought to an end by 'God, and Saint George, Richmond, and Victory' (in that order) when the providential reign of the Tudors is established. Both *Lear* and *Troilus* in contrast end on notes of desolate uncertainty (whichever ending of either play we accept).

Shakespeare had plenty of justification in his source material for seeing the ancient world in this light. Discussions of the sources nearly always concentrate on the narrative material that Shakespeare found and used, but Shakespeare must have been at least as interested in his authors' interpretations of the stories. Chaucer's great palinode, which has Troilus looking down from heaven and meditating on the vanity of the world, would not have gone unremarked:

> And down from thennes faste he gan avyse
> This litel spot of erthe, that with the se
> Embraced is, and fully gan despise
> This wrecched world, and held al vanite
> To respect of the pleyn felicite
> That is in hevene above; and at the laste,
> Ther he was slayn, his lokying down he caste.

And in hymself he lough right at the wo
Of hem that wepten for his deth so faste;
And dampned al oure werk that foloweth so
The blynde lust, the which that may nat laste,
And sholden al oure herte on heven caste.[28]

Shakespeare leaves these Christian assumptions implicit in the play, but surely much of Troilus' divine laughter permeates the play's demonstration not only of the vanity of worldly hopes, but of the pettiness with which such hopes are pursued.

Similarly in Lydgate, Shakespeare would be encouraged to see these pagan events from a Christian perspective. Book two of Lydgate's *Troy Book* opens with a meditation on the instability of this life:

The envious ordre of Fortunas meving,
In worldly þing, fals and flekeryng,
Ne will not suffre us in þis present lyf
To lyve in reste with-oute werre or striffe;
For sche is blinde, fikel, and unstable,
And of her cours, fals and ful mutable.
Who sit hiȝest, sche can down hym enclyne
Whan he leest weneþ bring hym to ruyne,
With awaites that gladly ben sodeyne,
And with hir face þat partid is on tweyne
Schewen most hool, when sche is leste to triste. . .[29]

This passage provides a prologue to the main account of the Trojan war which (like Chaucer's poem) is written essentially as an illustration of the *vanitas* theme. Lydgate reverts, even more explicitly than Chaucer, at the end of his long poem, to the Christian implications of his story:

In þis boke he may ful wel beholde
Chaunge of Fortune, in hir cours mutable. . .
How al passeth and halt here no soiour,
Wastyng a-way as doth a somer flour,
Riche and pore, of every maner age:
For oure lyf here is but a pilgrymage,
Meynt with labour and with moche wo,
þat ȝif men wolde taken hede þer-to
And to-forn prudently adverte,
Litel Ioie þei shuld han in her herte
To sette her trust in any worldly þing;
For þer is nouþer prince, lord, nor kyng,
Be exaumple of Troye, like as ȝe may se,
þat in þis lif may have ful surete.

þerfore, to hym þat starf uppon þe rode,
Suffringe deth for oure alder goode,
Lyfte up ȝoure hertis and þinke on him among:
For be ȝe nevere so myȝti nor so strong,
Withoute hym al may nat availle. . .[30]

It was one of Marston's major innovations to revive the tradition in which this theme is seen as essentially comic. Troilus, looking down on his tragedy in Chaucer's poem, comes to see that it was not a tragedy at all, but a farce. Marston's Paul's plays, *Jack Drum's Entertainment* (1600) and *What You Will* (1601) are comic treatments of the *vanitas* theme. He had given quasi-tragic treatment to the same theme in *Antonio and Mellida* and its sequel *Antonio's Revenge*. Traditionally the foolishness of trusting in the things of this world had been the subject of scorn and ridicule; Marston, with the conservatism of the new generation, restored that mood in both his formal satires and in his plays. He also – and this was his most radical innovation – evolved a dislocatory stage technique that was the formal expression of the theme of man's absurd delight in the inconsequential. He had been prompted to this by the very nature of the company he managed, for the acting of Paul's choirboys lent itself much more readily to parody and comic disruption than to the solemnities of either tragedy or romance. We have already seen, in the previous chapter, how this technique works in *Antonio's Revenge*, but a glance at one of the comedies that London playgoers would have seen at Paul's around the time of *Troilus*'s first performance will help to reinforce the point.

Marston's *What You Will* shares its title, curiously, with Shakespeare's *Twelfth Night* (January 1601), which has as its subtitle *Or What You Will*. Shakespeare uses his title casually to reflect the light-hearted nature of his play. If, as seems likely, it was a performance commanded by Queen Elizabeth[31] the 'you' may be addressed to the Queen herself. Marston's title is used in a rather more studied way – the title is repeated several times within the play – to reflect the central theme of 'opinion', the relativity of values in a fallen world. Not that Marston's play is markedly solemn, indeed he goes out of his way in the Induction to characterize the play as 'a slight toy' (88–9) while Quadratus refers to it in the epilogue as 'a slight-writ play' (2093).

Marston's play is noticeably less concerned with plot and narrative sequence not merely than Shakespeare's *Twelfth Night* (the last of Shakespeare's old-style romantic comedies) but than the dramaturgical methods evolved for the popular stage. There is a plot (derived indirectly from Plautus' *Amphitryo*) but this occupies only about half the play's stage time, which is otherwise concerned with a number of lightly satiric sketches, mostly built around the 'humours' characters of Lampatho Doria, in whom Marston deliberately parodies himself, and Quadratus, who has sometimes, on rather slender evidence, been thought to be a skit on

Jonson. Some scenes, such as III, iii, where a group of page-boys compare their varying roles, and an earlier classroom scene, II, ii, bear no relation to the main action, though both these scenes contribute to the play's main theme. The theme that runs through the play, though lightly treated, none the less gives unity to the work and justifies its apparently casual method. In the 'Amphitryo' plot the theme centres on the character of Albano, a merchant supposedly lost at sea, who returns to find his identity assumed by the perfumer Francisco. Francisco has assumed Albano's personality as a ruse to prevent Celia, the merchant's wife, from marrying again against the wishes of her brothers and he does so by the simple expedient of dressing up. A scene (III, i) where the assumption that the clothes make the man bears directly on the theme that the world constantly mistakes appearance for reality:

> I warrant you, give him but fair rich clothes,
> He can be ta'en, reputed anything.
> Apparel's grown a god, and goes more neat;
> Makes men of rags, which straight he bears aloft,
> Like patch'd-up scarecrows to affright the rout
> Of the idolatrous vulgar, that worship images,
> Stand aw'd and bare-scalp'd at the gloss of silks. . .
> (III, i, 937–43)[32]

That it is not just the 'idolatrous vulgar' that mistake appearance for reality becomes clear when the returned Albano tries to re-establish his identity. Albano fails to convince anybody (including his wife) that he is not the disguised Francisco. Ironically enough, one of the reasons Francisco has been persuaded to impersonate Albano is that Albano was readily defined by his clothes, as one of Celia's suitors recalls:

> O I shall ne'er forget how he went cloth'd,
> He would maintain't a base ill-used fashion
> To bind a merchant to the sullen habit
> Of precise black. . .
> (I, i, 281–4)

In this world of animated clothes, Albano comes to believe that identity consists in 'opinion', literally the view that others have of us:

> Doth not opinion stamp the current pass
> Of each man's value, virtue, quality?
> Had I engross'd the choice commodities
> Of Heaven's traffic, yet reputed vile,
> I am a rascal. . .
> (III, iii, 1247–51)

If this has a familiar ring we have only to turn to *Troilus* to see why:

> What's aught but as 'tis valued?. . .
> I take today a wife, and my election
> Is led on in the conduct of my will:
> My will enkindled by my eyes and ears,
> Two traded pilots 'twixt the dangerous shores
> Of will and judgement. . .
> *(T & C* II, ii, 53, 62–6)

For Troilus the world about us is constituted by what you will. Neither Troilus nor the disorientated Albano have the last word in their respective plays, but the problem of shifting values in an unstable world is a central preoccupation of both of them. *Troilus and Cressida* too has as a central image the dominance of clothes as an image of man's mutability, as when Troilus continues his argument that we must stick to the opinions we are committed to by an analogy with buying soiled silks (II, ii, 70) and Thersites sums up 'opinion' as a leather jerkin that may be worn on both sides (III, ii, 264–5). In Shakespeare's play the imagery of clothes becomes part of the action when Hector takes off his armour during battle to contemplate the rich trappings of the soldier he has just slain:

> Most putrefied core, so fair without,
> Thy goodly armour thus hath cost thy life.
> (V, viii, 1–2)

Palmer rightly invokes the gospels here (Matthew 23: 27), but the ultimate irony is that Hector himself loses his life at this very moment. Like Spenser's Red Cross Knight, he has been distracted by earthly shows into taking off the armour of his righteousness.[33]

Marston broadens his theme of the confusion between appearance and reality by having his surrogate 'Don Kinsayder' Lampatho Doria meditate on the theme of the vanity of human knowledge. 'Kinsayder' (i.e. gelder, 'mar-stone') had been Marston's adopted pseudonym in the formal satires that he had published earlier and he has this deliberately recalled in having Quadratus address Lampatho with the name (II, i, 531). Lampatho, however, is no firm authorial guide (unlike earlier surrogate figures like Chrisogonus in *Histriomastix*). As he himself explains, he has abandoned all trust in human ability to distinguish truth from falsehood. In a delightful account of his studies he tells us that at the end of it all he knew no more than his spaniel:

> philosophers
> Stood banding factions all so strongly propp'd,
> I stagger'd, knew not which was firmer part,
> But thought, quoted, read, observ'd and pried,

> Stuff'd noting-books; and still my spaniel slept.
> At length he wak'd and yawn'd, and by yon sky,
> For aught I know he knew as much as I.
>
> (II, ii, 866–72)

and he concludes:

> but now soft and slow,
> I know I know naught but I naught do know.
>
> (II, ii, 883–4)

The play's dramaturgical method is devised as a formal expression of this pyrrhonism. That Lampatho's (and Marston's) scepticism derives from Christian traditions of the vanity of earthly aspirations is made clear by Lampatho's earlier assertion of man's innate vileness:

> In Heaven's handiwork there's naught,
> None more vile, accursed, reprobate to bliss
> Than man, and 'mong men a scholar most.
>
> (II, ii, 821–3)

The phrase 'reprobate to bliss' has the ring of Calvinistic pessimism, while the attack on scholars sounds like a continuation of the infighting with the scholarly Jonson.

The relevance of Marston's exploration of Christian scepticism to *Troilus and Cressida* has already been suggested, but whereas Marston's play is designed as an expression of scepticism Shakespeare's play resists it. True the general picture we get of the world of *Troilus and Cressida* suggests a society vainly preoccupied with self-interest, with the ephemeral, but it also provides us with a critique of this relativism. Not only does the search for self-interest and self-gratification lead to disaster, most obviously in Troilus' loss of Cressida, but equally in the deaths of Patroclus and Hector and the prophesies of gloom that foresee the dissolution of Troy:

> The end crowns all;
> And that old common arbitrator, Time,
> Will one day end it.
>
> (IV, v, 223–5)

If time must have a stop it is because eternity succeeds it and the glimpse of the order that will then reign is given within the play, both in the Greek and Trojan camps. Among the Trojans the presence of order is felt above all in Hector's realism and his valiant courtesy, though like everything else in the fallen world of the play, it is a flawed virtue. Among the Greeks, Ulysses' noble appeal for order in society as an expression of a universal order, goes largely ignored and has been thought to be undercut by Ulysses' own behaviour, but it is a dull auditor who does not hear in it the cosmic harmony on which the Elizabethan rested his faith in a meaningful universe:

> The heavens themselves, the planets, and this centre
> Observe degree, priority, and place,
> Insisture, course, proportion, season, form,
> Office, and custom, in all line of order.
> And therefore is the glorious planet Sol
> In noble eminence enthron'd and spher'd
> Amidst the other; whose med'cinable eye
> Corrects the influence of evil planets,
> And posts like the commandment of a king,
> Sans check, to good and bad.
>
> (I, iii, 85–94)

In this spotty world such orderliness is only glimpsed at and striven for – so not surprisingly Ulysses himself fails to embody his own aspiration – but the power of the vision itself is unmistakable:

> Take but degree away, untune that string,
> And hark what discord follows. Each thing melts
> In mere oppugnancy; the bounded waters
> Should lift their bossoms higher than the shores,
> And make a sop of all this solid globe;
> Strength should be lord of imbecility,
> And the rude son should strike his father dead;
> Force should be right – or rather, right and wrong,
> Between whose endless jar justice resides,
> Should lose their names, and so should justice too.
> Then everything includes itself in power,
> Power into will, will into appetite,
> And appetite, an universal wolf,
> So doubly seconded with will and power,
> Must make perforce an universal prey,
> And last eat up himself.
>
> (I, iii, 109–24)

This is the play's principal riposte to Troilus' wilfulness. There is no fundamental disagreement in the two plays about the ultimate triumph of order, but the emphasis is very different: in the world of Marston's play, the eternal world only makes itself felt by its absence: it is the measure by which the chaotic, and so comic, world of appearances is silently to be judged. In Shakespeare's play the presence of this harmony is felt within the play itself. Compared to Heywood's play we are in a slippery world indeed, but compared to *What You Will* Shakespeare's older, more catholic faith in mankind's ability to reflect the divine orderliness shines out (if fleetingly) through the chaos.

As in the treatment of his theme, so in his dramatic methods Shakespeare in *Troilus and Cressida* reflects something of a compromise between old and new. The adoption of Marstonian methods, however, is more remarkable than the reflection of Marston's themes, because it signals a radical departure from Shakespeare's previous usages. We saw in the discussion of *Antonio's Revenge* in the previous chapter how Marston's dramatic technique emphasizes the artificiality of the stage. In contrast to Shakespeare's customary method of stimulating the audience's imagination into creating a sense of reality from the stage's creaky machinery, using the stage as a symbol of life, Marston goes out of his way to remind us we are in a theatre being entertained for a couple hours or so by a troupe of boys. Two of the scenes of *What You Will*, the conference of page boys where the roles of the different kinds of page-boys are discussed (III, iii) and the school scene (II, ii), give the boy actors boy roles to remind the audience at strategic intervals that all the characters are boys playing at being men and women. The 'theatrical' quality of the boy actors is also exploited by the inclusion of song and dance. Another function of these scenes is to break up the narrative so that we never settle long into a sense of sequential relationships – much, indeed, of the dialogue concerned with the two most prominent characters of the play, Lampatho Doria and Quadratus, is irrelevant to the main plot narrative of Albanus' return from being 'drowned'.

The dialogue within scenes, too, is often designed to suggest discontinuity. Half of Act IV, for instance, is taken up with a game of shuttlecock between Albano's wife Celia and her sister Meletza (neither of whom have appeared in the play up to this point). The game is (inevitably) lightly allegorized by Meletza as an image of her attitude to her suitors:

> Purr! just thus do I use my servants: I strive to catch them in my racket, and no sooner caught but I toss them away. If he fly well and have good feathers I play with them till he be down, and then my maid serves him to me again; if a slug and weak-wing'd, if he be down there let him lie.
>
> (IV, i, 1461–6)

Marston had clearly learnt much from Shakespearean comedy, but such inconsequentiality is nearly always in Shakespeare related sooner or later to consistency of character or narrative or usually both. In *What You Will* the inconsequentiality is more fundamental, more disruptive. Meletza's wooing is neither developed from or into anything else in the play. While her catalogue of suitors recalls similar moments in Shakespeare (*Two Gentlemen*, I, ii, 1–33; *Merchant of Venice*, I, ii, 35–115) the use made out of these similar scenes highlights the fundamental difference in dramatic method. In *Two Gentlemen* Julia's relation to her preferred suitor, Proteus, is to be central to the play's concerns, as is Portia's preference for Bassanio in *Merchant of Venice*; both scenes contribute to creating consistent character portraits and to the development of plot. In *What You Will* Meletza appears only in this scene and at the end of the play and there shows mild interest in Lampatho Doria, whom she had not mentioned in her roll-call of suitors. The game of shuttlecock too is introduced as much as a way of breaking up dialogue as of providing an emblematic reading. The opening of the scene illustrates the way in which Marston's dialogue suggests discontinuity – characters going their own way regardless – rather than any meeting of minds:

> *Celia*: Faith sister, I long to play with a feather. Prithee Lucea, bring the shuttle-cock.
> *Meletza*: Out upon him, light-pated fantastic, he's like one of our gallants at –
> *Lyzabetta*: I wonder who thou speakst well of?
> *Meletza*: Why of myself, for by my troth I know none else will.
>
> (IV, i, 1395–1400)

Meletza's self-absorption reflects the attitude of a world where what you will is given prior importance (a little later she tells Celia that her true husband is 'her will', 1448). Each character is essentially in a world of her own, without any but the most superficial contact with others. It is characteristic of the play that we never learn to whom Meletza is referring here.

Such a treatment of dialogue and plot is also inevitably reflected in Marston's attitude to character. It is no accident that Marston is attracted in his choice of main plot by a story of mistaken identities. Francisco, the perfumer, 'becomes' Albano, the missing husband, so that Albano, the play's hero, ceases to exist in his own right; at the centre of the action there is a non-person:

> If Albano's name
> Were liable to sense, that I could taste or touch
> Or see, or feel it, it might 'tice belief;
> But since 'tis voice and air, come to the musk-cat, boy:
> Francisco, that's my name, 'tis right, ay, ay.
> What do you lack? what is't you lack? Right, that's my cry.
>
> (III, ii, 1259–64)

Here we are truly in a world of Derridean deconstruction. As everyone insists that Albano is really Francisco in disguise as Albano, he might as well become Francisco, seeing that there seems to be no way in which he can communicate his true state to others. Appearance has become everything, identity is a matter of dressing up, so that becoming Francisco (as those he meets tell him he is) is simply a question of assuming a role created for him by other people. The outside view and the inside view of personality are completely discontinuous. Suitably enough, one of the requirements of the particular role that Francisco has to play to become Albano is to assume a speech impediment by which the dialogue is yet further dislocated. It is interesting to contrast Albano's acceptance, albeit reluctant, of his loss of identity with that of Antipholus of Ephesus in a similar situation in Act IV, scene iv of Shakespeare's *Comedy of Errors*. Certain of his own identity, Antipholus staunchly maintains it against a world which, in the person of Pinch the schoolmaster, assumes he's possessed by the devil and has him bound and carried off. In this earlier Shakespearean drama individual identity is a basic premise, in Marston it is seen as a continuum of uncoordinated moments. You make what you will of them:

> I'll f-f-follow, though I st-st-st- stut, I'll stumble to the Duke in p-p-plain language. I pray you use my wife well: good faith she was a kind soul and an honest woman once, I was her husband and was call'd Albano before I was drown'd, but now after my resurrection I am I know not what. Indeed brothers, and indeed sisters, and indeed wife I am *what you will*.
>
> (IV, i, 1715–20)

Albano is not exactly passive in this situation, but yet he, conveniently for Marston's purposes, loses sight of the fact that finally emerges in the last act: he has a distinctive mark on his breast. It is this that makes his identity readily demonstrable to his wife (V, i, 2025–30). Contrast Albano's ironic use of the resurrection metaphor with Shakespeare's imagery of rebirth in *Comedy of Errors* where the establishing of the truth is made to seem the point of entry into a new and more stable world of reality (*C of E* V, i, 400–6). To Marston the final establishment of the truth is merely a necessary end-game of the comedy, an accident that happens to relieve Albano of the more absurd consequences of his isolation.

Lampatho Doria, ironically enough Marston's spokesman in the play, is given similar disjunctive treatment. He is the chief fool in a world of fools; in a land where the governing Duke 'scorns all plaints, makes jest of serious suit' (I, i, 369) and uses the petition presented to him by Celia's brothers to light his tobacco pipe. Lampatho's relation to Quadratus is that of licensed fool, as Quadratus explains:

> he dogs me and I give him scraps and pay for his ordinary, feed him; he liquors himself in the juice of my bounty, and when he hath suck'd up strength of spirit he squeezeth it in my own face: when I

61

have refin'd and sharp'd his wits with good food, he cuts my fingers, and breaks jests upon me. I bear them, and bate him. . .

(IV, i, 1507–13)

When he first appears he is presented, like his author, as a railing satirist, a 'Don Kinsayder', but that this is merely one of several roles becomes clear later. At one point he stops in mid-harangue to attack the very role of railer he's just assumed:

> This is your humour only in request,
> Forsooth to rail. . .
> Who cannot rail? My humour's chang'd 'tis clear.

(III, ii.1144–5, 1149)

Such sudden and unpredictable changes of attitude destroy any sense of coherent characterization, as they are intended to, for we are in a world of essential incoherence. We need not be surprised later, therefore, when we find Lampatho assuming the role of infatuated lover in a sudden conversion (IV, i, 1639–41). All this does not prevent Lampatho from uttering words of wisdom, for indeed it is only through fragmentary glimpses of the truth that we receive guidance. We have already heard Lampatho expressing his author's scepticism concerning human knowledge, but that does not stop him from standing 'as confident as Hercules' in pronouncing on man's foolishness in thinking himself able to 'disturb the sway of providence':

> As if we had free will in supernatural
> Effects, and that our love or hate
> Depended not on causes 'bove the reach
> Of human stature.

(III.ii.1116–19)

to which Quadratus replies: 'I think I shall not lend you forty shillings now' (III, ii, 1120). In this way pertinency and impertinency are incongruously juxtaposed. The effect is essentially comic, but it is a comedy that expresses a radically pessimistic view of this world coupled with hopes for the hereafter.

Troilus and Cressida, too, opens in comedy, with Pandarus teasing the love-sick Troilus by pretending that he is no longer willing to act as go-between. The contrast between the passionate, earnest lover and the (apparently) disillusioned, weary helper provides a classic example of that clash of viewpoints that is at the heart of the comic. The comedy is sustained on and off throughout the play, the comic tone varying across the whole range from sardonic satire to benevolent fellow-feeling. Both the surviving versions of the play end with a comic epilogue spoken by Pandarus, though the comedy now has a bitter flavour that was absent at the beginning. The structure of the play has the diffuseness of comedy, allowing none of that sustained concentration on feeling that is characteristic of Shakespearean tragedy. There are, it is true, moments of intense emotion, as there are often in Shakespeare's comedies, but these are always undercut by alternative perspectives. The opening scene provides just such a double viewpoint, undercutting the seriousness of Troilus' lovesickness as Pandarus mutters, as much to himself as to Troilus, of the ingratitude of lovers and his determination not to meddle any longer. This comic double focus is achieved in several scenes by the structural device of representing a double action simultaneously on stage. The most notable example of this is at the moment of Cressida's betrayal of her lover (V, ii). Here the audience is required to watch Cressida's flirtation with Diomedes as Troilus, brought to the spot by Ulysses, observes and comments on his own betrayal. This double action is further complicated by the presence of Thersites, who, detached from both groups, provides a cynical commentary. The effect of so complex a structural device is to make it impossible for the audience to identify themselves emotionally with any one level of the action. The sympathy felt for Troilus is tempered by the inevitable absurdity of his concealment and by the presence of Thersites interposing his reductive comments throughout the scene. The audience is not likely to approve entirely of Thersites' point of view; he is the licensed fool of the play, not the choric voice, but his intervention not only breaks into the rhetoric of Troilus' emotion, but inevitably reminds us of the seamy side of Troilus' relationship with Cressida. 'How the devil Luxury, with his fat rump and potato finger, tickles these together! Fry, lechery, fry' (V, ii, 55–7) might be applied as much to the intoxicated sensuality of Troilus' love for Cressida as to her current affair with Diomedes. This, then, is a kind of comedy, for it presents a multiplicity of interpretations of a single event, but it is a perplexing, disturbing use of the comic. True comedy demands that the perspectives have similar validity, that one version of the events is as good (or bad) as another; here however, sympathy must principally lie with Troilus. The effect of the other perspectives is rather to prevent our fully engaging with Troilus' viewpoint; the comic element succeeds in frustrating the emotional impact of the scene without, however, releasing the laughter that would allow us to stand off from the emotion altogether. Is this design or accident? Is Shakespeare here attempting to explore some curious dramatic territory between tragedy and comedy or has the method adopted led to the blurring of the intended effect?

Certainly the pattern repeats itself in the play. In an earlier encounter between Troilus and Cressida (III, ii) which one would expect, on the models of *Romeo and Juliet* and *Antony and Cleopatra*, to present the lovers in the full flower of their emotional involvement, Shakespeare oddly intrudes the voyeuristic silliness of Pandarus to debase the emotional exchange. The scene starts with Troilus in full emotional flight:

No, Pandarus. I stalk about her door
Like a strange soul upon the Stygian banks
Staying for waftage. O be thou my Charon,
And give me swift transportance to those fields
Where I may wallow in the lily beds
Propos'd for the deserver! O gentle Pandar,
From Cupid's shoulder pluck his painted wings
And fly with me to Cressid.

(III, ii, 7–14)

It is true that the imagery of the underworld here already carries some ambiguity, but this seems to be momentarily dispelled as Troilus flings himself unashamedly into the prospect of unalloyed sexual fulfilment:

I am giddy: expectation whirls me round.
Th'imaginary relish is so sweet
That it enchants my sense: what will it be
When that the wat'ry palate tastes indeed
Love's thrice-repured nectar? Death, I fear me,
Sounding destruction, or some joy too fine,
Too subtle-potent, tun'd too sharp in sweetness
For the capacity of my ruder powers.

(III, ii, 17–24)

The ecstacy carries the seeds of its own destruction; there is a feeling of hysteria about the lines that are making it all too plain that Troilus is heading for his proverbial disaster. The psychological subtlety of the portrait cannot be overstressed. Shakespeare not only manages to convey in these lines the excitement of sexual anticipation, but equally the fragility and volatility of the psychological state that generates it. Here the *Hamlet*-master is clearly at work, creating a real psychological presence for his actor to play with. As so often in the love plot we seem to be back among the personal entities of the *Hamlet* world. Troilus, Cressida, Pandarus are each individual characters with a life overflowing the plot in which they function. Pandarus especially, brilliantly developed from Chaucer's own splendid creation, has something (but not everything) of the stage presence of that earlier 'historical' figure Sir John Falstaff. Yet Shakespeare uses Pandarus in this scene for a primarily negative purpose: to destroy any chance of the love scene taking on the lyrical magic that only Shakespeare could achieve, when he wanted, with total conviction. The sheer absurdity of Pandarus' prosings on Cressida's coyness derives as much from Pandarus' manner as from our memory of the brazen Cressida we saw in the second scene of Act I. This mocking, frivolous tone is again resumed, after a brief interval of under forty lines, in which the lovers are allowed to express an unconventional conventional exchange on the inability of lovers to realize love's potential (which Cressida characteristically interprets in terms of sexual competence). The dialogue of the lovers is itself rich in ambiguities, but Pandarus reduces these to the crudest mechanical level:

> if my lord get a boy of you, you'll give him me. Be true to my lord:
> if he flinch, chide me for it.

(III, ii, 103–5)

For the rest of the scene Pandarus remains looking on – with the occasional voyeuristic comment – as the lovers manoeuvre each other towards the bed chamber. Yet here again the effect is not primarily that of comic detachment, but rather a feeling of a thwarted love relationship meeting impenetrable barriers to its development.

Such constant deflationary interventions, which require the audience to stand back from emotional involvement at moments of emotional crisis, are certainly not accidental to the play. The interweaving of the love affair of Troilus and Cressida with the heroic matter of the Trojan war has a similar deflationary effect on the main action, for unlike Falstaff, who remains largely intrusive to the serious action and therefore must ultimately be repudiated, Pandarus is the tutelary genius of the whole play, as the revised ending, with Pandarus speaking the epilogue, clearly acknowledges. Like the love plot, however, the heroic plot is given considerable emotional substance. Once again Shakesepeare creates a perfectly credible substantial world of personalities in conflict. Hector on the Trojan side and Ulysses on the Greek in particular are both impressive figures, for all the reservations the play requires us to make about them. Hector, in spite of his chivalric magnanimity and intellectual clarity, ends by being deceived by what the Bible describes as 'lust of the eyes', while Ulysses, the defender of order in the state, stoops to rig the ballot that chooses Ajax as the Greek champion. For it is not just the juxtaposition of the two plots that undermines our confidence in the values of the heroic world. Again in the main plot (if it is the main plot) the deflationary techniques are at work and again with similar effect: not totally destroying the heroic world in mockery and parody, but blocking the full emotional impact it would otherwise have.

Even without the presence of Thersites, whose primary function is to throw doubt on the values of the heroic world, Shakespeare's presentation of both Greek and Trojan remains highly ambiguous. There are moments when, as with the love plot, we are called on to admire these epic figures. Both the grand debates of the Greeks (I, iii) and of the Trojans (II, ii) are marked by high seriousness and impressive rhetoric, while such chivalric encounters as that between Hector and Ajax (IV, v) or Troilus' final dedication of himself to avenge the murdered Hector are impressively presented. Certainly these are not scenes that inspire laughter and derision. Thersites' constant reductive comments simply will not do as a sane commentary on the action, though they inevitably leave their traces on our response. And yet in the centre of the play Shakespeare presents us with a scene whose main purpose is to suggest the hollowness at the heart of the action. In the one scene in which the direct cause of the war – Paris' infatuation with Helen – is directly represented, Pandarus is brought in to the main plot to emphasize the void over which the whole action is constructed.

Unlike Heywood's serious treatment of Helen, Shakespeare presents her as a minor comic character. In the little we see of her she is presented as a feather-headed woman who would seem totally incapable of inspiring anything but tedium, except possibly in bed. The one scene in which she appears (III, i) illustrates Shakespeare's newly found dislocatory method. It is placed almost exactly in the centre of the play (in terms of lines) and central to the scene itself is a song sung by Pandarus on the pleasures of sexual intercourse. This placing is not accidental, for it reinforces Thersites' earlier assertion that 'all the argument is a whore and a cuckold' (II, iii, 74–5) – where 'argument' would apply as well to the play's plot as to the historical quarrel between Greeks and Trojans. Nothing could be more reductive than the lyric Shakespeare provides for Pandarus in response to Helen's request for a song: 'let thy song be of love'. Paris prompts Pandarus by providing the title: 'love, love, nothing but love' and the lyric centres on that Elizabethan 'nothing', the female genitalia, describing, blow by blow, the 'shaft' tickling the 'sore' and the ecstacy of the lovers in their act of dying together.[34] The last lines of the song reduce language to little more than the ejaculatory sounds of sexual orgasm:

> These lovers cry O ho, they die!
> Yet that which seems the wound to kill
> Doth turn O ho, to Ha, ha, he!
> So dying love lives still.
> O ho, a while, but Ha, ha, ha!
> O ho, groans out for Ha, ha, ha! – Heigh ho!
> (III, i, 116–21)

As both Paris and Troilus at this point have exchanged the wounds of the battlefield for the 'wound' of the bedchamber, such a reductive view of the heroic would seem not inappropriate. Love-making has not only taken the place of warfare, but love-making itself is reduced to copulation.

Emptying the language of intellectual content is the most extreme form of the breakdown of communication that is illustrated in other ways throughout the scene, which opens with some comic patter between Pandarus and a serving man, in which the servant deliberately misinterprets Pandarus' intended meanings:

Pandarus: You know me, do you not?
Servant: Faith, sir, superficially.
Pandarus: Friend, know me better: I am the Lord Pandarus.

Servant: I hope I shall know your honour better.
Pandarus: I do desire it.
Servant: You are in the state of grace?
Pandarus: Grace? Not so, friend: honour and lordship are my titles.

(III, i, 9–19)

This kind of misunderstanding is, of course, characteristic of clownish patter, but it is typical of this play that the religious terms the servant plays with are without serious religious content, mere counters in verbal play, and the fact that they are Christian terms adds a level of incongruity that again contributes towards destroying any sense of ultimate coherence. In earlier Shakespearean comedy such a passage would go unremarked. Here it adds to the feeling of unsettlement that meets us at every turn.

The entry of Helen and Paris introduces another kind of verbal hiatus as Helen insists on one subject while Paris is pursuing another. Helen wants Pandarus to sing for her amusement, while Pandarus is anxious to convey to Paris a message from Troilus:

Pandarus: I have business to my lord, dear queen. My lord, will you vouchsafe me a word?
Helen: Nay, this shall not hedge us out: we'll hear you sing, certainly.
Pandarus: Well, sweet queen, you are pleasant with me. – But marry, thus, my lord: my dear lord and most esteemed friend, your brother Troilus –
Helen: My Lord Pandarus, honey-sweet lord –
Pandarus: Go to, sweet queen, go to – commends himself most affectionately to you –
Helen: You shall not bob us out of our melody; if you do, our melancholy upon your head. . .

(III, i, 57–68)

Pandarus' constant reiteration of meaningless adjectives adds a sense of vacuity to the disrupted dialogue, so that the whole encounter seems to be designed to avoid communication rather than further it. Not only does Helen fail to find out what Pandarus and Paris are discussing, but the audience has only a hazy impression of the purport of Pandarus' message, the manner of which seems as urgent as the content is trivial – a request that Paris will excuse Troilus' absence from the King's table at supper, a request, incidentally, that has no significance for the later action. The song itself is, of course, a further dislocatory device.

Here again, however, the effect is not primarily comic, but once again of the failure of feeling to communicate itself. The love of Helen and Paris for one another is not seriously in question, in spite of Helen's only half-serious suspicion of a flirtation between Paris and Cressida (III, i, 99). Paris' defence of keeping Helen in the Trojan council chamber is both serious and impressive, as Hector acknowledges (II, ii, 164). It is not surprising that, faced with such tonal ambiguities, the early editors were uncertain how to characterize the play. The uncertainty accurately reflects the tonal ambiguity, that the play has something both of the emotional dignity and commitment of tragedy and the multiplicity of focus and detachment of comedy. Is this tonal ambiguity, which clearly exercised Shakespeare's contemporaries, part of Shakespeare's intention then, another appeal to the 'wiser sort', or is it accidental?

We can answer this question best, I think, by looking more closely at the way Shakespeare uses 'Marstonian' effects in the play. I have already suggested that the theme of the play that Shakespeare picks up from his sources in Chaucer and Lydgate is peculiarly Marstonian: the vanity of a world dedicated to worldly glory and worldly lusts. In taking up this Marstonian theme it is not surprising that Shakespeare also experiments with Marstonian techniques in presenting it, whether out of a sense of co-operation or competition with the younger dramatist. The most striking of these techniques is the use of deliberate inconsistencies in character – as we have seen in such examples as Lampatho Doria's *volte-faces* in *What You Will*. The purpose of these dislocations in Marston is to illustrate the essential incoherence of human nature and undermine our trust in our own impressions of things – both fundamental elements of the Marstonian viewpoint. Shakespeare contrives a series of similar character lacunae in *Troilus*, the most notable being Hector's sudden change of mind at the end of his argument in favour of sending Helen back to the Greeks. He ignores the consequences of his own logic and capitulates to the viewpoint of Paris and Troilus, which he'd earlier described as superficial and immature, worthy only of young men 'whom Aristotle thought/Unfit to hear moral philosophy' (II, ii, 167–8):

> thus to persist
> In doing wrong extenuates not wrong,
> But makes it much more heavy. Hector's opinion
> Is this in way of truth: yet ne'ertheless,
> My spritely brethren, I propend to you
> In resolution to keep Helen still
> For 'tis a cause that hath no mean dependence
> Upon our joint and several dignities.
>
> (II, ii, 187–94)

It is not simply as Palmer explains it in his note,[35] that Hector distinguishes between an absolute moral standard and the practical code of 'honour' (it is in any case a strange concept of honour that defines it in terms of untruth), more important is the manner in which Shakespeare highlights the inconsistency, drawing attention to it by presenting it so starkly. If it were an isolated case we might dismiss it as some kind of error in textual transmission, but this is merely one example of several such striking inconsistencies. Troilus, for example, announces in Act I that he is not prepared to fight for so inadequate a cause as the possession of Helen: 'I cannot fight upon this argument' (I, i, 92), yet by the end of the scene he goes off with Aeneas to battle and later he makes it a central plank in his argument during the Trojan debate that honour requires us (as with Fortinbras) 'greatly to find quarrel in a straw'. Hector's inconsistencies too, do not consist only in the strange *volte-face* during the Trojan debate. The very first time we hear about him we hear of behaviour that is inconsistent with the Hector we actually meet and indeed has no bearing on the later development of the action:

> He chid Andromache and struck his armourer,
> And like as there were husbandry in war,
> Before the sun rose he was harness'd light
> And to the field goes he, where every flower
> Did as a prophet weep what it foresaw
> In Hector's wrath.
>
> (I, ii, 6–10)

The speaker (Alexander) explains this behaviour in terms of Hector's rivalry with Ajax, but when Hector and Ajax meet eventually in single combat (IV, v) the encounter is marked by Hector's outstanding courtesy and forbearance, as Ajax acknowledges: 'Thou art too gentle and too free a man' (IV, v, 138). It is odd too that if Ajax's renown on the battlefield is such as to stir Hector's wrath in Act I, Ulysses can use as his main argument in trying to stir Achilles to action, that Ajax is unknown as a soldier and will be given the chance to make himself famous if Achilles fails to respond to Hector's challenge (III, iii, 123–32). The description given of Ajax in the earlier scene, whose 'folly [is] sauced with discretion' (I, ii, 19–31), is also considerably at variance with the 'dull brainless Ajax' Ulysses describes during the Greek debate (I, iii, 381). This initial description of Ajax, indeed, is so at variance with the character we later see that it has been argued that the portrait of the first scene is intended as an *ad hoc* description of Ben Jonson put in the play as the 'purge' Shakespeare was thought, by the author of the second *Return from Parnassus*, to have administered his rival.

These are merely some of the contradictions in the presentation of character throughout the play, and there are others. Cressida, for instance, tells us in her soliloquy at the end of I, ii that wise women delay granting their favours to raise their price:

> That she belov'd knows naught that knows not this:
> Men prize the thing ungained more than it is.
>
> (I, ii 293–4)

69

but of all Shakespeare's heroines she is the least ready to wait until the bride price is right. Cressida becomes a byword (as we are reminded in the play) for duplicity. Here she seems to be deceiving herself rather than her lover. The point in all these inconsistencies is surely the same: human nature knows no constancy, we are an incoherent mass of desires, failing to know ourselves in the process of trying to manipulate others, 'Cressida is and is not Cressida'. In this world we are defined by opinion, 'what's aught but as 'tis valued'. In Marston the logic of these hiatuses is clear enough; in Shakespeare's play, however, they appear rather as lapses in an essentially mimetic realism. Shakespeare has not been able or willing to follow the full logic of Marston's Christian pessimism because he does not share it. It is not only Ulysses who articulates a vision of an hierarchical order that can be aspired to, if it cannot be reached; the play itself, in the dignity it affords (if fleetingly) to the participants in the midst of the world's confusion and in its refusal to dissolve into sardonic laughter, resists the devaluing of human endeavour. Shakespeare is here caught between his habitual affirmation of 'this goodly frame the earth' and the Marstonian formal experiments born of his need — at this moment — to keep up with the Jonsons and the Marstons. For there are other Marstonian intrusions: the play abounds in neologisms and difficult words of the kind Marston (in the person of Crispinus) is forced to eructate in *Poetaster* (V, iii, 463ff). A selection of unusual words in *Troilus* might include: 'unplausive', 'assubjugate', 'propugnation', 'violenteth', 'rejoindure', 'embrasures', 'maculation', 'mirable', 'multipotent', 'impressure', 'recordation'. Shakespeare always has a liking for the rich and strange in words as part of his rhetoric of wonder, but in *Troilus and Cressida* they function unusually. As in Marston's earlier plays (*What You Will* is not conspicuous for their use) Shakespeare here uses them to draw attention to the medium itself, to effect a gap between thought and meaning that is a verbal analogy to the thematic exploration of the gap between appearance and a transcendent reality. Like the other Marstonian devices they serve to distance the audience from the stage events; they are a specifically theatrical device for reminding the audience it is watching a play. Other characteristic Marstonian devices that we've already noticed include the tendency for dialogue to aspire to the condition of concurrent monologue, and also the sharp contrasts in stylistic levels between speakers that we can see in the contrast between Pandarus' prose and Troilus' poetry in the opening scene, or the contrast between Troilus' fondness for abstraction and Cressida's sensual practicality in the love dialogue of III, ii. The general tendency of the play to engage in abstract debate, most noticeable in the two council scenes, is in itself a device of dramatic alienation related to Marston's predilection for intellectual debate in his plays.

Troilus and Cressida's apparent failure on the popular stage, then, and the evidence that Shakespeare's contemporaries were uncertain about the play's generic status are a legitimate audience-response to a play of uncertain intention. Courageously, at the height of his career as a professional dramatist that had given him an unparalleled reputation and earned him a considerable fortune, in response to new rivalries he decides to experiment in his rivals' manner on a fashionable theme to which the new techniques could readily be accommodated, the ultimate vanity of the world. But after more than a decade of evolving a drama of the most brilliant character realism he cannot sufficiently jettison the experience of half a working lifetime. Tempted by one of his few rivals in the creation of character to translate Geoffrey Chaucer's Pandar on to the stage – as earlier he was led to create Juliet's Nurse from the brilliant sketch in Arthur Brooke's poem – he cannot resist depicting Pandarus as a rounded personality, nor of breathing mimetic life into the lovers. He cannot resist the temptation because at a deeper level he cannot accept the Calvinistic grimness of the Marstonian world. For all the silliness depicted in the world of *Troilus*, for all its contradictoriness, its betrayals, the play keeps catching glimpses of that brave new world that reflects the glory of God's handiwork. The play ends as an uneasy compromise between Shakespeare's deepest convictions and the new dramaturgical techniques he has the courage to explore.

3

'THE WORD. . .WILL BRING ON SUMMER': *ALL'S WELL THAT ENDS WELL* AND CHAPMAN'S MYTHIC COMEDY

Troilus and Cressida had not succeeded in answering the question it was designed for: how to hold the attention of the 'wiser sort' without alienating the more solid citizens of London. In 1602–3 the question still needed answering, for there was no sign that the boys' companies were weakening; on the contrary they were attracting the best of the older playwrights as well as the most talented of the new. Middleton was making his appearance at Paul's around now, as was Webster in collaboration with Dekker, both of whom were gravitating upwards from Henslowe's stables; Marston (exclusively a boys' company playwright) was in the process of moving to Blackfriars, for which Jonson had written *Cynthia's Revels* and *Poetaster*. But the most notable transfer from the public theatres to the 'private' was Chapman's. It has long since been forgotten that Chapman was the only serious rival to Shakespeare as a popular playwright in the second half of the 1590s scoring success after success, as can be seen both from the title-pages and Henslowe's receipt book, where between 1594 and 1597 *Humorous Day's Mirth* beats all comers (except, marginally, *Dr Faustus*) in its earning power, with *Blind Beggar of Alexandria* not far behind.[1] Chapman's decision to switch allegiances is not surprising, for he was by temperament a scholarly man with a fanatical belief in art's high calling, and the more fashionable and better-educated audiences of the 'private' theatres must have been as congenial to him as they were to his friend Ben Jonson.

Chapman had begun his new career at Blackfriars around 1601 with a comedy not unlike the one he had been writing for the Fortune, and indeed the play he wrote to inaugurate that theatre, *All Fools*,[2] was later transferred to Blackfriars. *May Day*, probably the first play written for Blackfriars, continues the style of intrigue comedy based on classical or neo-classical sources. Chapman, however, was a restless artist, constantly experimenting in new directions, and his next play, *Sir Giles Goosecap*, marks a change of style that inaugurates an interesting series of quasi-romantic comedies just as the fashion for satiric City comedies was establishing itself. *Sir Giles Goosecap* (autumn 1601) is not in itself a very

72

good play, but it begins a development towards a kind of mythic comedy that culminates in his two finest comedies *Monsieur D'Olive* (1604?) and *Widow's Tears* (1605?). For these plays he had found in his Blackfriars audience a fit auditory for the profounder truths it was his life's work to enunciate.

Having failed in one direction it was inevitable that Shakespeare should look towards the new work of his long-standing rival. He would find in Chapman's new experiments something closer to his own comic spirit than the pessimistic laughter of Marston. In *Troilus and Cressida* he had tried his hand at satire, but it was clear that however popular it was with the audience of the little eyases, satire did not go down well at the Globe. When, sometime in 1604, John Webster adapted Marston's *Malcontent* (a Blackfriars play) for the Globe, he wrote an introductory scene one of the purposes of which is to assure the audience they are not going to be inflicted with satire:

> Why, sir, 'tis neither satire nor moral, but the mean passage of a history; yet there are a sort of discontented creatures that bear a stingless envy to great ones, and these will wrest the doings of any man to their base, malicious applyment. . .[3]

Chapman's *Sir Giles Goosecap* and even more the comedy that immediately followed it, *The Gentleman Usher* (1602), provide new models that combine the romantic idealism which Shakespeare had so successfully cultivated in his earlier comedies with a more clearly defined, more philosophically oriented mythic pattern that adds intellectual depth and seriousness to the romance. The combination in *Sir Giles Goosecap* is unintentionally ludicrous, as the scholar-lover Clarence muses his way to the love of his lady Eugenia (signifying 'nobility') by way of neo-platonic riddles on the relationship of body to soul. These scenes of high-minded philosophizing mix, this time with intentional incongruity, with scenes of humours comedy centred on the zany Sir Giles, whose portrait was apparently successful enough to have become a byword for stupidity by the time (in 1603) that Dekker was writing his pamphlet *The Wonderful Year*.[4] But *Sir Giles Goosecap*, for all its inadequacy as a comedy, is particularly interesting because it can be seen as a kind of response (whether intended as such or not) to Shakespeare's *Troilus*.

G. L. Kittredge was the first to point out[5] that the Momford–Eugenia–Clarence plot in the play was not only based on Chaucer's *Troilus and Cresseyde*, but echoes Chaucer's poem verbally from time to time. It is a strange re-interpretation of Chaucer's trio, with Momford a high-minded Pandar bringing together the even more high-minded lovers, whose chief attraction for one another is their fondness for scholarly pursuits. Of all the attempts to re-interpret the tale this is probably the only one where the lovers are both chaste (although Eugenia, like her original, is a widow) and apparently concerned to make their union permanent (there is no equivalent to Diomedes in Chapman's play). It is probably not a coincidence that Chapman attempts this drastic rewriting of the tale at about the same time as Shakespeare is having his sardonic portrait of the lovers staged at the Globe, especially when we consider that *Troilus and Cressida* is itself a kind of satirical 'answer' to Chapman's *Seven Books of the Iliad* (1598).

There seems to have been an obscure kind of running rivalry between the two poets that may go back to the period of Shakespeare's earlier sonnets, for of all the candidates for the role of rival poet alluded to in the sonnets, Chapman seems best to fit the bill.[6] There is good reason why the two should have seen each other as rivals. Chapman was the only major dramatist of Shakespeare's precise generation to survive into the Jacobean period (all the other major figures were considerably younger) and, as I have already said, Chapman's comedies provided the one serious source of competition to Shakespeare in the second half of the 1590s. Temperamentally too, the two men seem to have been poles apart: Shakespeare the player, the professional man of the theatre, whose comparatively humble origins seem to have been reflected in both the modesty of his literary aspirations and the tendency to admire rank unduly that occasionally peeps through. Chapman, on the other hand, was 'gentry' who despised the common taste. He saw himself essentially as a scholar and man of learning for whom the stage provided a means of livelihood when more acceptable forms of patronage failed or proved inadequate. Shakespeare's practical good sense led him to a fortune: Chapman's high-minded devotion to scholarship kept him in poverty. It is probably not coincidence, then, that led Shakespeare to choose for his principal experiment in satire the story of the siege of Troy, Homer's poetic treatment of which Chapman was for most of his life attempting to expound as the most noble of man's achievements. In particular Chapman sees in Achilles the essence of heroic nobility, while for Shakespeare he is a combination of playboy and bovver-boy. Similarly in the treatment of the Chaucerian sub-theme, Shakespeare gives us a complex picture of sensual inebriation in Troilus and sexual opportunism in Cressida, where Chapman depicts in his comedy pure love as understood in neo-platonic doctrine. Where Shakespeare combines war theme and love theme as a means of devaluing both, Chapman treats war theme and love theme not merely in separate works, but in the distinctly different genres of exalted epic and lowly stage comedy.

The glaring differences, however, conceal more important similarities. In the last chapter I expressed the opinion that in *Troilus and Cressida* Shakespeare was working against the grain. Neither he nor Chapman shared the fashionable pessimism of the new city dramatists. Chapman and Shakespeare were closer to Spenser, with his characteristic faith in the omnipresence of God that found its expression in the neo-platonic belief in a world of God's reality, hidden, to be sure, from profane eyes, but to be discovered behind the surface glitter of appearances by the virtuous-wise. Bassanio understands this and gets his reward, and it is Desdemona's tragedy that her virtue in preferring Othello's mind to his visage gets no reward. The natural mode of discourse for this viewpoint is the allegorical journey, the search for the world of reality that enables the discoverer to move to a higher plane of being. Spenser had constructed his epic on a series of such journeys and the pattern recurs – if unobtrusively – in Shakespeare's earlier work, whether the brave new world that is reached is political, social or moral, or a combination of these.

Chapman's new series of comedies for the Blackfriars theatre, from *Sir Giles Goosecap* to *Widows' Tears*, all follow the pattern of allegorical journey. Each play becomes a refinement on the last, both in terms of dramatic technique and in the subtlety with which the theme of discovery is handled. *Sir Giles Goosecap* is by far the crudest, though it sets the basic pattern for the comedies that follow. Like *Gentleman Usher* and *Monsieur D'Olive* it sets out to contrast the world of appearances – a comic world of fools and knaves – with the romantic world of those serious seekers after knowledge whose wisdom is finally affirmed and justified. The opposing worlds of foolishness and wisdom are represented by distinct plots in all three plays and in each case the title of the play derives from the principal fool in the sub-plot. The main plot is for the 'understanders' of the audience as opposed to the mere hearers. In each of the four plays a journey is involved for hero (or heroes) and heroine (or heroines) towards enlightenment (in both *Monsieur D'Olive* and *Widows' Tears* this becomes literally a journey from darkness to light), under the guidance of a mentor who in the last two comedies is associated with the iconic saviour figure Hercules. In *Sir Giles Goosecap* Momford (the unlikely avatar of Pandarus) serves this function, guiding the young lovers towards a spiritual union that frees Eugenia from her frivolous companions and Clarence from his scholarly melancholy. This melancholy causes him to misunderstand the nature of love, which he interprets as a distraction from scholarship rather than a liberating spiritual force (III, ii, 39ff). One problem with the play, however, is that it is sometimes difficult to be sure how seriously we are meant to take this voyage towards spiritual discovery. Chapman is so keen to present Clarence as a learned man ('learning' having a particular force in Chapman's philosophy as a means for discovering the hidden 'reality') that a good deal of what he stands for is obscured by pedantry and intellectual pretentiousness. In Act IV, scene iii, for instance, Eugenia whitens her face so that she will not appear too distractingly beautiful to her lover. This anticipates the more drastic self-mutilation that Margaret undergoes in *Gentleman Usher* as a test of the lover's ability to see reality beneath the mere appearance of things. In *Gentleman Usher* this is a convincing test of Vincentio's love, in passing which he achieves the reward of Margaret's unexpected cure. In *Sir Giles Goosecap* Chapman is still sufficiently wedded to a naturalistic dramaturgy that he largely abandons in *Gentleman Usher*, to provide us with only a token mutilation which considerably weakens the force of the hero's response. Clarence's response is, in the event, confusing, for he launches into a paradoxical defence of face-painting (a subject that usually stimulates the kind of moral indignation Hamlet imbues it with) as an example of the triumph of art over nature. When Momford (acting the fall-guy here) suggests that the best authorities condemn it, alluding in particular to Daniel's attack on make-up in the *Complaint of Rosamond*,[7] Clarence flippantly says that Daniel was only trying to find a satisfactory rhyme (IV, iii, 60), but then launches into what appears to be a serious neo-platonic argument on the inner meaning of outer forms:

> For lightness comes from hearts, and not from looks;
> And if inchastity possess the heart,
> Not painting doth not race it, nor, being clear,
> Doth painting spot it:
> *Omne bonum naturaliter pulchrum.*
> For outward fairness bears the divine form,
> And moves beholders to the act of love,
> And that which moves to love is to be wish'd,
> And each thing simply to be wish'd is good.
> So I conclude mere painting of the face
> A lawful and a commendable grace.
>
> (IV, iii, 62–72)[8]

Not surprisingly Momford regards this as paradoxical, and it would certainly be difficult to know how seriously to take such pedantic posing without the much surer achievement of *Gentleman Usher* to guide us. All four plays need to be read together and in one important instance *Sir Giles Goosecap* throws light on the finest of these comedies, *Widows' Tears*, for Momford's advice to Clarence that boldness is the only guarantee of success in love, 'spirits wrastling with spirits, as bodies with bodies' (I, iv, 135–6), helps to explain the puzzling role of Tharsalio ('boldness') in the later play. The spirit of love is a dynamic force, as Botticelli shows it in his neo-platonic 'Allegory of the Seasons' – the so-called 'Primavera' – in depicting the wind god Zephirus inspiring the world with the dynamic of love and as Spenser shows at the hub of the world's generational processes in the Garden of Adonis.[9]

In *Gentleman Usher* Chapman decides to abandon the naturalistic dramaturgy that is otherwise observed in this mythic series. This leads to greater clarity of purpose and also allows Chapman to introduce a supernatural element into his theme, but it also makes the theme more remote from common experience and to that extent less vivid and plausible. In *Monsieur D'Olive* and *Widows' Tears* Chapman manages to combine a consistent and unequivocal exposition of his theme with a vivid sense of actuality, which makes these two plays outstanding contributions to the drama of the period. We are principally concerned here, however, with the two earlier plays because it is *Sir Giles Goosecap* and *Gentleman Usher*, especially the latter, which seem to have precipitated Shakespeare's next experiment in *All's Well that Ends Well*. It has to be admitted that the chronology of the three plays is somewhat uncertain. *Sir Giles Goosecap* is the easiest to date. The title-page of the first quarto, 1606 (published without Chapman's name on it) tells us that the comedy was 'presented by the children of the Chapell', which tells us that it must have been played between the opening of Blackfriars in 1600 and May 1603 when the theatre was closed on account of the plague. When it was reopened the name of the company had been changed to the Children of Her Majesty's Revels. A clear reference to Queen Elizabeth as still being alive (I, i, 140) points to a date of composition before March 1603. It seems likely that a reference to the presence in England of some of the 'greatest gallants. . .in France' (III, i, 48) is a topical reference to the resplendent embassy to London sent by the French, 5–15 September 1601, headed by the Duke of Biron, Marshall of France, a character who so impressed Chapman that he later wrote two plays with him as the central figure. The allusion would make more sense around the time of the visit and this therefore supports a date of autumn 1601 for the play's first performance. A date between 15 September and 11 November 1601 would seem to get confirmation from an obscure reference at the end of Dekker's *Satiromastix* (V, ii, 348–9) – which was entered in the Stationers' Register on 11 November – to a Lady Furnivall. This seems to be a topical reference and as the character who alludes to her, Captain Tucca, frequently alludes to plays, it seems likely that this is a reference to Chapman's play, where a Lady Furnivall played so notorious a part that the episode was censored in the printed version of the play.[10]

If we can feel fairly confident, then, that the first performance of *Sir Giles Goosecap* belongs to the autumn of 1601, this helps establish the date of *Gentleman Usher* as sometime during 1602. Parrott has shown how often *Gentleman Usher* echoes and refines on the earlier play[11] and there is one specific reference (II, i, 81) where Bassiolo (a goosecap of the play) calls a serving man Sir Giles Goosecap. It seems likely therefore that *Gentleman Usher* follows immediately after *Sir Giles Goosecap*, which would suggest a likely date for the first performance of around mid-1602. The Stationers' Register entry for the play is 26 November 1605 and the one edition, the quarto of 1606, contains no reference to the company that played it. *Sir Giles Goosecap* was reprinted in 1636 with a title-page informing that the comedy was 'lately acted with great applause at the private house in Salisbury Court', there was no reprint of *Gentleman Usher* and presumably no revival. The printing evidence suggests that *Gentleman Usher* was not an outstanding success, and it is not difficult to see why; it makes far fewer concessions to the audience in its retreat from the comic from Act III onwards and generally goes against the current fashion for down-to-earth satiric comedy.

The date of Shakespeare's *All's Well that Ends Well* is a good deal less easy to establish. The Arden editor, G. K. Hunter, dates it (tentatively) 1603–4,[12] mainly because of a close relationship he finds between it and *Measure for Measure*, which almost certainly dates from 1604. Hunter sees in *Measure for Measure* parallels with *All's Well* that suggest 'a slight development and clarification of the material'[13] as it is handled in the former play. The examples Hunter cites suggest some misunderstanding of Shakespeare's purpose in both plays – as I hope to explain. His argument that *All's Well* is to be dated before *Measure for Measure* is, I believe, correct, but probably a little earlier than he suggests. The strongest evidence for dating comes from the explicit allusions to *Troilus and Cressida* in the play. These not only suggest that the Troilus story had still not worked itself out of Shakespeare's head, but also, as I shall argue, show Shakespeare engaged in some sort of dialogue with his earlier play, for they are not merely casual mentions but seem to go to the heart of Shakespeare's purpose. There is above all the change of the heroine's name from Giletta in its source (William Painter's *Palace of Pleasure*) to Helena. That it is not an arbitrary change, I think, is clear from Lavatch's song reminding us of Helena's Greek namesake (I, iii, 67–76). The cynical view that Lavatch expresses here concerning women and the air of cynicism that pervades the song is a deliberate recollection of the Trojan world as Shakespeare depicted it, and it contributes to a powerful counter-theme that runs through the play in which male cynicism is finally overcome and eradicated by feminine virtue. Helena (as we shall see) redeems women from the curse placed on them on account of Cressida's proverbial falseness. In *All's Well* Ophelia's ghost is finally exorcised for Shakespeare. The frivolous Helen we see in *Troilus and Cressida* is to Helena as 'Eva' to 'Ave' in medieval lore, where anagramatically the curse on Eve was said to have been redeemed by Our Lady.[14] The other reference to *Troilus* in *All's Well* (II, i, 96) actually associates Helena with Cressida, as Lafeu, leaving her with the sick King, likens his own role to that of Pandarus:

> I am Cressid's uncle
> That dare leave two together.

Such an association would seem wildly inappropriate for the moment when Helena arrives to use her skill in medicine in an attempt to cure the mortally ill King, had we not already encountered Chapman's neo-platonic interpretation of the three roles. Here Shakespeare is taking a leaf out of Chapman's book, for Lafeu is playing a role not unlike Momford's in *Sir Giles Goosecap* as he leads the melancholy Clarence towards the cure that only Eugenia can bring him. Just as Eugenia ('nobility') redeems the name of Cressida in acting as the source of love's power, so too Helena's role is to

78

bring love to a maimed world. Even Shakespeare's title has its echo from the earlier play, for Helena's 'All's well that ends well; still the fine's the crown' (IV, iv, 35) is a triumphant Christian reply to the Sophoclean irony of Hector's 'The end crowns all' (*T & C* IV, v, 223).

While we cannot rule out the possibility that *All's Well* was written before *Gentleman Usher* was performed (though that seems unlikely) and that either *Sir Giles Goosecap*'s example or a spontaneous impulse to return to more congenial modes was enough to set Shakespeare on the road back towards romance and neo-platonic allegory, it seems unlikely to me that the striking parallels between the two plays' themes were the result of accident. It was always possible, of course, in the very small world of the London professional theatre of this time, that discussion of work in progress took place over a pint. Jonson and Chapman were close friends at this time, as can be seen from the fulsome commendatory verses Chapman supplied to *Sejanus*. Shakespeare too must have been in close contact with Jonson on an almost day-to-day basis, for Shakespeare's name is recorded in the cast list of the first performance of the same play in 1603. Jonson was not one to leave the production of his plays to others. In *Satiromastix* we learn that he was in the habit of interfering even during the course of a performance (V, ii, 298–301). Friendships seem to have flared up (like tempers) and to have died down with bewildering rapidity among the acting sort, then as now, and professional rivalry did not seem to preclude intimacy of acquaintance (as Jonson's relationship with Shakespeare testifies). The connections between *Gentleman Usher* and *All's Well* suggest influence by whatever means, rather than coincidence.

Like *Sir Giles Goosecap* before it and *Monsieur D'Olive* after, *Gentleman Usher* shows a contrast between a comic, foolish world of error and a romantic world in which the participants are engaged on a spiritual journey. Unlike the other two plays, however, Chapman does not separate the two parts into two separate and concurrent narratives, but hits on the unusual dramatic structure of a narrative which moves from comedy towards romance – a structure which Chapman may have developed from the 'antic-masque' or comic interlude that preceded the masque proper and which Jonson was later to develop into the antimasque. This may be yet another example where Chapman's experimentation led the way. At any rate *Gentleman Usher* not only begins in the chaos of comedy, but makes extensive use of the masque form within the play in the first two acts. The use of masque-like episodes in the first two acts is important, for it establishes the symbolic, non-realistic mode that requires its audience to interpret its signs allegorically. Thus the play opens with preparations being made for the Duke Alphonso, the ruler of a suitably vague 'Italian' state, to hunt boar. As the theme of the play is to be the transformation of earthly passion into spiritual experience, the reoccurrence of the hunt motif is suitably emblematic, for the boar was associated with wild passion and its death the assertion of control over passion. To Sandys, allegorizing the Erymanthian Boar slain by Hercules, the story symbolizes 'morally. . .the virtue of the minde, which subjects all terrors and difficulties'.[15] In another allegorization Sandys tells us the boar is 'the image of winter, savage, horrid, delighting in mire' and therefore a dangerous beast (the interpretation is given of Adonis's death).[16] This aspect is realized in the play when the virtuous Cynanche, wife of the nobleman Strozza, warns her husband of the dangers of the chase:

> My lord, I fancy not these hunting sports,
> When the bold game you follow turns again
> And stares you in the face. Let me behold
> A cast of falcons on their merry wings,
> Daring the stooped prey that shifting flies;
> Or let me view the fearful hare or hind
> Toss'd like a music point with harmony
> Of well-mouthed hounds. This is a sport for princes; [17]
> The other rude boars yield fit game for boors.

(I, i, 51–9)

Here Cynanche, who acts throughout as the messenger of divine truth, is pointing to the emblematic mode which is to be characteristic of the play and suggesting, in particular, the earthly preoccupations of the boorish Duke. The miry boar is only too apt to 'stare us in the face', to reflect our own beastliness, whereas the proper concern of mankind is to soar with the falcon into the higher world of the spirit, or participate in the lowlier harmony of the natural world (hence the rather quaint imagery of the hunting of hare and deer). We shall see both these themes enacted in the play: the soaring of the spirit in the spiritual journey her husband, Strozza, undergoes, and the achievement of harmony with the natural world in the story of the two lovers Margaret and Vincentio. The play will illustrate the working of love at the levels of spirit (represented by *Venere Celeste* or *Aphrodite Urania* in neo-platonic thought) and human nature (*Venere Volgare* or *Aphrodite Pandemos*).[18]

The Duke is a wayward man, not given either to the control of his passions or the overcoming of difficulties. At the beginning of the play we hear that he is infatuated with the young Margaret and is therefore a rival to his son, Vincentio, prompting the wise fool Pogio to ask: 'Will his antiquity never leave his iniquity?' (I, i, 31). His waywardness is first encountered when we hear that he has cancelled the hunt for the day and decided instead to have a pageant presented, in which a boar hunt is to be allegorized. The pageant itself turns out to be a chaotic amalgam and very wayward interpretation of several Ovidian boar myths. The Duke, who has been brought to see the pageant bound, to signify he is a prisoner of his love for Margaret, is represented as out hunting (in the pageant itself) when, like Adonis, he arouses a 'vast and dreadful boar' in a myrtle grove. The Duke confronts the boar 'like a second Hercules' (a reference to the Erymanthian Boar) and Strozza adds, for good measure, 'like the English sign of great St George' (I, ii, 92). This somewhat undignified reference to an inn sign stimulates a ribald aside from Vincentio: 'Plague of that simile' (though St George was often allegorized as a slayer of passion). The boar, however, suddenly and unexpectedly turns into the figure of Margaret 'like Diana arm'd' and, inappropriately for the goddess of chastity, turns the tables by directing a love arrow at the Duke's breast. This episode may derive from a redaction of the story of Meleager's slaying of the Caledonian boar in Book 8 of *Metamorphoses*. This tells of a boar sent by Diana to punish his countrymen that Meleager kills with the aid of the beautiful Atalanta, who is the first to inflict a wound on the beast to the chagrin of the male hunters. Whatever the origins of the pageant, however, we are given a precise allegorical reading of it when an Enchanter tells his audience that the boar signifies Margaret's cruelty, driven away by the Duke's love and defended by her own beauty (I, ii, 111–12). The Enchanter then asks Margaret to release the real Duke from his bonds (to signify, inappropriately, that she accepts his love), which she reluctantly does.

That this is a misuse of symbolic method is clear not only from Vincentio's ribald asides during the course of the recitation, but also by the blatantly coercive use to which the pageant is put. Art is here being prostituted to gratify selfish desire in a manner that elsewhere Chapman specifically warns against. When his allegorical poem *Andromeda Liberata* was allegorized by others in ways he had not intended, Chapman issued a defence of his allegorical method in a 'Justification' of the poem (1614). In this he both defends the practice of allegorizing ancient myth and attacks those who pervert their interpretations to their own wishes: 'giving up their understandings to their affections, and taking up their affections on other men's credits'.[19] The whole recitation had, indeed, got off to a bad start, for Duke Alphonso's henchman Medice had been meant to speak the lines, but when it comes to the point he is unable to remember them and the worthy Strozza has to take over. Medice's lack of eloquence and general lack of that Chapmanesque essential of the virtuous man, 'learning', defines him as the principal villain of the play. One of the signs of the Duke's depravity is that he befriends such a villain, while Vincentio's friendship with the virtuous Strozza equally serves to define his position in the moral hierarchy. We shall see that Shakespeare in *All's Well* adopts this device in using Parolles' friendship with Bertram to help define Bertram's moral immaturity. The close association between Vincentio and Strozza is expressed by the unusual device, at the end of the first scene, of having them speak in unison in an aside and exit line, promising to engineer Medice's downfall (I, i, 264).

81

The second act is also taken up with symbolic pageantry, this time, if anything, more absurd than the last. Bassiolo, the gentleman usher (chief steward) of the Earl Lasso, Margaret's father, has been ordered to prepare a pageant for the Duke's entertainment. Bassiolo (the usher of the title) is a curious figure, sometimes thought to be modelled on Malvolio, though he has a completely different function in his play. Bassiolo is one of the play's two fools, the other being Strozza's nephew, Pogio. The foolish have a special place in these late Chapman comedies; this play and both *Sir Giles Goosecap* and *Monsieur D'Olive* are named after the principal fool. In all three plays the figures of the foolish help to define the nature of the world of blindness which inflicts ordinary mankind, from which the spiritual voyagers must try to free themselves. Like Monsieur D'Olive, Bassiolo is so caught up with the things of this world that he is completely blinded to the world of the spirit, though like every part of God's creation he is an unconscious agent of the divine love. It is his role to bring Vincentio and Margaret together, but unlike Momford in his role as go-between in *Sir Giles Goosecap*, Bassiolo acts reluctantly and without understanding the significance of what he does. Margaret herself comments:

> he's not only
> My father's usher, but the world's beside,
> Because he goes before it all in folly.
> (IV, ii, 117–19)

The contrast between the two pandar figures is clearly seen in a very similar scene in the two plays, where the go-betweens agree to write letters from the ladies to their respective lovers. In *Sir Giles Goosecap* Momford tricks Eugenia into confessing her love more openly than she intends (IV, i, 140f). In *Gentleman Usher* it is Bassiolo who is fooled (III, ii, 380f). Bassiolo's letter on Margaret's behalf turns out to be totally incompetent, for he is much more interested in displaying his own stylistic ingenuity than in conveying her message, as he later admits to Vincentio (IV, ii, 8–9). Vincentio had earlier commented on Bassiolo's inability to distinguish form from substance: 'How serious apish souls are in vain form' (III, ii, 210). Bassiolo shares his linguistic incompetence with the villainous Medice and such incompetence is characteristic of Chapman's fools and knaves (as it is also of Pogio). Chapman in this is following Scriptural wisdom: 'for by thy words thou shalt be justified and by thy words shalt thou be condemned' (Matt. 12: 37). Again echoes of this doctrine are found in *All's Well*, where Parolles ('words') is characterized by his empty rhetoric and where in his exposure as a coward he is deceived by the pure nonsense of pseudo-Russian (IV, i, 64f). Dissatisfied with Bassiolo's absurd effort Margaret dictates to him a love letter whose significance he fails to understand, but which speaks plainly of her love for Vincentio. Her comment after he leaves her not only explains his role as conveyor of a wisdom that he does not understand, but also emphasizes another aspect of Chapman's theme that has strong echoes in *All's Well*, the dominance of women as the conduits of divine love (as again both Spenser in the *Faerie Queene*, Book III and Botticelli's 'Allegory of the Seasons' make plain):

> Pitiful usher. What a pretty sleight
> Goes to the working up of everything!
> What sweet variety serves a woman's wit!
> We make men sue to us for that we wish.
> Poor men, hold out a while and do not sue,
> And spite of custom we will sue to you.
>
> (III, ii, 508–13)

The last lines might almost be the epigraph of *All's Well*, for Helena, like Margaret, represents the power of love in the natural world overcoming those impediments to nature – Bertram's immaturity, Duke Alphonso's 'unnatural' love – that would interrupt the God-given rhythms of the natural world. Bassiolo, again speaking better than he knows, comments on the unnaturalness of Alphonso's love, but characteristically misapplies the insight in relating it to his own supposed friendship with Vincentio:

> But who saw ever summer mix'd with winter?
> There must be equal years where firm love is.
> Could we two love so well so suddenly
> Were we not something equaller in years
> Than he and she are?
>
> (III, ii.150–4)

Vincentio's 'love' for Bassiolo is entirely feigned in order to deceive him into acting as go-between (here Vincentio's virtue is defined in terms of his refusal to befriend the foolish Bassiolo), whereas the genuine, but unnatural, relationship between Bertram and Parolles is a sign of Bertram's unreadiness for an adult role. The relationship must be heterosexual because it involves (as in Spenser's Garden of Adonis) the rhythms of the generative processes. The theme of man's need to identify with the rhythms of the natural world is characteristically Chapmanesque and becomes most clearly stated in *Monsieur D'Olive* and *Widows' Tears*, where the impediment to the natural processes in both cases is an obsession with death. In *Monsieur D'Olive* (III, i, 1–50) the matter is discussed in some detail by means of heavy borrowing from Petrarch's *Secretum*, where St Augustine is represented in dialogue reproving Petrarch for his obsessive and unproductive love for Laura.[20]

Bassiolo is just as ready to usher in error as truth, for he is equally unable to distinguish either. Hence we see him in Act II busily engaged in organizing an entertainment which is again primarily intended to prostitute art to Alphonso's desires. The preparation of the entertainment appropriately includes a quarrel among the cast about what clothes shall be worn and by whom, for the actors here, who include Pogio, are more concerned with appearance than substance (again we recall that Parolles is a creature of clothes (II, iii, 202–4) as is Monsieur D'Olive in his play). The entertainment itself consists in a series of dances before Alphonso and Margaret (who is addressed by the Duke as his Duchess (II, i, 180) and who is required to sit on a throne next to the Duke). Each of the dances represents examples of feminine coyness in the face of male entreaty. These are then glossed by the deviser of the entertainment, the pedant Sarpego, as a warning to the 'quaint' Duchess not to refuse her Duke:

> This, lady and duchess, we conclude:
> Fair virgins must not be too rude;
> For though the rural wild and antic
> Abus'd their loves as they were frantic,
> Yet take you in your ivory clutches
> This noble duke and be his duchess.
> Thus, thanking all for their *tacete*,
> I void the room and cry *valete*.
>   (II, i, 291–8)

The linguistic incompetence here again helps to reveal the moral inadequacy, for the whole entertainment is a crude attempt at seduction. When Vincentio praises Bassiolo's efficiency in organizing the presentation he does so in ambiguous words that emphasize the prostitution of art that it has involved:

> That, even as in a turnspit call'd a jack
> One vice assists another. . .every different part
> Concurring in one commendable end. . .
>   (III, ii, 12–13, 15–16)

Its confused presentation is not only evident in the quality of its language, but in the absurdity of addressing Margaret as duchess and urging her to become one. Alphonso's comment on the entertainment: 'Generally well and pleasingly performed' places him as securely as Cynanche's wise comment places her when she remarks that Margaret's hand would better befit Vincentio than his father (II, ii, 317).

Pogio, who has played a part in this entertainment, differs in his foolishness from Bassiolo in being all too aware of his own folly. He is the Lavatch to Bassiolo's Parolles in the sense that he acknowledges his own absurdity: 'I am the veriest fool of you all' (III, ii, 221). To this Vincentio replies: 'Therein thou art worth us all, for thou know'st thyself.' In a world of blind men it is something to recognize one's own blindness and Vincentio is wise enough to realize that such recognition must precede the acquirement of transcendent wisdom. Bassiolo, on the other hand, likes to pride himself on his wisdom (as does Parolles), boasting of superior knowledge and understanding.

In the first three acts we have largely been in a world of make-believe, a world that is essentially fictional compared to the reality of the transcendent world to which we must now be introduced. From comic incompetence the play moves onwards and upwards to cosmic allegory. There is a hint of the marked change of tone that occurs in Act IV, in the short scene at the beginning of Act III where we hear Medice plotting to have Strozza (of whom he is envious) assassinated. At the beginning of Act IV Strozza is brought in, shot in the side during the course of the hunting that was to have taken place earlier. Here a 'real' arrow replaces the fictional arrow of the first entertainment as Strozza writhes in pain, unable to extract the arrow's barbed head from his body. Strozza's immediate response is to long for death to relieve him of his pain, which the physician Benevenius says he is unable to do anything about:

> I told you all that can be thought in art,
> Which since your lordship will not yield to use,
> Our last hope rests in Nature's secret aid,
> Whose power at length may happily expel it.
>
> (IV, i, 30–3)

Benevenius's human art must give way to a power beyond human understanding. Strozza's wife, Cynanche, reproves her husband for his impatience and urges him to assume 'a Christian part', accepting that God sends us suffering to wean us from earthly pleasures:

> 'tis said, afflictions bring to God
> Because they make us like Him, drinking up
> Joys that deform us with the lusts of sense,
> And turn our general being into soul. . .
>
> (IV, i, 62–5)

Again, a woman leads the way towards wisdom as she urges her husband to 'salve with Christian patience pagan sin' (IV, i, 86). When we next see Strozza, however (IV, iii), his mood has completely changed, he has accepted his wife's 'divine' advice, praising her as 'The weaker body, still the stronger soul' (IV, iii, 8) and describing her as like himself but 'divinely varied without change'. This may be intended to indicate that she is in harmony with the eternal patterns of nature (Spenser's 'eterne in mutabilitie') rather than or as well as being an assertion of the essential likeness of man and woman in spite of their accidental sexual difference. Her advice has led to the restoration of his health (IV, iii, 42) and his suffering has led to his spiritual purification:

> Leaves me nought else but soul, and so like her,
> Free from the passions of my fuming blood.
> (IV, iii, 51–2)

This triumph of spirit over matter, of which Cynanche is the type, has given Strozza special visionary powers that enable him to prophesy that in seven days the arrow will fall from his side. Cynanche is sceptical of this, for she lacks the visionary knowledge that Strozza's suffering has given him. Strozza summons Benevenius, the physician, in order to impress upon him the superiority of God's power over human:

> I'll teach my physician
> To build his cares hereafter upon heaven
> More than on earthly med'cines. . .
> (IV, iii, 71–3)

The arrow does in fact come out of the wound precisely as Strozza predicts and a miraculous cure is effected.

The role of Benevenius is an important one. J. H. Smith has shown that the source for the story of the miraculous cure of Strozza is in an early sixteenth-century medical work by Antonio Benivieni, from whose name Chapman's Benevenius obviously derives.[21] The work was posthumously edited in 1507 by Antonio's brother, Girolamo, who was an important figure among the Florentine neo-platonists. He was a friend of the neo-platonist philosopher Pico della Mirandola and author of the *Canzone dello Amore* on which Pico wrote a commentary developing his own thoughts on love. Chapman had no doubt come upon the medical work in the course of his neo-platonic studies, whose influences, and that of Ficino in particular, abound in this play and elsewhere. Cynanche's advice to Strozza, for instance, that he should endeavour to take the opportunity of his suffering to overcome the weakness of the flesh 'And turn our general being into soul', exactly accords with Ficino's admonition that the aim of the wise is: 'to make oneself incorporeal, in other words, to separate one's mind as much as possible from corporeal movement, perception, passion and imagination'.[22] Similarly Cynanche's exhortations to patience as a means of overcoming suffering and identifying oneself with the divine will is a reflection of Ficino's philosophy:

> Oh admirable power of patience! Other virtues fight against fate in some way; patience alone or chiefly among them overcomes fate. For those things which fate has decided to be unchangeable and necessary, patience, agreeing with the will of divine Providence, changes in such a way as to make them voluntary rather than necessary.[23]

Even Chapman's change of the name of the sufferer from Gaspar in Benivieni's narrative to Strozza ('throat') gets a useful gloss from Ficino:

86

We are all thirsty for the true goods, but we all drink dreams. While we absorb the deadly waves of the river Lethe through our open throats, we scarcely lick with our lips a shadowlike bit of nectar and ambrosia.[24]

The name of Cynanche ('collar') suggests the discipline of true doctrine for the thirsty Strozza. George Herbert's poem 'The Collar' uses the same image in a similar way. A recurring idea in Chapman, that we have already discussed in connection with *Gentleman Usher*, is the association between evil and ignorance. This connection can again be found in Ficino's view that 'the cause of evil is the stupidity and ignorance of men'.[25] Yet another important connection between Ficino's thought and *Gentleman Usher* (in this case shared with *All's Well*) is in Ficino's belief in miraculous cures. Jean Jacquot points out that Ficino's father was a physician and that Ficino believed that his father had prophetic gifts. Ficino himself claimed that he had had foreknowledge of a miraculous cure of his own sickness. He also believed that when the soul became liberated from its ties with the body, in consecrating itself entirely to God it became the instrument of the divine will, receiving the power of prophecy and the ability to change the natural course of things.[26] Both Ficino and Pico make the power of God's love the dynamic principle of all life. *Gentleman Usher* and *All's Well* assert an intimate connection between the power of love and a miraculous cure.

Benevenius, however, as we have seen, is not allowed to apply his art to Strozza's case. When later Margaret is suffering from her self-inflicted mutilation, his skill is efficacious, for he applies a remedy, as he says, from the 'little storehouse of great Nature' (V, iv, 123) and cures her completely. This contrast between the supernatural curing of Strozza and the natural cure Benevenius provides for Margaret is deliberate and highlights Chapman's theme of the double workings of divine love, through the spirit and through the natural world – a contrast that Spenser makes in his representation of the twin sisters Belphoebe and Amoret in Book III of the *Faerie Queene*.[27]

Margaret's self-inflicted wound provides several parallels as well as this basic contrast with Strozza's ordeal. Vincentio and Margaret are at last brought together in Act IV, scene ii with the aid of Bassiolo, who advises Vincentio on the proper way of wooing a lady, to the amusement of both the lovers. Margaret, in this philogynous play, now takes the initiative in swearing a solemn oath of marriage to Vincentio to prevent Alphonso from achieving his aim of marrying her himself. She argues that the formal marriage ceremony is merely the outward sign of an inward truth that can be asserted without such formality:

> Are not the laws of God and Nature more
> Than formal laws of men? Are outward rites
> More virtuous than the very substance is

> Of holy nuptials solemniz'd within?. . .
> My princely love, 'tis not a priest shall let us,
> But since th'eternal acts of our pure souls
> Knit us with God, the soul of all the world,
> He shall be priest to us. . .
>
> (IV, ii, 133–6, 140–3)

Both this and Vincentio's reply, in which he devises a solemn ceremony committing themselves to one another, are imbued with neo-platonic imagery (as Smith comments).[28] At the end of the ceremony Vincentio asks Heaven to bless their union:

> And now, fairest heaven,
> As thou art infinitely rais'd from earth,
> Diff'rent and opposite, so bless this match,
> As far remov'd from Custom's popular sects
> And as unstain'd with her abhorr'd respects.
>
> (IV, ii, 196–200)

Margaret's appeal to the laws of 'God and Nature' against the laws of men is not (as it might at first appear) in contradiction to Vincentio's assertion that heaven and earth are opposites, for Margaret is appealing to those laws of the natural world that are themselves an expression of the nature of the divine being. It is right that she should appeal to God's natural laws, for her sexual union with Vincentio will be an expression of those natural laws – God's will working through nature. The contrast Vincentio is asserting is between those obeying the God-given laws of the natural world and those who obey the world's laws, devised by men – the essential contrast is that between the City of God, where God's will prevails and the City of Men, in which man asserts his own will against divine intention. In true neo-platonic fashion, then, the lovers' sexual union is to be an expression of God's spiritual laws.

Margaret and Vincentio have still to overcome the Duke's hostility, however, and before their love is finally consummated, like Strozza's spiritual awakening, it must be tested by suffering. Act V is largely devoted to this process. Duke Alphonso gets wind of the lovers' intentions and arranges with Medice and Margaret's father, the Earl Lasso, to spy on them. When they discover the truth of the situation, Margaret is seized and imprisoned, while Vincentio manages to escape. Medice is sent in pursuit with orders not to harm him, which he ignores, and Vincentio is brought in severely wounded. Margaret, meanwhile, in despair, threatens suicide in words that echo Strozza's earlier (V, iii, 6–8; IV, i, 72–4). The echo is deliberate, because we are being asked to see both scenes of suffering as part of an initiation rite into the world of the spirit. Margaret, indeed, proves the stronger of the two, for whereas Strozza was given the decisive support ('collar') of his wife Cynanche, Margaret has to suffer the ordeal, not merely unaided, but against the sly insinuations of her warder and anti-type, Corteza. Like all the evil figures in the play, Corteza is presented as an essentially comic character. Margaret cannot, in the event, bring herself to commit suicide, but she does succeed in mutilating her face with an antipilary ointment supplied by Corteza. Both Vincentio and Margaret, therefore, like Strozza, undergo a process of physical suffering for their spiritual welfare. Margaret's self-mutilation provides another element in the initiation rite, for it tests Vincentio's willingness to see through the superficialities of bodily beauty to the spiritual beauty Margaret evinces; a test that he triumphantly passes.

The play, of course, ends happily. The evil act Medice commits in causing Vincentio to be wounded redounds on his own head. Duke Alphonso is so grieved by his son's injuries that he renounces his opposition to the wedding and Medice is finally condemned for his crimes. Evil, being essentially negative, has been unable to prevail against the force of love and undoes itself. Benevenius, the doctor, has an important role in this triumph of love, for it is he who provides ointment out of the 'little storehouse of great Nature' to cure both Margaret of her disfigurement and Vincentio of his wounds. Because the love of Margaret and Vincentio is a manifestation of the natural world, Benevenius's natural skills can effect a cure, whereas God's direct intervention is required for the miraculous cure of Strozza. At the end evil is expunged, not only in the exposure of Medice, but in the comic exposure of Bassiolo's divagations, for Bassiolo has attempted and failed to repudiate his role in bringing the lovers together and he is brought before the Duke, as Pogio assures him, to be 'chopp'd in pieces'. He is (of course) pardoned, but his foolishness is too fundamental to be susceptible of cure. Pogio, on the other hand, as the wiser fool, takes on himself the responsibility of seeing Medice finally expelled from the Court.

As I have said, we cannot be absolutely sure that *All's Well that Ends Well* appeared after *Gentleman Usher* had been presented at Blackfriars, though it seems highly probable. The important point about the comparison of the two plays, however, is not to discuss the possible influence of the one on the other, but to compare the work of the two playwrights writing at around the same time in similar modes of comedy. Shakespeare's play has perpetually puzzled its critics because its mode seems so alien to Shakespeare's habitual handling of romantic material; it is a romance seemingly deprived of romance. But a comparison with Chapman's late comedies establishes its mode clearly and provides an entry into what has commonly come to be regarded as Shakespeare's 'unfortunate comedy'.[29] Both *Gentleman Usher* and *All's Well* are essentially mythic comedy and both describe spiritual journeys. To understand the nature of the myth helps to establish *All's Well* as one of Shakespeare's most impressive achievements in the comic mode.

Its most obvious similarity with Chapman's play, apart from its setting in France, Chapman's favourite location, is that the plot links the triumph of love with a miraculous cure. In *All's Well* the connection is achieved much more economically by making the heroine, Helena, the principal figure in both actions and by ingeniously giving the hero, Bertram, the dual (and opposite) roles of lover and blocking figure. The result is much neater plotting, avoiding much of the diffuseness of Chapman's comedy. The theme of the two plays is even more remarkably similar – the triumph of love in both the spiritual and natural worlds – but here again Shakespeare's closer integration of the two themes leads to a neater dramatic structure. For in giving Helena the role both of God's agent in the miraculous cure and of romantic heroine, he is able to show the interrelationship of spirit and nature as expressions of the divine love,[30] if obscuring, to some extent, the clarity of the neo-platonic distinction that Chapman's play is careful to maintain. Generally Shakespeare goes for dramatic effectiveness, Chapman for thematic clarity. This is equally true in the handling of the comic, though again there is remarkable similarity of treatment as well as some significant difference. In both plays the comic represents the negative, what has to be repudiated (unusual for Shakespearean comedy) and in both plays a distinction is made between the wise foolish (Lavatch/Pogio) and the foolish foolish (Parolles/Bassiolo). This latter distinction is rather clearer in Chapman than in Shakespeare. Both plays, too, tend to associate foolishness with men and wisdom with women, though here Shakespeare makes the distinction clearer. The sexual aspects of this distinction derive from neo-platonic thinking where the power of love (represented by Venus) is associated with femininity, while its anti-type is Mars. In the famous Botticelli depiction of Mars and Venus (now in the London National Gallery) Venus is shown in splendid triumph over Mars; love and femininity is shown quite obviously triumphing over war and masculinity.[31] In Shakespeare's play this opposition (a *discordia concors*) is very precisely and clearly represented in the contrast between those places dominated by women (Rossillion, the widow's house in Florence) and the chaotic and/or enfeebled world of the martial male (Paris, the Italian battlefield).

Shakespeare probably found the story he uses for his play in William Painter's *Palace of Pleasure*, a work, oddly enough, somewhat confusingly and indirectly alluded to in *Gentleman Usher*.[32] Painter had translated his story from Boccaccio's *Decameron*, but Shakespeare seems to have gone to the English source, which he'd probably used earlier in writing *Romeo and Juliet*. The collection of stories was ready to hand and Shakespeare follows his source fairly closely. All this, as too the epilogue, suggests the play was intended in the first place for the Globe audience, for it did not involve what we would now call the special 'research' required by two of the plays on either side of it, *Troilus* and *Measure for Measure*. There are other features of the play that would have appealed to a popular audience, notably the ever popular bourgeois theme of the superiority of virtue to birth. Helena's rise in the world from poor physician's daughter to countess, through her own enterprise, is made more emphatic than in the source material, where Giletta, the heroine, is the daughter of a physician who is both famous and wealthy. The treatment of this theme, however, is sentimental rather than ideological; no class points are scored, for the preference of virtue to birth is shared by the king of France and the Count's mother (the latter a Shakespearean addition). Yet this is neither sentimental comedy nor comedy of manners. Both sentimental and social conventions are flouted in making the hero, Bertram, the principal stumbling-block to the heroine's happiness, while the heroine herself (described by H. B. Charlton as 'a nymphomaniac succeeding in her quest')[33] has qualities that range far beyond those of the conventional romantic heroine. The governing principle is myth: the use of romantic material to demonstrate a higher truth. This was a highly suitable vehicle in appealing to the two levels of his audience, those who wanted principally to be entertained and those wiser sort, the 'understanders', who expected doctrine with their delight.

Perhaps the feature that marks off *All's Well* most clearly from Shakespeare's earlier romantic comedies is its restlessness.[34] All the earlier comedies present us with a sense of place, usually a romantic 'Italy' that imparts a glamour to the recognizably Elizabethan. Each of the earlier comedies gives the sense of a settled community in better-than-average surroundings, sometimes courtly, sometimes bourgeois. Only *Two Gentlemen of Verona* of the earlier comedies gives the same sense of unsettledness, depicting as it does a movement not only from Verona to Milan and the wild wood where Valentine becomes an outlaw, but also the suggestion of an allegorical journey for the two gentlemen from youthful immaturity towards adult responsibility. In the figure of Proteus, too, *Two Gentlemen* manages to combine the roles of romantic hero and villain. But *Two Gentlemen* remains firmly centred in its romantic conventions, creating an aura of fantasy which guarantees the triumph of the pleasurable. *All's Well* is much more fundamentally unsettling in throwing a cooler light on the mating processes that has suggested to some commentators that the word 'cynical' best describes its tone.[35] It is, however, an odd cynicism where the Christian God figures so strongly.

The spacial restlessness of the play is not merely a matter of scene changes as we move from Rossillion at the beginning, to the King's court in Paris in the second scene, alternating between Rossillion and Paris in subsequent scenes until II, ii-v settles for a time in Paris. By the beginning of Act III we are in and around Florence, but again with lightning trips to Rossillion at III, ii and III, iv. Act IV finds us alternating between Florence and an army camp somewhere between Florence and Siena and then Act V takes us once more back to Rossillion via Marseilles. Sometimes the visits to Rossillion seem to add nothing to the progress of the plot, as in the short scene between the Countess and Lavatch (II, ii) which is almost totally devoid of narrative content; the Countess gives Lavatch a letter to convey to Helena in Paris, but we never hear what the letter contains or get the answer Helena is urged to send back. The scene serves primarily to bring us back to Rossillion in order to keep the Countess's presence constantly before us; for the action always refers back to Rossillion and the Countess, from which it begins. We are never allowed to forget her presence as the pivotal point of the play's action and it is she who provides the point of reference from which the dynamic of the plot's movement gets its meaning: it is she who remains the fixed point in a turning world.

This constant movement away from and around Rossillion (for the action of the play eventually describes a complete geographical circle) has also a very clear allegorical dimension, it is not merely a matter of scene changing. The play opens with a double farewell in Bertram's opening line: 'And I in going, madam, weep o'er my father's death anew'. A metaphor is achieved in which parting at one level is associated with death at another. Bertram's restlessness is the restlessness of youth, but it is also, more profoundly, the restlessness of the world's larger cycle that expresses itself in the constant change of life into death, death into life. The hero's restless instability is also brought out in Helena's anticipation of his sexual experimentation when he arrives in Paris:

> There shall your master have a thousand loves,
> A mother, and a mistress, and a friend,
> A phoenix, captain, and an enemy,
> A guide, a goddess, and a sovereign,
> A counsellor, a traitress, and a dear. . .
>
> (I, i, 162–6)

The whole range of the male's relationship with femininity is here displayed, including that need for mothering that Bertram in his boyishness is seeking to escape from. Commentators have been puzzled by 'mother' in this Petrarchist context,[36] but like the inserted Rossillion scenes it is another reminder that maturity involves acknowledging the dependence born of our birth, an emotional dependence that earlier Shakespeare had vividly portrayed in one of his sonnets (no. 143). The play depicts the male in flight, but Helena's reminder that the mother is an omnipresent aspect of a man's experience shows the futility of the attempt, which is also what the main action of the play is to illustrate. Spenser had dealt at some length with the fleeing male in Book III of *The Faerie Queene*, most notably in the figure of Marinel ('he will not marry'), who is described as 'loves enimy', who 'ever from fayre ladies love did fly'.[37] Spenser had also made central to this book the myth of Adonis, the type of the fleeing male, whom Shakespeare had himself made the subject of an earlier poem which recounts the tragic flight of Adonis from the predatory Venus.

No sooner has Bertram arrived in Paris than he is restlessly contemplating flight to Florence and the wars, where he can escape from women altogether, and it is again for largely negative reasons: to avoid having to consummate his marriage with Helena. This feeling of restlessness, of refusing to settle down, is, then, central to the play's dominant theme of the need of all of us to be in harmony with nature's (and so God's) purposes, a theme also central to Chapman's thought. Bertram is unwilling to take on the burden of emotional commitment, but his flight is as doomed to failure as it is for Marinel, for it is an attempt by a weak man to defy love's power, the dynamic at the centre of the neo-platonic universe.

Because he wants us to enter a mythic world through the portals of the here and now, Shakespeare combines in this play (in the manner of Chapman) a worldly-wise realism with an elusiveness of intention that adds still further to the sense of unsettled restlessness in the play. We appear to be moving across the map of France and Northern Italy, but there are strange and unsettling incongruities. Helena mysteriously announces to the Countess in a letter (letters are frequently, in Shakespeare, a sign of confusion) that she has set out for 'Saint Jacques'— that is, presumably, the Spanish town and shrine of Santiago de Compostela. This might be thought to have been intended by her as a ruse to cover her tracks if we did not find her in the next scene in Florence announcing that she is bound for 'Saint Jacques le Grand' (III, v, 34), being assured by the Florentine widow that she can join a group of penitents who have gathered in her house on their way to the shrine (III, ii, 93–4). The visit to Saint Jacques, clearly not in or near Florence, is again reiterated by the First Lord's account of Helena's 'death', which is supposed to have taken place there (IV, iii, 46–51). It is inconceivable that Shakespeare made a mistake (as the Arden editor supposes) about the position of the most famous shrine in western Christendom, and when we examine Helena's curious letter to the Countess we find it is couched in language as mysterious and mystifying as the reference to the shrine itself. Not only is the letter in a gnomic form of verse, but it also has the tone of ritualistic prayer:

> Bless him at home in peace, whilst I from far
> His name with zealous fervour sanctify. . .

and ending with the couplet:

> He is too good and fair for death and me;
> Whom I myself embrace to set him free.
> (III, iv, 10–11, 16–17)

The last couplet has a veritably Delphic ambiguity, for the 'death' she appears to be embracing turns out to be, in fact, the 'he' of the previous line (Bertram) whom she sets free from his own immaturity by literally embracing him in a Florentine bed, where she conceives his child. It is thus Bertram who escapes 'death', a Chapman-like death of the soul from which Helena's love saves him. The religious tone is no accident, any more than the pilgrimage to Saint Jacques is a mistake; for all the play's air of matter-of-factness Shakespeare wants us to be constantly aware of another level of meaning, a mythological level in which a divine reality gives a more permanent reading to the uncertainties of the literal text.

There are other examples of this geographical vagueness in the middle of apparent certainty: the Sienese war, for instance, in which Bertram does such valiant service, is represented on stage by two night scenes of uncertain location, in which we find ourselves in the presence of 'Russian' soldiers speaking a pseudo-Russian language (IV, i and IV, iii). These scenes are primarily fantasy played out for Parolles's benefit and to expose him as a victim of a largely verbal nonsense, suitable enough for one whose wordiness is the principal example of vacuity in the play. They disorientate more than Parolles, however, for they show a farcical world of empty noise (suitably emblemized by the drum Parolles is in search of) that both images Bertram's state of mind (as well as that of his friend) and contrasts with the secure world of Helena's purposeful love.

Time is treated in a similar way to space in the play. There is all the appearance of precision, both on a general scale (we are presented with a Renaissance French king who seems to belong to the present, but on whom no precise identification can be fathered) and on the local scale of Parolles's 'Ten a'clock. Within these three hours 'twill be time enough to go home' (IV, i, 24–5). Yet in this apparently modern world we are introduced to a miraculous cure of the King by a combination of divine aid and the magical properties of herbs that (like Helena's riddle-solving later) suggests much more readily the world of myth and legend. It is a combination, again, that we have found in Chapman's mythic comedies. And like the treatment of space, time comes to have a further meaning in this play, apart from its function in marking out the chronological progress of the narrative. Commentators have noted how sharply the generations are contrasted and separated in the play. The old generation is dying – the play opens with the reminiscence on the death of Bertram's father and we learn shortly that Helena's father too is recently dead – the King is on his deathbed, recalling, with the aged Lafeu, a time when he and Bertram's father were in their pride of life. And while the passing of one generation is in progress, the extreme youth and inexperience of the new generation is equally stressed, not only Bertram and his frivolous henchman, Parolles, but also the boyish French aristocrats who restlessly take on other people's wars out of a sense of boredom at home (a Renaissance equivalent of the football hooligan):

It well may serve
A nursery to our gentry, who are sick
For breathing and exploit.
                    (I, ii, 15–17)

A 'nursery' it certainly seems, for the war scenes concern themselves with a drum and a nursery language that is without adult meaning.

But the purpose of the play is not to contrast the wisdom of the old with the foolishness of the young. Lafeu, for instance, has his share of foolishness and we hear that the Countess keeps her fool Lavatch mainly because his foolishness was popular with Bertram's father (IV, v, 61–2). The King too needs to be rescued from a foolish despair by the youthful Helena. Clearly neither youth nor age has a monopoly of foolishness in the play. Rather the contrast of the generations draws our attention constantly to the passage of time, its inescapability, its continual movement. The effects of time are constantly rehearsed in the play:

Even so it was with me when I was young;
If ever we are nature's, these are ours; this thorn
Doth to our rose of youth rightly belong;
Our blood to us, this to our blood is born:
It is the show and seal of nature's truth,
Where love's strong passion is impress'd in youth.
By your remembrances of days foregone.
Such were our faults, or then we thought them none.
                    (I, iii, 124–30)

Again the gnomic language, this time of the Countess, points to the sacredness of the theme. The passage of time that so concerns the Countess is irreversible but not irredeemable, for each generation renews the processes that time destroys. For each individual time is inexorable – 'to be young again if we could' sighs the Countess (II, ii, 37), but nature and, above all, the power of love, working through our sexuality (and the Countess' wisdom expresses itself in a lively awareness of the sexual imperative) constantly replaces what is lost. To the King Helena is Nature's 'immediate heir' (II, iii, 132). Again we have 'eterne in mutabilitie'.[38] Here the imagery of the natural world links humanity to the changing seasons and the great cycles of time, of birth and decay. Participation in these cyclic rhythms is not without its tribulation, woman's love is thorn as well as rose (the sexual connotations of 'thorn' and 'rose' are not unintentional and recur more explicitly at IV, ii, 18–19), and the pain not without fault, for the pains of childbirth are the punishment for Eve's transgression. But they are also part of God's purpose and as such only to be avoided in defiance of the divine will. So we are reminded of the power of time to renew as well as destroy:

95

> But with the word the time will bring on summer,
> When briars shall have leaves as well as thorns,
> And be as sweet as sharp: we must away,
> Our wagon is prepar'd, and time revives us,
> All's well that ends well, still the fine's the crown. . .
>
> (IV, iv, 31–35)[39]

Helena echoes the Countess's earlier words to assert love's triumph in her conception of Bertram's child. The phrase 'with the word' has caused considerable difficulty for the commentators here (including the Arden editor, who takes 'word' to mean 'motto' and re-punctuates). The context, however, shows it must mean 'the word of heaven' (as in *Measure for Measure* I, ii, 114 and elsewhere in Shakespeare),[40] for Helena is asserting that all will be well in God's good time. Here God's time and nature's time are brought explicitly together as different aspects of the same process. The phrase 'the time revives us' suggests more than merely that a solution will appear when she arrives in Rossillion: time is conceived as taking an active role in bringing about revival. We are here close to Chapman's assertion, in his comedy *Monsieur D'Olive*, that only in participating in the temporal rhythms of the natural world can we fulfil God's intentions for us. The last line's echo of the Latin tag *'finis coronat opus'* confirms the religious connotations, for the phrase is constantly associated with Christian adjuration to 'remember thine end' and 'in the beginning is thine end'; the title of the play itself points to the importance of the religious dimension. Timing is of the essence, as Helena makes clear in her reply to Parolles in the first scene on the loss of virginity: 'not my virginity yet' (I.i, 161).

Helena and the Countess are by no means the only characters concerned with the passage of time in the play. The King greets Bertram at the Court in Paris with a detailed reminiscence of his friendship with Bertram's father and a comparison (and contrast) between past and present virtue (I, ii, 24ff). Whereas time is associated by the women with natural growth, however, the King's views are negative and despondent, smelling of death:

> Such a man
> Might be a copy to these younger times;
> Which, followed well, would demonstrate them now
> But goers backward.
>
> (I, ii, 45–8)

Where Helena sees renewal and growth, the diseased mind of the King sees retrogression. This negativity reaches its logical conclusion in the King's wish that he were dead:

> I, after him, do after him wish too,
> Since I nor wax nor honey can bring home,

I quickly were dissolved from my hive
To give some labourers room.

(I, ii, 64–7)

Chapman in *Gentleman Usher* twice associates the death wish with spiritual
torpor and centres his two last comedies on the rescuing of characters,
through love, from a kind of death-in-life. The King here says nothing
about renewal, nothing about who shall succeed him, his thoughts are on
the past and show an attempt to blot out time. Hunter remarks that the
image of the hive here is particularly apt since 'the Elizabethans assumed
the queen bee to be a king'.[41] The full implication, however, is clearly that
the King's comparison is inapt, because no worker bees can flourish
without their head.

The King's constant reference to his own sickness again emphasizes the
male negativity that it is the role of love to overcome. It is typical of him
that while he tells Bertram he would have called on Helena's father to cure
him, were he still alive (I, ii, 72), he at first has no faith in the physician's
live daughter, partly of course because she is a woman and partly because
she is young. When he is first told of her arrival at Court his immediate
response is an absolute refusal of help. Lafeu asks: 'will you be cur'd/Of
your infirmity?', to which the King replies with a single 'No' (II, i, 68).
Lafeu hints, albeit jokingly, that the problem is the mythic 'king's disease'
(impotence) in a bawdy joke about the girl's likely powers of stimulation:

> I have seen a medicine
> That's able to breathe life into a stone,
> Quicken a rock, and make you dance canary
> With sprightly fire and motion; whose simple touch
> Is powerful to araise King Pippen, nay,
> To give great Charlemain a pen in's hand
> And write to her a love-line.

(II, i, 71–7)

Lafeu had earlier explained the King's sickness as a 'fistula' (I, i, 31) but
here he is anticipating the miraculous results of Helena's cure in bringing
life out of death. The pun on 'stone' (testicle) and the sexual implications of
dancing the canary 'with fire and motion'[42] suggest a more traditional
king's disease than an abscess. An even more elaborate (and obscure) sexual
reference is contained in the reference to King Pippen and 'great
Charlemain's' pen. Shakespeare had earlier (and unmistakably) used 'King
Peppin' to refer to the male sexual organ in the notorious 'hit it' sequence
of *Love's Labours Lost* (IV, i, 116ff), while Charles the Great's 'pen' needs
little exposition.[43] The point of this elaborate bawdy (characteristic of the
play) is to associate the miraculous cure with the power of feminine
sexuality and in particular the power of virginity, as well as to suggest the

97

legendary royal ailment. Helena's function is not merely to revive the dying King, but to renew the cycle of generation, as she does triumphantly in her pursuit and capture of Bertram (as Venus captures Adonis and transforms him in Spenser's garden).[44] It is not by accident that Lafeu sees himself in the role of Pandarus as he ushers Helena into the King's presence (II, i, 96–7).

After the King's cure has been effected Lafeu celebrates it again in explicitly sexual terms: 'why your dolphin is not lustier' he says of the King to the uncomprehending Parolles and again 'Lustique, as the Dutchman says. I'll like a maid the better whilst I have a tooth in my head. Why, he's able to lead her a coranto' (II, iii, 41–3). Lafeu is equally concerned to emphasize the miraculous nature of the cure, attacking those rationalists who speak as if the age of miracles is past (II, iii, 1–6) and ascribing the cure to 'the very hand of heaven' (31). Throughout the dialogue Parolles, like Chapman's fools, is much more concerned with the sound of the words than with their meaning: 'Nay, 'tis strange, 'tis very strange; that is the brief and the tedious of it; and he's of a most facinerious spirit that will not acknowledge it to be the –' (II, iii, 27–30). And here even the syntax breaks down into nonsense, to be rescued by Lafeu as Medice's verbal incompetence is rescued by Strozza. It is typical of the play that this sense of divine revelation should have to struggle to express itself through the recalcitrant material of the fallen world, whether in Parolles's inanities or Bertram's obduracy.

The King's cure is a precondition for the health of his kingdom and frees time to pursue its proper course. At the end of the play the King presides over the quickening of time as he hastens Bertram to what purports to be his second marriage:

> Let's take the instant by the forward top;
> For we are old, and on our quick'st decrees
> Th'inaudible and noiseless foot of time
> Steals ere we can effect them.
>
> (V, iii, 39–42)

The supposed death of Helena cannot defeat the due processes of time and the now healthy King sees his role as furthering these processes: 'The time is fair again' (V, iii, 36) he announces to the regenerate Bertram. There are impediments to come; Bertram has still to purge his contempt of Diana, but he is finally brought to acknowledge his role as husband in his conditional promise to love the resurrected Helena 'ever, ever dearly' (the condition that she demonstrates 'clearly' that she has his ring and bears his child is the last bleep of the recalcitrant male). The King finally fulfils his role as lord of fertility in turning to Diana ('yet a fresh uncropped flower') and offering her a dowry as soon as she too has chosen her husband. This ending is important for it suggests Helena's initiative is no special case, but the enactment of a law of nature, which Diana in her turn is required to fulfil. It also, in this cyclic play, returns us to our starting point. The chaste earth nymph Chloris is to undergo the inevitable transformation into Flora once again.[45]

That this power of regeneration is an expression of the divine intention is the principal assertion of the two central scenes of the play concerned with the curing of the King. Helena insists that it is not she who will achieve the miraculous cure, but God working through her:

> It is not so with Him that all things knows
> As 'tis with us that square our guess by shows;
> But most it is presumption in us when
> The help of heaven we count the act of men.
> Dear sir, to my endeavours give consent;
> Of heaven, not me, make an experiment.
>
> (II, i, 148–53)

This is the kind of 'boldness' that Chapman associates with love's wisdom – a confidence like that of Strozza and Margaret born of absolute knowledge and faith in God's purposes. It is strange how often this aspect of Helena's role as divine agent has been ignored or played down by commentators,[46] yet it could hardly be made more explicit. The prosaic tone, which the play shares with Chapman's late comedies, is partly to explain for this, adopted deliberately by both playwrights as the gauze to protect the beholder from too dazzling a display of truth.[47] Helena's role as divine agent is crucial to our understanding not only of the function of her character in the play, but, inevitably, of the play as a whole, and it obviates all those misdirected objections to any impropriety in her conduct as romantic heroine.

Helena's metaphysical 'boldness' is suitably complemented by her personal modesty (and here again we have a parallel with Chapman's Margaret). When we next see her with the King (II, iii) the cure has been effected and we find her protesting: 'I simply am a maid'. But Shakespeare devises the scene, in which she insists on Bertram as her husband in fulfilment of the King's promise that she shall have a choice of whomever she wishes, in a ritualistic manner. This is again to emphasize the 'allegorical' level of interpretation appropriate for the scene. Helena moves deliberately from one young man to the next, commenting on each in the name of Love, whose votary (she says) she has become (II, iii, 75). Lafeu interposes into these formal and measured words comic remarks that show he has misunderstood (with a male perversity typical of the play) the import of the scene, for he seems to think the young men are each in turn refusing Helena's offer of marriage. When she finally chooses, she chooses Bertram with becoming modesty: 'I give/Me and my service. . .Into your guiding power' (II, iii, 102–4).

Adonis-like, Bertram's instinct is to flee and like Adonis, he flees into a male world of reckless (and destructive) activity. Having been refused permission to join the Florentine army because of his youth, he defies the King, breaks the marriage vows that have been extracted from him and proceeds to Italy without consummating his union with Helena. Bertram rejects the rites of Venus to follow the god of war:

> This very day,
> Great Mars, I put myself into thy file;
> Make me but like my thoughts and I shall prove
> A lover of thy drum, hater of love.
>
> (III, iii, 8–11)

That he does 'most honourable service' in this war is a necessary condition for Venus's ultimate triumph; Mars must be worth the entanglement. Mars' usual trumpet, however, is here suitably substituted by the empty vessel of a drum – and the drum is to be the central symbol of war in the play. The 'honourable service' of the war is not shown, merely reported briefly; instead we are presented with two war scenes where we see grown men haggling over a drum. To the empty-headed Parolles ('Tom Drum' as Lafeu calls him, V, iii, 315) love is the frivolity as he contemptuously reduces the male generative organs to a nursery plaything:

> He wears his honour in a box unseen,
> That hugs his kicky-wicky here at home,
> Spending his manly marrow in her arms,
> Which should sustain the bound and high curvet
> Of Mars's fiery steed. To other regions!
> France is a stable. . .
>
> (II, iii, 275–80)

The sexual meaning of 'stable' here ('standing place')[48] identifies France as a country dominated by women, where men are reduced to the role of satisfying women's pleasure. For Parolles sexuality is a frivolous diversion, as he makes clear in his advice to Helena to lose her virginity as soon as she can because it is against nature to preserve it. Helena's reply 'Not my virginity yet. . .' (I, i, 161), as I remarked earlier, shows a very different view of sexuality as having its appropriate times and seasons. Whereas for Parolles and Bertram sex is a casual amusement subject to no times or laws except those of appetite, to Helena it is a sacred trust, sanctified in marriage by divine law. This contrast in male and female attitudes runs through the play. Whereas to Diana marriage vows are a pledge to God (IV, ii, 28–9), to Bertram they are simply a means to a temporary cure of his 'sick desires' (IV, ii, 35) and both Helena and the Widow stress the 'lawfulness' of the bedroom exchange that will bring husband and wife together, the mystery of God's ways being suitably presented in Helena's riddling summary:

> Let us assay our plot; which, if it speed,
> Is wicked meaning in a lawful deed,
> And lawful meaning in a lawful act,
> Where both not sin, and yet a sinful fact.
>
> (III, vii, 44–7)

Bertram's 'wicked meaning' is miraculously to be translated into divine law, his sinfulness to be transmuted into divine virtue, his 'sick desires' cured as the King's were cured. We have seen how even the wise Lafeu in his bawdy interprets sexuality in terms of the incongruous, and this same male frivolousness is evinced by the lowly Lavatch, also an adept at the bawdy joke, who declares himself no longer satisfied with his humble Isbel now he has encountered the court ladies (III, ii, 12–14). It is odd that a play singled out (apparently)[49] for its bawdy by a later contemporary should have as a major theme the sacredness of sexuality.

It is not to sexuality itself that Bertram objects. As Parolles rightly remarks, Bertram is 'a foolish idle boy, but for all that very ruttish' (IV, iii, 207). We find Bertram perfectly willing to spend his 'manly marrow' in the process of seducing the chaste Diana in Florence. Bertram's objection is specifically to marriage, as the King pronounces: 'Wives are monsters to you' (V, iii, 154). Bertram himself prefers the male world of warfare to domestic obscurity: 'War is no strife/To the dark house and the detested wife' (II, iii, 287–8), which Parolles caps with the proverb: 'A young man married is a man that's marr'd' (II, iii, 294). The play rests on the Spenserean contrast between illicit, lawless sexuality out of wedlock and marital sexuality, which is an expression of the divine love. The images of darkness which both Bertram and Parolles associate with sexuality are images of emptiness. It is also characteristic of Bertram that he expresses his refusal to consummate his marriage with Helena in convolutedly negative terms: 'Till I have no wife, I have nothing in France' (III, ii, 99), and in a letter to his Mother he writes punningly of his marriage that he has 'sworn to make the "not" eternal' (III, ii, 21). Bertram has to be cured of this negativity as the King was of his. For Helena and the Widow, however, the darkness is God-given and the night-tryst that Helena makes with Bertram in Diana's bed part of heaven's purpose:

> Doubt not but heaven
> Hath brought me up to be your daughter's dower,
> As it hath fated her to be my motive
> And helper to a husband. But, O strange men!
> That can such sweet use make of what they hate,
> When saucy trusting of the cozen'd thoughts
> Defiles the pitchy night. . .
>
> (IV, iv, 18–24)

The hidden world of femininity is only a hostile world to male lawlessness and egocentricity. As part of God's cyclic rhythm it promises rebirth; Adonis must die in order to be perpetually reborn in Spenser's garden. Bertram finds himself participating in this process in spite of himself, saved from himself by Helena's love for him. His act of rebellion against God is, unknown to himself, a participation in God's purposes:

> *Second Lord*: He hath perverted a young gentlewoman here in Florence, of a most chaste renown, and this night fleshes his will in the spoil of her honour; he hath given her his monumental ring, and thinks himself made in the unchaste composition.
> *First Lord*: Now, God delay our rebellion! As we are ourselves, what things are we!

(IV, iii.13–19)

The two French Lords here touch on a central concept of the play: that all human activity contributes to the divine purpose and our very sinfulness comes to be used by God for His purposes. We are nothing in ourselves, everything in being part of the divine purpose. So Bertram finds, for all his wayward efforts to avoid his responsibilities as a husband, that he has unwittingly slept with his own wife and that she has conceived his child. It requires a final return to the maternal home however, for all this to become clear, and even at the end he is a reluctant, though inevitable, participant in the cycle of renewal.

If the empty drum is the central symbol of male irresponsibility in the play, the ring is the central symbol of femininity. It is through the recognition on his finger of the ring given to him by Helena that Bertram is finally brought to his senses. He is literally secured by his wife's ring, just as Strozza is secured by his wife's collar. The ring is, of course, a particularly appropriate symbol of femininity, as Lavatch makes clear in a characteristically bawdy disquisition on appropriateness, where he takes 'Tib's rush for Tom's forefinger' to be a symbol of perfect integration (II, ii, 22). Lavatch reflects the habitual male frivolity in seeing such fitness as a joke. The ring is more than simply a device of the plot, its circularity dominates the very structure of time and space in the play, which turns back on itself in the keeping of the Countess of Rossillion. It is a ring of the Rossillion family 'of six preceding ancestors' (V, iii, 195) that exposes Bertram's treachery to Diana, reminding us not only of the futility of Bertram's attempt to avoid the ring's logic, but also the repeated pattern of the ring's use. Like the ring that binds Donne and his wife in the compass image of 'Valediction Forbidding Mourning' so the rings of *All's Well* remind us of the centre which both gives meaning and direction to human activity: the erring male brought round to a sense of the divine stability of a moving world.

All's Well then, is the enactment of a myth of regeneration that takes its audience on a pilgrimage of grace. Lavatch, in his foolish wisdom, describes Helena as 'the sweet-marjoram of the sallet, or, rather, the herb of grace' (IV, v, 15–16) and Helena herself confidently offers the King:

> The greatest Grace lending grace,
> Ere twice the horses of the sun shall bring
> Their fiery coacher his diurnal ring. . .
> (II, i, 159–61)

God's time is, of course, independent of the cyclic pattern of sublunary nature. With Bertram we are taken on a journey which brings us back to our source in the love that binds us to one another. The play sees a central opposition between a femininity which has the guardianship of love's power and the wayward male whose destructiveness expresses itself in terms of comic frivolity. The stage evidence (such as it is) would suggest that it was not a particularly successful play, perhaps because its mythic content is expressed in a rather matter-of-fact way that to some extent hides its mythic purpose. As with Chapman, God's truths must be contemplated veiled lest they dazzle. Even the language of the play takes on a gnomic, enigmatic quality (not unlike Chapman's, as Tillyard remarked)[50] which creates a barrier to be penetrated. It was only in the later mythic plays – especially *Winter's Tale* and *Tempest* – that Shakespeare evolved a lyrical quality that expressed its religious mysticism more openly and more obviously. *All's Well* succeeds so well in hiding its art that it has never achieved satisfactory exposition. Yet its quasi-realistic mode expresses exactly that sense that the mysterious is to be discovered in the everyday world that is at the heart of neo-platonic thought[51]. Such transcendence as this play has to offer is not easily available (it is characteristic of the play that it is the foolish Parolles who speaks emptily of 'great power, great transcendence', II, iii, 34). Yet the play is a remarkable exploration of a mode that, if Shakespeare was later to endow with a more noumenal power, he was never to surpass in terms of dramatic presentation.

4

OTHELLO: A MAN KILLED
WITH KINDNESS

The probabilities are that having finished *All's Well* in the second half of 1602 Shakespeare began writing *Othello* early in 1603. The first production of *Othello* we hear of is at Court on 1 November 1604, to be shortly followed by the first recorded performance of *Measure for Measure*, also at Court, in December 1604. These two plays have one very important thing in common; they both derive from short stories in Giraldi Cinthio's series of moralized tales entitled *Gli Hecatommithi*, first published in 1565. It seems likely that Shakespeare read both these tales in Italian, for there is a probable verbal echo in the Disdemona story in the Moor's demand for ocular proof of his wife's infidelity (III, iii, 361) and Cinthio's Italian: 'If you do not make me. . .see with my eyes' ('se no mi fai. . . veder cogl'occhi'). No English translation seems to have been available, though Shakespeare could have made use of a French version of both tales. It seems certain that the two plays were written close together and that *Othello* must be the earlier. The main reason for concluding this is that *Measure for Measure* is unmistakably a Jamesean play and must have been begun after the accession of James I to the English throne in March 1603. It makes very extensive use of themes close to James's heart and in particular of James's book on kingship, *Basilikon Doron* (as we shall see in the next chapter) and it seems possible that the performance on 26 December 1604 was its first presentation. *Othello* also shows some influence of the King in Shakespeare's introduction of the war between Venetians and Turks in and around Cyprus that James had commemorated in his poem *Lepanto*, reprinted in 1603. Cinthio's story makes no mention of the Turkish wars and it seems likely – as Emrys Jones has argued[1] – that Shakespeare introduced the war theme as a complimentary gesture towards the new monarch. There is no actual echo of James's poem in *Othello* (Shakespeare derives his details of the war from Richard Knolles's *General History of the Turks* (1603), a book Knolles had dedicated to James). The connection between *Othello* and the King is therefore distinct, but peripheral, whereas the reflection of the King's ideas in *Measure for Measure* is far-reaching and fundamental. A reasonble conjecture would be that Shakespeare conceived and started writing *Othello* just before the accession of James and then included the Turkish connection as an early afterthought. Its first public performance would necessarily have to be delayed until after March 1604 when the theatres reopened after a year's closure because of the plague.[2]

Measure for Measure was certainly made to the King's measure, whereas *Othello* was not. On the contrary, its unusually domestic emphasis would suggest a popular audience[3] and in particular it would suggest a Globe reply to Heywood's apparently highly successful[4] domestic tragedy, *A Woman Killed with Kindness* at the Rose in late February or early March 1603 – just before the King's accession. In terms of its dramaturgy, *Othello* is the most clearly 'popular' play since *Hamlet*. We can conjecture, I think, on the evidence of its subsequent stage history, that *All's Well that Ends Well* was not a success; its mythological treatment of romance was probably neither romantic enough nor spectacular enough in its employment of myth to suit the less sophisticated of the Globe audience. A return to affective tragedy – a mode that had provided Shakespeare with his last unequivocal success – was therefore to be expected, especially with Heywood demonstrating so convincingly its appeal in a rival theatre. *Othello* follows *Hamlet* in appealing both to the more sentimentally inclined and to the wiser sort – indeed in its combination of heart-rending pathos and in its highly sophisticated aesthetic patterning, *Othello* shows Shakespeare at his most professionally skilful in catering for the full range of his audience.

It is sometimes argued that there is a special connection between *All's Well* and *Measure for Measure*[5] and both have come to be incorporated under the misleading (and misconceived) label of 'problem plays'. The emphasis of *All's Well* is not on problems, but on solutions, as we have seen, nor is it in any sense problematic; *Measure for Measure* on the other hand delights in the pursuit of rather esoteric theological problems, no doubt to the approval of the pedantic James. Clearly the two plays are not unrelated, but similarities have been exaggerated. There is some resemblance in tone between the two plays in the sense that they both have a somewhat disillusioned air, but whereas this is apparent in *All's Well* it is real in the later play. There is little, if anything, of the mythic quality of *All's Well* in *Measure for Measure*, which explores its intellectual themes with a more determined realism and a greater concern for its characters as personalities. Nor have the heroines more than a superficial resemblance: Helena is essentially a symbol of God's power in her play, while Isabella is all too human a figure, who, like Bertram, has to undergo a voyage of spiritual change that will lead her to becoming a different person at the end of the play from the woman we see in the beginning. Dramaturgically *All's Well* is essentially mythic, *Measure for Measure* thematic in structure. The affinities between *All's Well* and *Othello* are, on the other hand, more fundamental. Both plays centre on the discord between love and war, both alike identifying love with femininity and war with masculinity. Both plays show the feminine as constructive, the masculine as destructive. Othello, like Bertram, is a man who has not come to terms with the world of domesticity, and is a stranger to it:

> For since these arms of mine had seven years' pith,
> Till now some nine moons wasted, they have us'd
> Their dearest action in the tented field,
> And little of this great world can I speak,
> More than pertains to feats of broil, and battle. . .
>
> (I, iii, 83–7)[6]

In Othello's case the sexual immaturity is all the more alarming because he is no boy and lacks the easy malleability that reconciles Bertram to his sexual responsibilities. The outcome is, therefore, tragic; for Othello, who cannot bend, must break, and breaks not only himself but the wife who has too readily accepted the romantic view of the heroic world that her husband projects.

The thematic preoccupations of *Othello* are, then, remarkably similar to those of *All's Well* and suggest a continuation of that marriage debate that converts the frivolous Helen of the Trojan war to the life-bringing Helena and now re-explores the tragedy of sexual mistrust between men and women that had been a sub-theme of *Hamlet*. It was no doubt this that attracted Shakespeare to the *Hecatommithi*, whose introduction proclaims the intention of demonstrating that human love can only find its true expression in marriage. Giraldi presents the stories as contrasting examples of 'how peace in love may be obtained'.[7] Don Fabio, the leader of the group of five men and five women who tell the tales on the way from Rome to Marseilles, starts the debate by asserting that true love can only be found in marriage:

> And because I do not see any love among us. . .which is not wholly appetite except that which is between husband and wife, I hold without any doubt that in the love of which we speak there cannot be a quiet and reposeful life except where husbands and wives. . .join together, seeking wisdom and prudence, and desiring honest repose so as to live peacefully in this mortal state.[8]

Don Fabio is challenged by Don Ponzio, who claims that marriage may be fraught with unhappiness:

> In this more than in any other affair it is needful to take reason and counsel for guide, and with discerning eye to consider the quality, manners, life and habits of the men or women, their mothers, fathers, families, antiquity, rank, and other such factors which are manifest signs of the natures and lives of other people.[9]

The stories told by each of the party in turn illustrate a variety of problems round this central theme, some supporting Don Fabio's viewpoint, some against. The theme of the third day is 'The infidelity of husbands and wives' and it is in the course of this day's story-telling that Don Curzio tells the story of Disdemona.

If the thematic preoccupations of *Othello* show continuity and progression, the dramaturgy does not. In dramatic technique *Othello* completely abandons the myth-making purposes of *All's Well*, indeed Shakespeare goes out of his way to demythologize his material in this play (as we shall see), to centre his dramatic interest in the play of personality. In this *Othello* is partly a return to well-tried methods, for here Shakespeare returns to his predilection for treating characters as people and asks us to respond to his fictional world with real emotion. But there is also a very important shift in Shakespearean technique in this play, a moral detachment appears that sees the tragedy of the lovers not so much as part of a system of praise and blame, as of aesthetic contrast: the black and white opposition of the play, in all its subtlety, is an accurate indication of an aesthetic dominance.

Shakespeare's rejection of symbolic characterization is nowhere clearer than in his treatment of Desdemona. In *All's Well* the heroine not only plays an exceptionally active role as symbol of love's power, but she is also presented, as we saw, without too much regard for either romantic convention or even psychological plausibility in her combination of personal humility with confident determination. Desdemona, in contrast, is not only an exceptionally passive heroine, resembling Ophelia in her willingness to suffer the hero's vituperations with little complaint, but she is also presented in strongly personal terms as a suffering human being. The scene (V, iii) in which Emilia prepares Desdemona for what proves to be her death bed is surely one of the most affecting scenes in all Shakespeare, rivalling in pathos Ophelia's mad scene in *Hamlet*. It is noticeable how particular and how domestic Shakespeare keeps this scene between the two women:

Emilia: I would you had never seen him!
Desdemona: So would not I, my love doth so approve him,
That even his stubbornness, his checks, his frowns, –
Prithee unpin me, – have grace and favour in them.
Emilia: I have laid those sheets you bade me on the bed.
Desdemona: All's one, good faith: how foolish are our minds!
If I do die before thee, prithee shroud me
In one of those same sheets.
Emilia: Come, come, you talk.
Desdemona: My mother had a maid call'd Barbary,
She was in love, and he she lov'd prov'd mad,
And did forsake her; she had a song of 'willow',

An old thing 'twas, but it express'd her fortune,
And she died singing it. . .

(IV, iii, 18–30)

The small domestic details – the unpinning of the gown, the instruction about the precise sheet to go on the bed, the reference to the maid called Barbary and then the discussion of the Venetian ambassador Lodovico as what some modern ladies would call 'male crumpet' that follows – all suggest a real and actual world which we are invited to share. Heywood's tragedy shows a similar concern with domestic minutiae. But it is not only that we are encouraged to believe in the world of *Othello* as a world of solid actuality, we are equally invited to respond to the emotions of the two characters. Desdemona's premonitions of the disaster to come and the 'willow' lament that she cannot get out of her head are charged with a pathos that conveys itself directly to the audience. The contrast between the sensitive Desdemona, sensing a tragic outcome that she has not yet consciously defined, and the coarser-grained but well-meaning Emilia, chattering about women's rights, is a poignant reminder of the gap between justice and power that emerges from their particular personalities.

This sense of particularity is all the more remarkable because Desdemona's pedigree dramatically would seem to relate her to the exemplary role of obedient wife, beloved of Elizabethan theory. Shakespeare had no doubt glanced, during his work on *Othello*, at the newly printed quarto of *Patient Grissil* of 1603. There is some slight hint of a connection between the two plays, both in the conversation between Babulo, the clown, and Laureo on the subject of monsters, in which creatures are described as 'without heads, having their eyes, nose and mouths in their breasts' (V, i, 25)[10] and also in the incongruous Welsh of the termagant Gwenthyan, who has a fondness for swearing by Iago (St James). Written jointly by Dekker, Haughton and Chettle for the Admiral's Men, *Patient Grissil* was first performed early in 1600 (probably at the Rose playhouse) and was, in Professor Hoy's words 'evidently successful'.[11] In it Shakespeare could not only have found the archetypal obedient wife, but also a strongly affective treatment in the Dekkerian manner. The play retains its function as an 'exemplum' of patience: 'Patience hath won the prize' we are assured in the final scene (V, ii, 273), but the exemplary element does not preclude a strong emphasis on the pathos of Grissil's suffering. The most notable example of this affectiveness in the play does not involve Grissil (whose role almost inevitably invites pathos) but the wayward and tyrannical Marquis, Grissil's husband. One of the trials Grissil is forced to undergo as a test of her Christian patience is to have her twin babies taken from her. In the beginning of Act IV, scene i (by Chettle, according to Hoy)[12] we find the Marquis troubled that he must inflict suffering on his wife and, in a sentimental manner we would not usually associate with Elizabethan paternity, expressing his joy in fatherhood:

108

Marquis: Give me this blessed burthen, pretty foole
  With what an amiable looke it sleepes,
  And in that slumber how it sweetly smiles,
  And in that smile how my heart leaps for joy. . .

(IV, i, 3–6)

The transformation of the stern marquis of the Chaucerian exemplum into sentimental hero shows how far the popular stage had taken to heart the Shakespearean lesson by 1600. *Patient Grissil* is not by any means the only play to portray the patient wife around this time, indeed a whole spate of plays adopted the theme, such as Middleton's *Phoenix* (1603–4), Heywood's *Wise Woman of Hogsden* (c.1604), Marston's *Dutch Courtesan* (c.1604); and the anonymous plays *London Prodigal* and *Fair Maid of Bristow*, the last two being Globe plays of around 1604. *Patient Grissil*'s printing may have helped generate the fashion.

Desdemona takes obedience almost to the exemplary lengths of Grissil, but while Shakespeare exploits her passivity to the full for its pathos, he studiously avoids associating it with the theme of Christian patience, which is an explicit theme of Dekker's play. *Othello* characteristically avoids such mythologizing. Desdemona is not presented as a type of Christian fortitude, but as a woman desperately struggling to come to terms with a male violence whose causes she cannot imaginatively comprehend. That the drama is one of psychological mismatch, not of ideology, is equally and more surprisingly demonstrated by the use to which Christian ideology is put in the play's patterning.

It has frequently been remarked how dominant the images of the morality drama are in *Othello*. Repeatedly the play makes use of the terminology of the psychomachia. The application of these references too are consistent and clear, with Desdemona presented as the angel of light in opposition to Iago's diabolical darkness, and with Othello the figure of Everyman, for whose soul the war between good and evil is waged. A process akin to beatification of Desdemona seems to take place in the course of the play, beginning with Cassio's greeting of the 'divine Desdemona' (II, i, 73) on their arrival in Cyprus:

> Ye men of Cyprus, let her have your knees:
> Hail to thee, lady! and the grace of heaven,
> Before, behind thee, and on every hand,
> Enwheel thee round!

(II, i, 84–7)

As Ben Jonson remarked on another occasion: 'if it had been written of the Virgin Mary it had been something'. The sense that Desdemona has a semi-divine status gathers strength towards the end of the play, especially in Othello's references to her. To Emilia any thought against Desdemona's fidelity should bring divine retribution on the accuser (IV, ii, 15–16). To

Othello, life without Desdemona's love is 'perdition' and 'chaos' come again (III, iii, 91–3) and, more extraordinary, her death is seen as an apocalyptic moment in which the whole of nature is disrupted:

> O, insupportable! O heavy hour!
> Methinks it should be now a huge eclipse
> Of sun and moon, and the affrighted globe
> Should yawn at alteration.
>
> (V, ii, 99–102)

It was Theobald in the eighteenth century who first suggested an allusion here to the Crucifixion and certainly the association is not forced. Desdemona, it seems, is in the process of deification, a process that has arrived, at least for Othello, by the time he recognizes his tragic mistake and that Desdemona was indeed – as Emilia asserts – 'heavenly true' (V, ii, 138). As he prepares to kill himself he sees her judging him from Heaven:

> when we shall meet at count,
> This look of thine will hurl my soul from heaven,
> And fiends will snatch at it: cold, cold, my girl,
> Even like thy chastity; O cursed slave!
> Whip me, you devils,
> From the possession of this heavenly sight,
> Blow me about in winds, roast me in sulphur,
> Wash me in steep-down gulfs of liquid fire!
>
> (V, ii, 274–81)

Othello is in a state of total hysteria when he utters these lines, he has not long since been cursing Desdemona:

> *Othello*: She's like a liar gone to burning hell,
>   'Twas I that killed her.
> *Emilia*: O, the more angel she,
>   And you the blacker devil!
> *Othello*: She turn'd to folly, and she was a whore.
> *Emilia*: Thou dost belie her, and thou art a devil.
> *Othello*: She was false as water.
>
> (V, ii, 130–5)

Here the language of the morality play is shared equally by Othello and Emilia, yet its function is not to establish Desdemona's or Othello's true place in a mythology of good and evil, but to reveal the irony that Othello's derangement has completely reversed normal values. One function of this simplifying pattern of Christian images is to make possible, by its very clarity, a spectacular play of paradoxical oppositions with a common base in the black/white opposition of the hero and heroine. In these terms the paradox here is that the white Desdemona should be

110

accused of blackness by the black Othello (whose inner whiteness has been blackened by the black white man, Iago – and so on).[13] In this way the moral problems that the play confronts are constantly diverted towards aesthetic ends. We ought to note that Shakespeare got a hint of this play of opposites in Giraldi's treatment of his tales in *Gli Hecatommithi*, where at one point after demonstrating 'it is better burying women than marrying them'[14] Don Fabio comments : 'che non é cosa nel mondo così buona, ne così santa che non habbia le sue contradittioni' (for there is nothing in the world so good or holy that does not have its contradictions). Othello is clearly not a devil, but a man caught up in a perplexity of contradiction from which he cannot free himself, a victim not an initiator of evil. The morality pattern is here being used – as it is throughout the play – not to assert the myth of good and evil, but to highlight the gap between perception and truth. Othello's 'she was false as water' is particularly revealing here, for it reverses the mythic expectations that associate water with cleansing and regeneration. Othello's image is an image of subconscious as well as conscious mistrust. Desdemona is seen as belonging to a hostile medium, the female element of water, where a man can have no firm footing. The later remark 'Cold. . .even like thy chastity' (V, ii, 275–6) is similarly revealing, for it suggests a psychological hostility in Othello, a puzzlement concerning female sexuality that belies (presumably) the actual facts of his sexual relations with her. Her sexuality is 'cold' because (unlike a man's) it remains undemonstrated in crude physiological terms. Shakespeare develops a kind of counterpoint throughout the play in which the complexity of actual character is seen against a grid of clear and simple moral typology. The assertion of Desdemona's 'divinity' is a reminder that she is completely innocent, even though her actual behaviour is sometimes indiscreet and compromising. Take the scene, for instance, immediately after Cassio's ecstatic greeting of Desdemona (II, i, 85–8). No sooner is the greeting over than Shakespeare gives us a bawdy interchange between Iago and Desdemona in which she deliberately encourages Iago to express his cynical view of women. The contrast between the holy Desdemona and the sexually alert young woman is a deliberate demythologizing that reminds us that we are not dealing with the Virgin Mary here, but with a young bride whose admiration for her black husband has led her to defy her father and insist against her husband's initial judgement on accompanying him to the wars (I, iii, 235–59). This does not invalidate Cassio's ecstatic comments; on the contrary Cassio's reverence keeps us aware of the basic truth that Desdemona, for all her womanly actuality, is essentially a woman of virtue and purity. The mythological grid helps us chart our way through the complexities of the actual world, where devils can appear honest and angels are seen as whores. In *Othello* myth is at the service of actuality; the method of *All's Well* is reversed. This can again be illustrated in Desdemona's dying words: 'A guiltless death I die' (V, ii, 125) which would, taken strictly in mythic terms, imply a purity that no Christian could claim. This is not, however, mythic statement, but the assertion that essentially Desdemona is innocent of the charges that Othello has brought against her. The mythic language simplifies and clarifies the actuality. In *All's Well* the significance of the actual events can only be understood in terms of the underlying myth: in *Othello* the mythic references can only be understood in terms of the psychological reality.

The language of myth also has a subtler role to play in *Othello* and this is to reinforce the sense of incompatibility between the sexes. The association of Desdemona with the angelic and the pure, and increasingly, the association of Othello with darkness and evil, heightens the sense that female and male are separated by an unbridgeable divide that eventually becomes, in Othello's mind, the vision of his being hurled at the Last Judgement into hell-fire by a glance from the beatified Desdemona. This opposition between 'dark' and 'white' sexuality had made its appearance years earlier in one of the most famous of the Dark Lady Sonnets. In Sonnet 144, however, the roles are reversed; it is feminine sexuality that is seen as dark and diabolic and male as white (fair) and angelic:

> The better angel is a man right fair,
> The worser spirit a woman colour'd ill.
> To win me soon to hell, my female evil
> Tempteth my better angel from my side,
> And would corrupt my saint to be a devil,
> Wooing his purity with her foul pride.

Here the same patterns of dark and light emerge with an effect that is not primarily aesthetic, but psychological: the hell to which women constantly tempt men and that leads to the 'firing out' of venereal disease, expresses a profound hostility to the hidden nature of women's sexuality. The dark/light opposition is an emphasis on sexual difference, made all the more emphatic by the sexual sameness of the friend. The 'otherness' of femininity is vividly expressed in the sonnet by the revival of the medieval identification of the vagina with the mouth of hell[15] in the line: 'I guess one angel in another's hell'. In *Othello* the opposition remains as firmly entrenched, only the gender values have been reversed. The male/female opposition is again seen as absolute, but now that opposition is expressed in terms of female 'whiteness' and angelic purity against the demonic and dark forces of male sexuality and violence. There is also in *Othello* an important shift in Shakespeare's response to the contrast, which is treated less as a subject of moral outrage and more as a subject of aesthetic patterning, much as Renaissance painters liked to hit off colour contrasts in the painting of male and female flesh.[16]

Certainly this sense of male and female contrast dominates the play.

112

Even Cassio, who is clearly both attractive to women and attracted by them, ('He has a person and a smooth dispose. . .fram'd to make women false', I, iii, 395–6) shows his essential hostility to female 'otherness' in his contemptuous treatment of the infatuated Bianca (IV, i, 106ff). The most acute expression of this opposition is in Iago's relation to Desdemona. Desdemona's world is presented in markedly domestic terms, in a preoccupation with bed-linen, needlework (IV, i, 197), her fan, her gloves and mask (IV, ii, 8), her nightclothes – and it is yet another of the play's paradoxes that it is a handkerchief that brings her downfall. What other Shakespearean heroine would argue her case in terms of looking after her husband's health: .

> Why, this is not a boon,
> 'Tis as I should entreat you wear your gloves;
> Or feed on nourishing dishes, or keep you warm,
> Or sue to you, to do a peculiar profit
> To your own person. . .
>
> (III, iii, 77–81)

Iago's world, like that of the other principal male figures in the play, is the army, the world of war. Shakespeare is yet again exploring the Mars/Venus conjunction. But whereas Othello's lack of domesticity has led him into seeing women in romantic terms, Iago has an explicit hostility to women. If Othello tends to see women as saints, Iago sees them unequivocally as whores:

> since I could distinguish between a benefit and an injury, I never found a man that knew how to love himself: ere I would say I would drown myself, for the love of a guinea-hen, I would change my humanity with a baboon.
>
> (I, iii, 312–16)

Iago frequently uses animal imagery to describe sexual relationships. He had earlier described Othello's relationship with Desdemona to Brabantio as 'an old black ram. . .tupping your white ewe' (I, i, 88–9) and again as 'you'll have your daughter covered with a Barbary horse' (I, i, 111–12). Later he conjures up a picture of Cassio and Desdemona together in similar terms: 'as prime as goats, as hot as monkeys, /As salt as wolves, in pride. . .' (III, iii, 409–10). He sees sexual intercourse as essentially a dehumanizing process in which the female body is an instrument for working off the sensual madness that man's reason fails to control:

> If the balance of our lives had not one scale of reason, to poise another of sensuality, the blood and baseness of our natures would conduct us to most preposterous conclusions. But we have reason to cool our raging motions, our carnal stings, our unbitted lusts; whereof I take

this, that you call love, to be a sect, or scion.

(I, iii, 326–33)

Not surprisingly Freudian interpretations of the play have seen in Iago the attitudes of the male homosexual and Lawrence Olivier gave a homosexual reading of the part (with advice from Ernest Jones) in a production of the 1930s.[17].Certainly the depths of Iago's hostility towards Desdemona and his contemptuous attitude to his wife – a contempt that ends in her murder – are best explained in psychological terms as paranoia. There is also a marked contrast between the animal imagery he habitually uses to describe heterosexual intercourse with the almost lyrical description he gives homosexual foreplay in his account of the imagined' encounter in bed between himself and Cassio:

> And then, sir, would he gripe and wring my hand,
> Cry out, 'Sweet creature!' and then kiss me hard,
> As if he pluck'd up kisses by the roots,
> That grew upon my lips, then laid his leg
> Over my thigh, and sigh'd, and kiss'd, and then
> Cried 'Cursed fate, that gave thee to the Moor!'

(III, iii, 427–32)

Whether we interpret this as a sign of Iago's latent (or actual) homosexuality, or simply as Iago's imaginative skill in working on Othello's insecurity, the effect of the hostile references to feminine sexuality is to create a sense of the essential opposition between the sexes. Iago's hostility to women generates a sense in the play of two hostile worlds of male and female which Othello finds himself unable to bridge. Iago plays constantly on Othello's ignorance of women and their ways in presenting Desdemona as both incomprehensible and 'unnatural':

Othello: And yet how nature erring from itself –
Iago: Ay, there's the point: as, to be bold with you,
 Not to affect many proposed matches,
 Of her own clime, complexion, and degree,
 Whereto we see in all things nature tends;
 Fie, we may smell in such a will most rank,
 Foul disproportion; thoughts unnatural.
 But pardon me: I do not in position
 Distinctly speak of her, though I may fear
 Her will, recoiling to her better judgement,
 May fall to match you with her country forms,
 And happily repent.

(III, iii, 231–42)

Here Iago manages to insinuate both that there is an essential

114

incompatibility between Othello and Desdemona in terms of 'clime, complexion and degree' (points Othello clearly takes to heart a little later, III, iii, 267–70) and that there is something perverse and unnatural in Desdemona's sexual preferences. The intense language suggests a nausea towards feminine sexuality in general: 'we may smell in such a will most rank,/Foul disproportion'. Moreover the tortured language here suggests an impossibility of speaking rationally on the subject of women's sexuality. The last sentence in particular, whether we accept the punctuation of the folio (and Arden) as here, or place a semi-colon after 'Distinctly speak of her' (as in the New Cambridge Shakespeare) is particularly tortuous and seems to be both suggesting that 'haply' Desdemona's judgement may chance ('fall') to coincide with her marital obligations and contradictorily casting doubt on it at the same time ('though I may fear her will'). The doubt becomes more insistent because of the sexual overtones of 'will' and especially of 'country forms' (we recollect Hamlet's 'country matters').

Just as Desdemona is associated with the imagery of heaven, so Iago, throughout the play, is attended by images of hell. But again these references have a metaphorical rather than literal function: Iago is like the devil in his behaviour, but he is not the devil, simply a man possessed by hatred, especially of women. Othello makes the distinction himself:

> I look down towards his feet, but that's a fable,
> If that thou be'st a devil, I cannot kill thee.
>
> (V, ii, 287–8)

Othello's phrase 'but that's a fable' reveals the demythologizing principle that characterizes the play. In promptly wounding him Othello demonstrates in action what his words have asserted, that the language of heaven and hell is merely illustrative and that the reality lies in the everyday world of mortal men and women. The diabolical role that Iago assumes is essentially that, a part assumed to express a state of mind:

> How am I then a villain,
> To counsel Cassio to this parallel course,
> Directly to his good? Divinity of hell!
> When devils will their blackest sins put on,
> They do suggest at first with heavenly shows,
> As I do now. . .
>
> (II, iii, 339–44)

'As I do now' suggests difference as well as similarity: Iago will behave as if he were a devil in adopting diabolic stratagems. Accordingly Shakespeare is careful to suggest human motives for Iago's behaviour: Othello has passed him over for promotion in favour of Cassio, he even claims at one point to be a rival for Desdemona's love (II, i, 286) and (less plausibly still) he claims that he suspects Othello of adultery with his wife:

> I hate the Moor,
> And it is thought abroad, that 'twixt my sheets
> He's done my office; I know not if't be true. . .
> Yet I, for mere suspicion in that kind,
> Will do, as if for surety. . .

(I, iii, 384–8)

It is true that the hatred expressed here does not seem commensurate with the suspicion, but this suggests some hidden psychological prompting such as the thwarted homosexuality some have read into the relationship. The reasons Iago gives for his hatred of Othello look like rationalizations, but that merely confirms them as of psychological, not supernatural import. You cannot demythologize, however, without evoking mythic patterns. Something of Iago's diabolic descent from earlier drama remains and Iago is closer to his mythic origins than either Othello or Desdemona.

Whatever obscurities lie in Iago's motivation, there is nothing obscure in the workings of Othello's mind – as Iago himself recognizes:

> The Moor a free and open nature too,
> That thinks men honest that but seems to be so:
> And will as tenderly be led by the nose. . .
> As asses are.

(I, iii, 397–400)

It is Iago's function to exploit the great differences in background, age, race, between Othello and Desdemona in expressing his comprehensive contempt for mankind. This is made comparatively easy by Othello's ignorance of women and conversely by his confidence in his assessment of men:

> This fellow's of exceeding honesty,
> And knows all qualities, with a learned spirit,
> Of human dealing: if I do prove her haggard,
> Though that her jesses were my dear heart-strings,
> I'ld whistle her off, and let her down the wind,
> To prey at fortune. Haply, for I am black,
> And have not those soft parts of conversation
> That chamberers have, or for I am declin'd
> Into the vale of years – yet that's not much –
> She's gone, I am abus'd, and my relief
> Must be to loathe her: O curse of marriage,
> That we can call these delicate creatures ours,
> And not their appetites! I had rather be a toad,
> And live upon the vapour in a dungeon,
> Than keep a corner in a thing I love
> For others' uses. . .

(III, iii, 262–77)

116

As with Iago, beneath the level of plausible explanations for his hostility – his colour, his age, lack of domesticity – lies a much more fundamental sense of women's 'otherness'. Even Othello himself feels the inadequacy of the rationalizations in the dismissive 'yet that's not much', half-recognizing, through the imagery of revulsion, the more potent antagonism in the nature of feminine sexuality itself. Significantly Othello (like Iago) resorts to animal images to express his sense of Desdemona's wildness in the image of the hawk (the role of the male is, ironically in the circumstances, seen as to domesticate, to tame the wildness) and this then becomes subtly intertwined with more sinister images. The hostility aroused by the thought of the contrast between feminine 'delicacy' and the unbridled sexual appetite that this delicacy conceals leads to the image of the toad living upon the vapour of a dungeon. The toad/dungeon imagery, ostensibly referring to Othello himself, is suggestively juxtaposed with the sexual imagery of corner/thing/uses,[18] which associate sexuality, and female sexuality in particular, with the unsavoury and the unhealthy. Iago, Othello assures Emilia, 'hates the slime/That sticks on filthy deeds' (V, ii, 149–50), again setting up an underlying antithesis between the clean and sanitary male and the slippery, unhealthy world he encounters in consort with the feminine. The romantic view of women that prompted Othello's elopement is here shown to be the sentimental side to a hostility to femininity he shares with Iago. Nowhere does Othello reveal his preferences more clearly than in the alacrity with which he prepares to abandon Desdemona for the wars (I, iii, 229–39) and in his willingness to forgo the trivialities of love for the 'serious. . .business' of war. For all Othello's function as victim of Iago's diabolical scheming he is revealed at a more fundamental psychological level to be one with Iago in his incomprehension of female 'otherness'.

Here again, then, the mythological role of 'everyman' that Othello could be expected to assume in the morality pattern of the play is fundamentally undermined by the emphasis on individual psychology. As 'everyman' figure, at the centre of the war between good and evil for the possession of his soul, we might expect that his natural, instinctive leanings would be towards the good, whereas we find a superficial attraction to Desdemona that conceals a latent incomprehension and hostility. Equally the morality pattern would lead us to expect that Othello must face a fundamental choice between good and evil, for if there is no choice there can be no sin. Heywood's *Woman Killed With Kindness* makes that particularly clear. Again *Othello* defies the logic of this pattern. The very depth of his hostility pre-empts any possibility of choice, he is already at the beginning of the play 'of the devil's party without knowing it'.

It is partly for this reason that Othello, in all logic (if not in natural sympathy) cannot be held fully responsible for killing his wife, in the light of his conviction that in doing so he is protecting other men from similar deception ('she must die, else she'll betray more men' – V, ii, 6). This

117

thought may be mad, but it is not strictly criminal. The strange logic of Othello's mind has convinced him that femininity itself is the enemy that must be extirpated to free men for the healthy pursuit of war, which paradoxically he associates with peace and contentment:

> I had been happy if the general camp,
> Pioners, and all, had tasted her sweet body,
> So I had nothing known: O now for ever
> Farewell the tranquil mind, farewell content:
> Farewell the plumed troop, and the big wars,
> That makes ambition virtue: O farewell,
> Farewell the neighing steed, and the shrill trump,
> The spirit-stirring drum, the ear-piercing fife;
> The royal banner, and all quality,
> Pride, pomp, and circumstance of glorious war!
> And, O ye mortal engines, whose wide throats
> The immortal Jove's great clamour counterfeit;
> Farewell, Othello's occupation's gone.
>
> (III, iii, 351–63)

The opening image of the hidden 'pioners', moling it in the dark of Desdemona's body is starkly contrasted with the open male world of light and healthy energy surrounding the activities of glorious war. Here again, and massively, are the dark/light paradoxes at work. It is difficult to realize fully that the splendid image of the 'mortal engines' that challenge comparison with divine thunder refer to the cannon that wreak such destruction on the battlefield; and this in spite of some undercutting of the pomp and circumstance in the punning return to sexual imagery at the end.[19]

It is interesting that we do not immediately reject what is after all a particularly perverse view of war, as Othello describes it. On the contrary the tendency of our sympathy is to support war's 'healthiness' against the treacherous world of human sexuality. Were this not the case Othello would seem little better than a madman. Shakespeare achieves his paradoxical feat largely by keeping strictly moral considerations in the background throughout *Othello*. We are not being asked to judge war for what it is, so much as admire its spectacle as an aesthetic event, and this is thoroughly characteristic of the play. The very treatment of the character of Othello illustrates the same tendency. It is a commonplace of *Othello* criticism that the hero constantly seems to be dramatizing himself, adopting some heroic role that he sees himself fulfilling.[20] So the reason he gives for Desdemona's love for him is that she 'pities the tale of him' (to adapt Sidney's phrase):

> She lov'd me for the dangers I had pass'd,

And I lov'd her that she did pity them.
(I, iii, 167–8)

Critics have felt the need to explain this self-dramatization in psychological terms as a sign of Othello's immaturity and this testifies to the sense of individuality that the characterization encourages throughout the play. But equally important is the distancing from too close an identification with the hero that this technique achieves. This is in marked contrast to Shakespeare's presentation of Hamlet. One clear indication of the difference between the two plays in this respect is in Shakespeare's use of soliloquy in *Othello*. Whereas in *Hamlet* soliloquy serves to bring us close to the inner workings of Hamlet's mind, in *Othello* soliloquy is used more as we saw it in *Hamlet's* rivals, *Lust's Dominion* and *Hoffman*, as a means of defining the speaker's role rather than revealing inner thoughts. Thus Iago, the prime mover of the action, is given rather more soliloquy than Othello, as, for instance, when he explains to the audience his intentions towards Othello at the end of Act I (I, iii,, 381ff), lays out his plot (II, i, 281ff) or both defines his role and further explains his plotting (II, iii, 327ff). Othello is given only one extended soliloquy, in which he presents his inner thoughts (III, iii, 262ff) and even this is quite unlike a Hamlet set-piece, serving to record the conclusions Othello has come to rather than (as with Hamlet) presenting the inner tensions and dilemmas which prevent decisions from being made. We are not, that is, being invited in *Othello* to share the hero's bafflement, but rather being given information that points us towards the denouement. Moreover this particular soliloquy in Act III is closely bound up with the action in ways that the positioning of Hamlet's soliloquies preclude. Iago has just left Othello, having sown the seeds of doubt in Othello's mind, and we watch Othello trying to adjust to the new information in preparing for the entry of Desdemona twenty-two lines later. Similarly the short soliloquy Othello is given on his entry into Desdemona's bedroom, prior to her murder, is closely bound up with the action of the murder, a dramatic pause before the onslaught, which is superbly effective in heightening the pathos but does nothing to close the emotional gap betwen the protagonist and the audience.

Shakespeare's dramaturgy in this play, then, while insisting on the individuality of the characters and exploiting the action affectively, also contrives an element of detachment that leaves us as much spectators of the ironic pattern of events as emotional participants in them. In Hamlet we readily identify ourselves with the hero: in Othello we sympathize with a man who is essentially different from ourselves. This is partly because the play presents Othello as an outsider and misunderstandings caused by his status as an outsider are a crucial element in his downfall. It is even more to do with that rhetorical presentation, that 'Othello music', that wraps around him and prevents the reader penetrating beneath the public

119

carapace, as one can with Hamlet. Even the moments of intense passion are peculiarly theatrical. It is thoroughly appropriate that his distress at the thought of his wife's infidelity should express itself in the melodramatically visual form of an apoplectic fit. That it is the Shakespearean method of presentation of character in the play, rather than the peculiar circumstances of his isolation, that creates the distance between the expressed emotions and the audience can be illustrated from our response to Desdemona. She, like her husband, is a figure with whom we can very readily sympathize, but with whom it is extremely difficult to identify. She too possesses a 'stagey' quality in her almost fanatical refusal to challenge her husband's fantasies, which in the event kills him with her kindness. This gives her an heroic quality that complements her husband's, but it emphasizes her difference from us. Like Othello, she conforms to the Aristotelian requirement (in what is in some respects a remarkably Aristotelian play) that the major figures of tragedy should be 'better than average'. Here the pattern of Christian references (the 'myth grid') plays a crucial role. Associating Desdemona with the angelic constantly reminds us of her difference from the ordinary, which her whiteness, in opposition to her husband's blackness, helps to reinforce in aesthetic terms.

This element of detachment is not so strong that we find ourselves standing in indifferent aloofness from the participants, and the Victorian lady who is supposed to have shouted from the gallery 'Oh you great black fool, can't you see, can't you see?' was genuinely (if apocryphally) responding to a play that presents character in vividly human terms. Nor is the feeling of detachment sufficient to prompt the clarity of moral judgement that is characteristic of the kind of satirical alienation we find in Jonson's plays. At the end of the play no clear moral judgement of the hero emerges; this is largely because he is presented so much more as a victim than as an instigator of the tragedy. Othello's flaw is, in moral terms, something of a virtue: to believe too readily and too naïvely in Iago's 'honesty'. The decision to kill Desdemona is made in good faith. The essential error is one of ignorance, not moral turpitude. Here again Shakespeare, whether consciously or not, adopts Aristotelian criteria, for in Aristotle's discussion of fear and pity he declares his approval of tragic plots in which 'the character should act in ignorance and only learn the truth afterwards'[21] and the concept of *hamartia* seems to involve the hero's ignorance rather than wilful perversity. Aristotle also, in the same section of the *Poetics* advocates plots

> when the sufferings involve those who are near and dear to one another, when for example brother kills brother, son father, mother son, or son mother, or if such a deed is contemplated, or something else of the kind is actually done, then we have a situation of the kind to be aimed at.[22]

The killing of a wife would presumably fit this category, and this is unique to *Othello* among Shakespeare's tragedies. Certainly the ending of *Othello* evinces more unequivocally than any of his other tragedies that evocation of pity and fear that Aristotle claims to be the necessary emotions for achieving that mysterious 'catharsis' that he sees as the end of tragedy.

The lack of serious moral conclusion was one of the principal objections to *Othello* put forward by Thomas Rymer in his attack on the play in the *Short View of Tragedy* (1692) where he complains that the play teaches little more than that ladies should look after their linen.[23] His objections may be somewhat provocatively expressed (though later endorsed by T. S. Eliot) but they rightly bear witness to the play's refusal to yield a satisfactory pattern of moral statement. Had Rymer (a classical scholar) been as much of a neo-classicist as some of Shakespeare's contemporaries, he would have applauded Shakespeare's 'Aristotelianism' here too, for the aesthetic, rather than the moral, effect of tragedy is emphasized by the Italian theorist Castelvetro in his commentary on Aristotle's *Poetics* of 1570.[24] It is unlikely that this Aristotelianism was accidental, for *Othello* was written at a time when the Jacobean popular stage was just beginning to come to terms with the new classicism, led by George Chapman (whose experiments in a more austere classical tragedy were about to commence) and the proselytizing of Jonson. One of the influences on Shakespeare in this respect was undoubtedly Jonson's recent experiment in classical tragedy, *Sejanus*, a play for which the neo-classical rules are specifically invoked.

We cannot be as certain that Shakespeare had attended a performance of Heywood's *Woman Killed With Kindness* as we can that he was intimate with *Sejanus*, but a study of the two plays is equally instructive in the light it throws on *Othello*, in terms of similarity as well as difference. Shakespeare could easily have seen Heywood's tragedy at the Rose playhouse (probably), which was only a stone's throw from the Globe in Southwark, sometime late in January, February or early March 1603. He was very unlikely to have been able to read it in preparing *Othello*, for it did not appear in print until 1607. He would have wanted to see a successful play by a rival firm on his doorstep (the second quarto of 1617 tells us the play 'hath been oftentimes acted') and there is enough in common between his only attempt at domestic tragedy (*Romeo and Juliet* is not quite that) and Heywood's to make it plausible that *Woman Killed With Kindness* was a seminal influence on *Othello*. If he had joined the audience of the Rose for one of these early performances he would have been immediately struck by the play's domesticity, which marks it out from almost all other Jacobean tragedies. It is not that this is tragedy of the lower classes, for the central figures are indeed (like those of *Othello*) all gentlefolk; we are assured in the first scene that the husband and wife, John and Anne Frankford, at the centre of the tragedy, are 'both. . .descended nobly' (i, 68) and Frankford

121

himself later boasts 'I am a gentleman. . .a king's no more' (iv, 3, 4). In spite of this insistence on class status, which Heywood exploits for comic purposes in his contrasted handling of the servants, the overall impression given by the play is of spectacularly ordinary people going about their daily tasks. Even the tragedy itself, if it leads to unusual consequences, is the result of the kind of temporary infatuation between wife and lodger that has hardly ever rated as especially newsworthy in any age. That this impression of ordinariness is deliberate Heywood makes clear from the prologue, which warns its audience:

> Look for no glorious state, our Muse is bent
> Upon a barren subject, a bare scene. . .

Nor is this ordinariness merely a matter of its homely setting in Yorkshire and its down-to-earth references to domestic detail, though these are important features of the play; it also rests in Heywood's view of his characters. These are distinguished mostly by a common sense and decency that (as so often in real life) break down under the stress of momentary passion. Even the villain (though in a theatre fraught with machiavels and bloody revengers the term seems inappropriate for Wendoll) attempts valiantly to resist his infatuation for his host's wife, before he plunges into a sin that can hardly be thought of as out of the ordinary:

> I am a villain if I apprehend
> But such a thought; then to attempt the deed –
> Slave, thou art damn'd without redemption.
> I'll drive away this passion with a song.
> A song! Ha, ha! A song, as if, fond man,
> Thy eyes could swim in laughter, when thy soul
> Lies drench'd and drowned in red tears of blood.
> I'll pray, and see if God within my heart
> Plant better thoughts. Why, prayers are meditations,
> And when I meditate – O God, forgive me –
> It is on her divine perfections.
>
> (vi, 1–11)

Far from wallowing in his evil, Iago-like, Wendoll appears increasingly as a pathetic, faintly ludicrous figure as he runs across the stage in his nightshirt, caught in the bedroom act with Frankford's wife. His last despairing appeal and rejection by the penitent Anne Frankford affords him our considerable sympathy:

> She's gone to death, I live in want and woe,
> Her life, her sins, and all upon my head,
> And I must now go wander like a Cain
> In foreign countries and remoted climes. . .
>
> (xvi, 124–7)

It is typical of a Heywood character, however, that even this grief and remorse is to be put to sensible use, for Wendoll's last words are to assure us that he'll make good use of his time abroad learning foreign languages, so 'At my return I may in court be rais'd' (xvi, 136). Heywood has much in common with Defoe, both in his willingness to record people as they are and in his unshakeable faith in the basic decency and common sense of humanity.

Clearly *Othello*'s domesticity is a very different affair from this. The deliberately low-key presentation of character through a linguistic medium that is (Defoe-like) as unpretentious as it is efficient, contrasts vividly with the tone of the *Othello* music. Othello's splendid rhetoric, his grandeur as an heroic figure, is as important in creating a sense of tragic dignity for this play as it is for creating that perceptible distancing effect we discussed earlier. Yet, as we saw, the insistence on dramatic detail characteristic of both plays gives to both a sense that we are dealing with real people in real places. It is true that Venice and Cyprus provide an exotic background for the action that again tends to heighten the dignity of the tone by removing it from everyday English experience, but the Venetian world depicted is genuinely historical, a world of Doges and argosies, of Turkish invasions and Venetian counter-diplomacy, very different – say – from the symbolic Babylonian Venice of *Volpone*. In Heywood's play factual detail – whether it is the marks made by the hobnail boots on the hall floor by the dancers (i, 90) or the stage directions at the beginning of scene viii instructing the servants in detail on the clearing of the dinner-table, or, most poignantly, Frankford's sending of Anne's lute after her into exile because he cannot bear that it should remind him of her (scene xvi) – help to create that world of the familiar, everyday life of its audience that must have made it a most unusual theatrical experience in its day, for such homely detail was normally confined to comedy. In *Othello* the domestic detail is used more sparingly and more subtly to distinguish Desdemona's world of the feminine from Othello's 'pomp and circumstance of glorious war', but in both plays a sense of actuality is created that fixes the action of the play in the here and now of human experience. And just as Shakespeare uses his mythological Christian references to guide us through this world, so Heywood's Christianity is essentially at the service of the realism. Like *Othello*, *Woman Killed With Kindness* abounds in Christian reference. In Heywood's tragedy – much more than in *Othello* – the characters live (as Elizabethan man clearly did) in a world of constant Christian awareness. In crises especially, they resort to the comforts (or discomforts) of their religion as readily as we resort (for similar reasons) to our televisions; whether it is the servingman Jenkins praying that his mistress, Anne, may be preserved from sin: 'God keep my mistress chaste and make us all His servants' (xii, 13–14) or Anne herself realizing the consequence of her sin: 'O what a clog unto the soul is sin' (xi, 103). Indeed the consciousness of sin, of the doctrine of the fall (explicitly referred to in Anne's first consciousness of her shame: 'Women that fall not quite bereft of grace/Have their offences noted in their face', vi, 156–7) provides the basis of the tragedy. In this sense the Christianity is far more deeply embedded in the morality of Heywood's play than it is in *Othello*, where, as we saw, Othello's 'guilt' is largely unrelated to an awareness of sin. In *Woman Killed With Kindness* choice betweeen good and evil is a condition for all men, as is made explicit when Wendoll is at the point of being swept away by his passion:

> I will not! Zounds, I will not! I may choose,
> And I will choose. Shall I be so misled?
> Or shall I purchase to my father's crest
> The motto of a villain?
>
> (vi, 93–6)

Yet Heywood also uses Christian reference in his play as Shakespeare does in *Othello*, to highlight a character's standing and point up the ironies inherent in the action. So Susan, the heroine of Heywood's sub-plot and Anne Frankford's foil, is described (rather like Desdemona) as 'an angel in a mortal shape' (vii, 100), while Wendoll's role as villain is (somewhat unfairly) given emphasis and clarity by associating him with the devil. To Nicholas the serving man, for instance, Wendoll *is* the devil: 'The Devil and he are all one in my eye' (iv, 88). As in *Othello*, these references to psychomachia roles can be used to point up ironies, as when Frankford, detecting the sexual innuendo between his wife and Wendoll, remarks: 'My saint's turn'd devil' (viii, 151) or when he acknowledges he must resort to trickery 'To try two seeming angels' (xi, 2). This use of psychomachia language is not unusual in Jacobean drama, but it differs from the genuinely allegorical use of psychomachia roles that we find, for instance, in Middleton's comedies, most notably in *Mad World*, but also elsewhere. In *Woman Killed With Kindness* and *Othello* the language of the morality play comes to be used as a guide to the nature of actuality depicted on stage – in both plays the metaphysical system is at the service of the realism rather than a representation of an alternative reality. Indeed Heywood's determination to keep his play firmly anchored in middle-earth can be illustrated from one of the very rare excursions his play makes towards a transcendental reality. Frankford, with his world falling apart, imagines the possibility of recalling past time to reconstitute the world of innocence that is now lost for ever:

> O God, O God, that it were possible
> To undo things done, to call back yesterday;
> That Time could turn up his swift sandy glass,
> To untell the days, and to redeem these hours;

Or that the Sun
Could, rising from the west, draw his coach backward,
Take from the account of time so many minutes,
Till he had all these seasons call'd again,
Those minutes and those actions done in them,
Even from her first offence; that I might take her
As spotless as an angel in my arms.
But O! I talk of things impossible,
And cast beyond the moon. God give me patience.

(xiii, 52–64)

Frankford (and Heywood) are far too sensible and practical to see this flight of the imagination as anything other than fantasy, though it is interesting that Heywood — as a practical man of the theatre — indulges in just that 'impossible' double time for which *Othello* is notorious. For, like *Othello*, *Woman Killed With Kindness* syncopates an actual time (running over several years) into a sense of concentrated stage time, a phenomenon that is clearly illustrated by the introduction, in scene xiii, of two children of the Frankford marriage, which had taken place in the first scene of the play.

Another important feature that links both plays is the central role of paradox. In Heywood's tragedy the ironies that are highlighted by psychomachia references are used with less skill and appropriateness than in *Othello*: Iago makes a convincing surrogate for the devil, whereas Wendoll does not, but in both plays this verbal simplification into black and white enables the playwrights to explore the central paradox of the contrast between intention and result. The very title of Heywood's play points to the central paradox that Frankford's good intention in forgiving his wife ends by killing her, while the pun on 'kindness' (consanguinity) introduces the further paradox that she is killed by her nearest and dearest. The paradox that kindness can be crueller than cruelty is equally illustrated by Desdemona's response to Othello. Heywood explores his paradox not only in the main action, but in the sub-plot where Sir Charles Mountford's crime of murder is met by the generosity of his enemy, Sir Francis Acton, in paying the debts Sir Charles incurs in his successful defence at law. In both cases forgiveness paradoxically places an intolerable burden of guilt on the forgiven, as Sir Charles makes explicit when he persuades his sister Susan to agree to sleep with Sir Francis in repayment of the debt:

Thy honour and my soul are equal in my regard,
Nor will thy brother Charles survive they shame.
His kindness like a burden hath surcharged me,
And under his good deeds I stooping go,
Not with an upright soul.

(xiv, 61–5)

125

Similarly Frankford's forgiveness of his wife in the main plot inflicts a psychological burden of guilt that she cannot sustain and so she starves herself to death from shame. The outcome of the sub-plot provides thematic contrast in ending happily with Sir Francis Acton doing the decent thing and agreeing to marry the impoverished Susan. Heywood's exploration of paradox in the main plot lacks the dazzling clarity and therefore the aesthetic effectiveness of Shakespeare's manipulation of paradox in *Othello*. Instead Heywood throws out paradoxical suggestions that the action fails to explore. Anne's initial reaction to her husband's kindness is paradoxically to accuse him of failing in his moral duty:

> He cannot be so base as to forgive me,
> Nor I so shameless to accept his pardon.
>
> (xiii, 139–40)

This suggestion is again taken up by Anne's brother, Sir Francis Acton, only to be set aside:

> My brother Frankford show'd too mild a spirit
> In the revenge of such a loathed crime;
> Less than he did, no man of spirit could do.
> I am so far from blaming his revenge
> That I commend it.
>
> (xvii, 16–20)

Here, interestingly, Acton assumes Frankford's leniency is not Christian kindness but a subtler kind of revenge, and strictly Frankford's decision to exile his wife rather than kill her is revenge, not forgiveness, as Frankford himself at one point seems to acknowledge:

> I'll not martyr thee
> Nor mark thee for a strumpet, but with usage
> Of more humility torment thy soul
> And kill thee even with kindness.
>
> (xiii, 153–6)

This sublety would become a machiavel, but Frankford is not seriously criticized in the play and indeed the presentation of his character makes it clear that we are genuinely meant to see his behaviour as an act of Christian kindness. Nevertheless Heywood suggests a further paradox here, that forbearance can be a more effective form of revenge than open aggression. Heywood hints at a clash between two (or more) value systems – the Christian doctrine of patience and the pagan doctrine of honour – but is content to leave the problem as the kind of problem inherent in day-to-day living rather than as a subject for intellectual examination. This is the technique of *Hamlet*, not of *Othello*, and indeed in its constant appeal to the audience's emotion *Woman Killed With Kindness* comes closer than is usual

126

with Heywood (in spite of the characteristic pace of its action) to the affective drama of Shakespeare's earlier period.

Shakespeare's use of paradox in *Othello* is both clearer and more profound than Heywood's and ultimately contributes to that sense of distancing that is such a particular feature of the play. At times *Othello* might almost be a paradoxical and ironic comment on the action of *Woman Killed With Kindness*. Frankford's bitter feelings as he stands by the bedroom door ('that door that's bawd unto my shame') leading to his 'polluted bedchamber,/ Once my terrestrial heaven, now my earth's hell' (xiii, 15–16) are, as it were, the actuality mirrored in Othello's fantasies as he accuses Desdemona of adultery and bids Emilia turn the key on 'the gates of hell' she guards (IV, ii, 94). The interview between Frankford and his servant Nicholas, in which Nicholas reveals his suspicions of Anne, has a similar relationship to the malicious fantasies of Iago as he torments Othello with accounts of Desdemona's unfaithfulness. Frankford's tormented response to the truth works at the level of Othello's dreams:

> Thou hast kill'd me with a weapon whose sharp'ned point
> Hath prick'd quite through and through my shivering heart.
> Drops of cold sweat sit dangling on my hairs
> Like morning's dew upon the golden flowers,
> And I am plung'd into a strange agony.
>
> (viii, 56–60)

Othello provides a constant ironic commentary on the central assumptions of the male world of *Woman Killed With Kindness* where the 'treasure' of Susan's chastity that Charles successfully barters to free himself from obligation to Sir Francis Acton, becomes the 'pearl' that Othello throws away, like the base Indian. The action of Shakespeare's tragedy is a sustained and malign fantasy created by Iago out of the kind of actuality represented in Heywood's play. None of this, of course, proves, or is intended to prove that Shakespeare had seen a performance of *Woman Killed With Kindness* before writing *Othello*, but a comparison of the two plays highlights qualities in Shakespeare's tragedy that help to clarify the nature of Shakespeare's achievement.

Heywood's tragedy and Jonson's *Sejanus* are as far apart in dramaturgy as the popular Elizabethan stage would allow. In place of Heywood's intricate double plotting we have a play observing neo-Aristotelian unity of action (if not of time) and minutely observant of its classical sources, which deal with exalted matters of state; in place of Heywood's unashamed appeal to the audience's emotions on behalf of ordinary, decent, English folk like themselves, we have a dry-eyed moralistic tragedy, sardonic in tone, concerning extraordinary people depicted at a particular moment of history remote from the audience's experience in time and place. Yet *Sejanus*, dating, like *Woman Killed With Kindness*, from 1603 was certainly an

127

influence on *Othello* and has to be taken into account in understanding the dramatic climate in which *Othello* was conceived and executed. That a later contemporary associated the two plays together is clear in Leonard Digges's contrast (published in 1640) between Jonson's failure and Shakespeare's success:

> oh how the Audience,
> Were ravish'd, with what wonder they went thence,
> When some new day they would not brooke a line,
> Of tedious (though well laboured) *Catiline*;
> *Sejanus* too was irkesome, they priz'de more
> Honest Iago, or the jealous Moore.[25]

The audience referred to here was certainly the Globe because one of the contributors to the 1605 quarto of *Sejanus* (a certain Ev.B.) mentions seeing it there and also its hostile reception.[26] We know that Shakespeare was intimately acquainted with Jonson's play because the folio edition (1616) gives us a cast list of the 'principall Tragoedians', eight in all, in which Shakespeare's name heads the second four-man column. This edition also tells us that the play was acted 'in the year 1603' and 'by the Kings Majesties Servants'. As Herford and Simpson point out in their edition of the play, the theatres were closed (probably) from 19 March 1603 until March 1604 and, as Shakespere's company did not become the King's Men until 19 May 1603, we must assume the 1603 performance was a private one if we are to take the statement as an accurate record of the company's title at the time of the first performance. It does seem possible, however, that the play had had a public performance (by the then-named Chamberlain's Men) in early 1603, that is, at virtually the same time as *Woman Killed With Kindness*. In any case we can be fairly sure first that *Sejanus* was written for the Globe and second that Shakespeare had an important part in its first performance. Herford and Simpson conjecture that Shakespeare played the part of Tiberius Caesar.[27] Jonson's lines must certainly have been running in Shakespeare's head at this time, but in spite of this it is remarkable that we can detect little verbal influence of *Sejanus* on *Othello*, a measure both of Shakespeare's verbal exuberance and the stylistic gap between the two dramatists. It is also possible that Shakespeare's was that 'second pen' that Jonson tells us, in his address to the reader, 'had good share' in the stage version of the text,[28] a contribution that, characteristically, Jonson excised in preparing the play for the press. Chapman has also been suggested as the contributor, but Chapman, as far as we know, never worked for Shakespeare's company and in any case would be more likely to collaborate at the literary level Jonson would respect and preserve, than at the level of popular stagecraft.

We can regard *Sejanus*, I think, as a product of that (mostly) friendly rivalry-cum-cooperation between Shakespeare and Jonson that lasted until

Shakespeare's death, which, in one version, we are told, was occasioned as a result of a drinking bout between himself, Jonson and Drayton.[29] For *Sejanus* is a kind of purist's 'answer' to *Julius Caesar* in exhibiting a treatment of Roman history that gives greater priority to both historical accuracy and moral statement, part of a rivalry that culminated in that most splendidly classical of all Jacobean plays, *Coriolanus*. The challenge to *Julius Caesar* is deliberate in *Sejanus* where the contrast between the 'old liberty' (I, 404) of the late Republic and the present Tiberian tyranny is an important part of Jonson's theme. The historian Cordus is arraigned before the Senate in Act III for making this contrast. One of the accusations is:

> Comparing men,
> And times, thou praysest Brutus, and affirm'st
> That Cassius was the last of all the Romanes.
> (III, 390–2)

– a charge that Cordus is willing to accept and defend (III, 449–60). Afer, the government orator, sees this praise of Brutus and Cassius as a deliberate attack on the current regime:

> To have a Brutus brought in paralell,
> A parricide, an enemie of his countrie,
> Rank'd, and preferr'd to any reall worth
> That Rome now holds. This is most strangely invective.
> Most full of spite, and insolent upbraiding.
> Nor is't the time alone is here dispris'd,
> But the whole man of time, yea Caesar's selfe
> Brought in disvalew. . .
> (III, 396–403)

The play as a whole clearly supports Cordus against Tiberius and his lickspittles, giving a decisive moral stance to the play in condemning tyranny and timeserving and upholding the rule of law. We need not be surprised that the play ran into trouble with the authorities.[30] All this is an implicit criticism of Shakespeare's treatment of the same theme, where the presentation of Julius Caesar, Brutus and Cassius is remarkably even-handed. Jonson would no doubt regard this as moral irresponsibility, for he complains in the prefatory material of *Volpone* of 'the present trade of the stage' and seeks to counter in his own play those critics who (with some justification, he implies) 'crie out, we never punish vice in our enterludes'.[31]

Jonson's faithfulness to Rome in *Sejanus* is more a matter of historical than dramaturgical allegiance, in spite of the address to the reader which paraphrases Giraldi Cinthio's defence of Seneca in claiming 'truth of Argument, dignity of Persons, gravity and height of Elocution, fulness and frequency of sentence'.[32] This is a clear echo of Giraldi's argument that

Seneca's tragedy excels the Greek 'nella prudenza, nella gravità, nel decoro, nella maesta, nelle sentenze'[33] (it is notable that Jonson omits mention of 'maesta'). Shakespeare's *Othello* conforms to these requirements in gravity of tone, 'dignity of persons' (decoro) and 'majesty' rather more convincingly indeed than *Sejanus*, where in practice Jonson has emphasized 'truth to argument' above other considerations. It is characteristic of Jonson, however, that his critical defence should be at odds with his actual practice. We have to get behind this habitual critical smokescreen to try to see the play as Shakespeare saw it when he accepted it for production at the Globe (for we can assume that his opinion on what went on there and what didn't was decisive at this stage of his career). We need to remind ourselves that the play that the King's Men actually played was not the same as the *Sejanus* we now read and Jonson's explanation of this seems to suggest that the contributions of the 'second pen' were quite substantial:

> I would informe you, that this Booke, in all numbers, is not the same with that which was acted on the publicke Stage, wherein a second Pen had good share: in place of which I have rather chosen, to put weaker (and no doubt lesse pleasing) of mine own, then to defraud so happy a Genius of his right, by my lothed usurpation.[34]

This seems to imply also that the material substituted for that of the 'second pen' was new, not a reversion to previously written copy. Whether Shakespeare (or whoever it was) began on the collaboration from the beginning or required changes in preparation for the production is not clear, though the latter seems more likely as Globe plays (unlike those of the other playhouses) were not often collaborative efforts at this period. This is all the more likely because clearly Jonson spent a considerable time writing the play (his previous play, *Poetaster*, dates from the spring of 1601) and Jonson is said (by a contemporary diarist) to have shut himself off from the world at the time he was preparing his tragedy.[35]

What, then, would Shakespeare have seen in the play to justify his accepting it for the King's Men, a decision, incidentally, that turned out to be an error of judgement in view of its hostile reception? Certainly any actor would relish the part of Tiberius, it is the best acting part of the play, with its combination of hypocritical humility and cunning ruthlessness. The relationship between Sejanus and Tiberius, where Sejanus constantly attempts to weave textures of deception around his master, must have provided more than a few clues in developing the relationship of Iago and Othello. Iago and Sejanus are both machiavels, both adept at manipulating others for their own purposes, yet both are presented in realistic terms as real people, not Grand Guignol monsters. One obvious difference in the relationship is that Iago succeeds, whereas Sejanus is completely outwitted by the superior cunning of Tiberius (a relation of villain to super-villain developed further in the Mosca–Volpone relationship and then in the

Alchemist in the combination of Subtle and Face). In terms of the theatre (though few people have the opportunity of seeing it on stage) Tiberius and Sejanus dominate the play, and this is one of the problems with it. For Tiberius is not a tragic figure and Sejanus is only tragic in the superficial sense that he dies at the end of the play. Tiberius, indeed, must be played as a comic part, for his duplicity, his skill at saying one thing and meaning another, is of the essence of the double focus out of which the comic is generated. In creating Sejanus and Tiberius, Jonson, for all his Senecan intentions, falls back on the long native tradition exploited in the morality plays of the essential comedy of evil. The first appearance of Tiberius illustrates the point. As he enters 'one kneels to him' (as the stage direction requires), at which Tiberius launches into a characteristic exercise in false humility, to the hypocritical compliments of Sejanus and the fierce moralistic asides of Arruntius:

> *Tiberius*: Wee not endure these flatteries, let him stand;
>   Our empire, ensignes, axes, roddes, and state
>   Take not away our humane nature from us:
>   Looke up, on us, and fall before the gods.
> *Sejanus*: How like a god, speakes Caesar!
> *Arruntius*: There, observe!
>   He can indure that second, that's no flattery.
>   O, what is it, proud slime will not beleeve
>   Of his owne worth, to heare it equall prais'd
>   Thus with the gods?

(I, 375–83)

This is good comic stuff, because both Tiberius and Sejanus know as well as we do that they don't believe a word of what they say. The passage recalls most readily, not the grim solemnities of Senecan tragedy, but those scenes of comic villainy where Shakespeare has Richard of Gloucester and Buckingham act out their deceits before the citizenry of London in *Richard III*. The discrepancy between Sejanus' obviously acceptable flattery and Tiberius' pretended humility is so palpable that Arruntius' intervention is clumsy and otiose. The effect of Arruntius' moralizing – which continues throughout the play – is to spike the laughter, so that the immense comic potential of the play is never achieved. This is at the root of the play's failure; the audience are invited to a comic spectacle and then not allowed to laugh. Jonson himself obviously realized something was wrong, for in his next play, *Volpone*, he uses a similar pair of crooks, but exploits them brilliantly for comic purposes, and he achieves this partly by suppressing the voice of virtue which proves such a clog to the comic energies of *Sejanus*. Jonson is so determined in the tragedy to apply the 'Senecan' principles of 'dignity of persons' and 'gravity' and to make explicit the moral purpose that the comedy is dissipated and repressed. The conflict is,

131

in a sense, one between Jonson's neo-classical dogmas and those natural instincts as both man and dramatist that express themselves best through the native forms. Arruntius' phrase 'proud slime' is instructive here, for Arruntius is talking the language of Christian humility (the Douay Bible translates the Vulgate 'Formavit igitur Dominus Deus hominem de limo terrae' from Genesis 2: 7 as 'And the Lord God formed man of the slime of the earth'). The equivalent passage of Juvenal's fourth satire, Book I (from which Jonson's lines derive) merely says, referring to the Emperor Nero: 'nihil est quod credere de se/non possit cum laudatur dis aequa potestas' – 'there is nothing godlike power will refuse to believe of itself when it is praised'.[36] For all its strict dependence on classical sources the ethos of the play stems from Christian notions of sin and redemption. Jonson's contemporaries quickly saw the relevance of his Rome to their own times and country, for Jonson tells Drummond that he was 'called befor the Councell for his *Sejanus* and accused both of popperie and treason'.[37] Presumably the government felt the play's preferences for the 'old liberty' of the Roman republic had unwelcome modern implications. Chapman's commendatory verses for the play see in it an admonition to statesmen:

> Thy Muse yet makes it the whole sphaere and lawe
> To all State lives; and bounds Ambitions strife. . .[38]

Even the stridency of Arruntius' virtue derives at least in part from comic example, for his satiric commentary on the play's action follows the pattern set by such earlier satiric voices as Asper and Macilente in *Every Man Out of his Humour* and Crites in *Cynthia's Revels*. Arruntius' language often partakes of the colourful excess of these predecessors, ironically adding to the impression of grotesque perversity the play gives, rather than to the 'gravity and height of Elocution' the address to the reader promises:

> Way for my lord! proclaime his idoll lord-ship,
> More then ten cryers, or sixe noise of trumpets!
> Make legs, kisse hands, and take a scatter'd haire
> From my lords eminent shoulder! See Sanquinius!
> With his slow belly, and his dropsie! looke,
> What toyling haste he makes! yet, here's another,
> Retarded with the gout, will be afore him!
> Get thee *liburnian* porters, thou grosse foole,
> To beare thy'obsequious fatnesse, like thy peeres. . .
>
> (V, 451–9)

Nor is the language of scurrility confined to Arruntius. One of the most notable of the opposition to Tiberius' tyranny, Caius Silius, who commits suicide in the Senate asserting his innocence, can equally sound this comic note on the same subject (largely taken from Juvenal), the flatterers of great ones who:

> Laugh, when their patron laughes; sweat, when he sweates;
> Be hot, and cold with him; change every moode,
> Habit, and garbe, as often as he varies;
> Observe him, as his watch observes his clocke;
> And true, as turkise in the deare lords ring,
> Looke well, or ill with him: ready to praise
> His lordship, if he spit, or but pisse faire,
> Have an indifferent stoole, or breake winde well. . .
>
> (I, 33–40)

Even Agrippina, around whom the opposition gathers, like Silius deliberately made more virtuous than the sources suggest by Jonson's careful selectivity, nevertheless contributes to the grotesqueness of the *Sejanus* world:

> Were all Tiberius body stuck with eyes,
> And ev'ry wall, and hanging in my house
> Transparent, as this lawne I weare or ayre;
> Yea, had Sejanus both his eares as long
> As to my in-most closet: I would hate
> To whisper any thought, or change an act. . .
>
> (II, 450–5)

Jonson has a special delight in the grotesque, the incongruous, that gives these passages a vitality that the language of virtue in the play conspicuously lacks. Virtue, indeed, can often sound both pretentious and silly, as, for instance, when a little earlier in this same scene the subject turns on the mundane matter of Silius' wife, Sosia, staying with Agrippina:

> *Agrippina*: Sosia stayes with us?
> *Silius*: Shee is your servant, and doth owe your grace
>   An honest, but unprofitable love.
> *Agrippina*: How can that be, when there's no gaine, but virtu's?
> *Silius*: You take the morall, not the politique sense.
>
> (II, 431–5)

Vitality in *Sejanus* courses through the veins of the evil more than of the good, and especially in the character of Sejanus himself, whose 'scoffing with ambiguous words' might well have supplied Milton with his model for Satan. In addition to his skill as the machiavel schemer of the play, he too shares the comic zest for the incongruous that oddly links him to his opponents. In the process of corrupting the physician Eudemes, for instance, when he persuades him to act as pandar between himself and Livia, wife to the virtuous Drusus, whom Sejanus poisons, he jokes at length in the language of the moral satirists on the traditional subject of women's vanities:

Why, sir, I doe not aske you of their urines,
Whose smel's most violet? or whose seige is best?
Or who makes hardest faces on her stool?
Which lady sleepes with her owne face, a nights?
Which puts her teeth off, with her clothes, in court?
Or, which her hayre? which her complexion?
And, in which boxe she puts it?

(I, 304–10)

In such a grotesque world, whose almost total corruption is frequently lamented, the rogue hero holds sway, and all the more so because in *Sejanus* the supreme rogue, Tiberius, remains in possession of his empire at the end of the play.

How then did Shakespeare view all this? Presumably he saw in the play a picture of a society dedicated to evil of the kind that he himself had depicted in *Richard III*, but here refined and justified by its classical credentials. Certainly it must have stimulated him to think again about the implications of neo-classical theory, with the result, as we have seen, that *Othello* is far more thoroughgoing in its Aristotelianism than anything Jonson attempted, for all his declared respect for the neo-classical 'laws' in *Sejanus* (as later in *Volpone*, where he asserts that 'from no needful rule he swerveth').[39] *Othello* also fulfils the 'Senecan' requirements for tragedy as Giraldi enunciates them better than Seneca himself. At the same time, playing opposite (or at least close to) Burbage's Sejanus must have revived Shakespeare's moribund interest in the machiavel rogue, while he transformed the part he himself perhaps played by creating Othello under the influence of the noble figure Tiberius pretends to be. The choice of a sympathetic and noble hero opens up the possibility of genuine tragedy not available to Jonson's rogue-centred play. The choice too of an heroic figure whose downfall principally involves not gross sin, but a fatal error of judgement, leads to that effect of detachment-with-sympathy that is essentially Aristotelian in character. Perhaps too *Sejanus* helped Shakespeare to re-focus on the problem of aesthetic distancing, adding fear and wonder as well as pity and woe to produce the cathartic effect of his tragedy, for such distancing is at the core of Jonson's dramaturgy. Certainly *Sejanus* must have been one of the strongest of those influences that set Shakespeare on a course of exploration into classical methods that was to bear such fruit in *Lear* and *Coriolanus* and, in a radically different way, in *Antony and Cleopatra*.

It is probably no coincidence that Jonson's next unaided play, *Volpone*, performed at the Globe in 1606, was also set in Venice, though a Venice markedly different from Shakespeare's. Jonson's choice of setting is not dictated by his sources and is all the more remarkable for coming shortly after the production of a revised version of *Every Man in his Humour* which changes the original Italian setting to London. E. K. Chambers suggests that the new version was made for a Court performance in February 1605.[40] The prologue to the new version, moreover, fairly obviously cocks a snook at Shakespeare's romantic dramaturgy and declares that, in contrast, his own play aims at a dramatic realism, with

> deeds and language such as men do use,
> And Persons such as Comedy would choose
> When she would show an image of the times. . .

The London setting, subsequently adhered to in all Jonson's later comedies except *Volpone* (if we include *New Inn*'s 'Barnet'), plays its part in this new realism. In this context the choice of Venice for *Volpone* has special significance, for it suggests that Jonson's city of sin was chosen in corrective contrast to the romantic and glamorous world of *Othello, the Moor of Venice*, whose concern with aesthetic effect must have smacked for Jonson of the escapism and moral irresponsibility castigated in *Volpone*'s 'Address to the Universities'.

5

ROYAL MEASURES: *MEASURE FOR MEASURE* AND MIDDLETON'S COMEDY OF DISILLUSIONMENT

On 19 March 1603, new style, all the London theatres were closed by order of the Privy Council; the Queen was dying and the nation awaited the eclipse of the mortal moon. She died on 24 March and before the mourning was over and the new king installed ominous signs of plague appeared and a virulent visitation began in April and continued throughout that year and into the next. The theatres remained closed, except possibly for a short period in late April and early May. Shakespeare, like most other rich men who were able, would certainly have left London and probably found himself with unwonted leisure to concentrate on the completion of *Othello* and the contemplation of its successor. On 19 May King James bestowed the title of 'King's Men' on the hitherto Chamberlain's Company and made a gift of £30 to the company for 'mayntenance and releife, being prohibited to present any playes publiquelie in or neere London by reason of the plague'.[1] The money was probably not important, for the King's Men were in the best position of the playing troupes to survive a long lay-off, and in any case the company did some touring in the provinces during the London closure.[2] Much more important was the prestige brought by the seal of James's approval.

James's interest in the theatre may have been somewhat intermittent, but in these early years in England he (and even more his Queen) seem to have been enthusiastic playgoers. Elizabeth I had enjoyed watching plays, but there is a notable increase in Court appearances by players in the early years of James's reign and in addition large sums of money were spent staging Court masques.[3] In spite of remaining, throughout his life, a 'regal Calvinist',[4] James saw in the theatre both usefulness and legitimate entertainment. In *Basilikon Doron* he defends the stage, without irony, as a harmless pastime:

> For I cannot see what greater superstition can be in making playes and lawfull games in Maie, and good cheere at Christmas, then in eating fish in Lent, and upon Fridayes, the Papists as well using the one as the other: so that alwayes the Sabboths be kept holy, and no

unlawfull pastime be used: And as this forme of contenting the peoples mindes, hath beene used in all well governed Republicks: so will it make you to performe in your government that olde good sentence, *Omne tulit punctum, qui miscuit utile dulci.*[5]

The importance of James's interest in the theatre cannot be overstressed, because coming as it did when the London stage had reached an unprecedented height of sophistication, it provided a climate in which the vigorous growth could continue and develop. The development, it is true, in this time of royal encouragement, continued the tendency towards a more elitist theatre and this in the long run turned out to contain the seeds of decay as well as the immediate promise of more fruit.

Given the new King's interest in the theatre, it is not surprising to find the playwrights competing for his attention. The play Shakespeare began work on, probably sometime in the year of the King's accession, was *Measure for Measure*. This play shows unmistakable evidence of a concern to interest (and flatter) the King, both by reflecting his ideas (notably as expressed in his book on the conduct of a king, *Basilikon Doron*)[6] and by representing his monarch in an idealized manner on stage in the character of Duke Vincentio. Duke Vincentio is not a portrait of James I. No playwright in his right mind would have the temerity to attempt such a thing, even if the censorship would have allowed it (which it wouldn't), but he provides a sufficiently close reflection of James's views and attitudes to make the representation clear and flattering.[7] Like *Macbeth*, *Measure for Measure* is an exercise in delicate sycophancy, which no doubt succeeded in confirming James's approval of the Chamberlain's Men and Shakespeare's ultimate triumph over his rivals. The demise of the boys' companies in particular turned out not to be far off.

Shakespeare's triumph at this time is now clear to us, but was probably not so obvious to him. Accordingly *Measure for Measure* shows as much concern with current theatrical developments as the previous plays. Even if the play was written in the first instance for Court performance Shakespeare would want to transfer it to the Globe as soon as possible. By the time of the closure of the playhouses it was becoming clear that a different kind of comedy was coming into vogue, a comedy of moral disillusionment that was (after the reopening) to lead to that outburst of comedies of London life of which Thomas Middleton was the most successful exponent. As usual Ben Jonson quickly got on the bandwagon, converting the Italian setting of *Every Man in his Humour* to the new taste and adding a new prologue in the name of fashionable 'realismo'. This use of comedy to record the seamier side of the here and now was not fully under way in 1603, although already early in that year George Chapman (always the innovator) had put a play about a current London scandal on the boards in the lost play the *Old Joiner of Aldgate*, while Middleton's early play, the *Family of Love*, also touching on aspects of contemporary life, may date from around the same time. The difficulty of dating these early London plays exactly makes it impossible to chart the precise way the comedy of disillusionment developed. By 1603, however, the older romantic comedy, in which Shakespeare had excelled, had clearly given way to a comedy where the more sordid activities of low life were displayed. Perhaps we ought to refer to a *revival* of satiric comedy, for examples of comic realism, such as *A Knack to Know a Knave* (*c.*1592) and *A Knack to Know an Honest Man* (*c.*1594), both using the device of the disguised traveller to expose vice, provide some link between the new Jacobean satire and the satire of the old morality plays. In the latter play, for instance, the joint hero, Sempronio, disguises himself as 'Penitent Experience' (compare Middleton's Penitent Brothel) to become the agent of justice. Dekker's *Blurt, Master Constable* can be taken as an early example of the new fashion; written for Paul's Boys in 1602 it is set in Venice and combines a romantic element with a great deal of seedy comedy, much of which centres on a brothel. Similarly Middleton's *Phoenix* (1603/4), another Paul's play set in Italy, gives a jaundiced view of a world of corruption that, like Dekker's play, is more English than Italian. *Phoenix* is particularly interesting in using the device of the ruler-in-disguise; for Prince Phoenix, son of the reigning Duke of Ferrara, has the role of satirical observer as he moves about the Dukedom incognito. This same device, central to *Measure for Measure*, is found in Marston's *Malcontent* which also probably dates from 1603, in this case just before the closing of the theatres in March. Shakespeare certainly knew this play well, for it was transferred from Blackfriars, for which it was written, to the Globe, probably after the reopening in 1604.

Marston's play is worth looking at in some detail, not just as a possible influence on *Measure for Measure*, but as an example of the current fashion in comedy as Shakespeare began work on his play. Like *Blurt* and *Phoenix*, it is set in Italy, but concerns itself exclusively with Court life (Blackfriars was much patronized by courtiers). 'Courtly', however, means something quite different here from the idealized courtly world of earlier Shakespearean comedy, for the atmosphere is one of sordid intrigue and sexual aberration. *Malcontent* marks a new trend in Marston's work. Compared to the early comedies written for Paul's Boys, the play is coherently plotted, indeed its structural ingenuity is one of the more remarkable things about it. For in it Marston solves a structural problem that Jonson had found insuperable in his 'comicall satyre' up to this time: how to integrate the satirical commentator into the main action. Marston achieves this by having his hero, Altofronto, assume the role of the malcontent, Malevole, as his means of disguise. Altofronto thus becomes both the disaffected satiric commentator and the intrigue hero. Because the inchoate structures of his earlier comedies were themselves symbols of Marston's theme of the essential incoherence of human life, such a radical change in plotting marks

138

an equally radical change in theme. Accordingly, *Malcontent* abandons the Christian pessimism of the earlier plays for a more orthodox (and banal) statement of the earthly triumph of virtue. There are still times, however, when the Duke (in his role as Malevole) can strike the earlier lugubrious note:

> Think this: this earth is the only grave and Golgotha wherein all things that live must rot; 'tis but the draught wherein the heavenly bodies discharge their corruption; the very muck hill on which the sublunary orbs cast their excrements. Man is the slime of this dung pit. . .
>
> (IV, v, 107–11)[8]

It is difficult to give this grim view of man much weight here, not only because it is presented as a deliberate affectation, adopted by Altofronto as part of his disguise, but also because it is not ultimately borne out by the pattern of the play's events. *Malcontent* is essentially a romance, in which the forces of virtue, headed by Altofronto-Malevole and including the loyal courtier Celso and the saintly Maria, Altofronto's wife, triumph over the evil Mendoza and the usurping Duke, Pietro. The evil reign of Duke Pietro is characterized by the political manoeuvrings of the base Mendoza and pervaded by the sexual immorality represented by the adulterous Aurelia, Pietro's wife, and the bawd Maquerelle, who sets the seedy tone of the court.

Malcontent, in its combination of decadent atmosphere and chocolate box morality, is a kind of sentimental re-run of the earlier Senecan tragedy *Antonio's Revenge*, which also tells of a usurping duke (who, more interestingly, is also a psychopath) and a disguised revenger. In the earlier play the atmosphere of violent perversion is a suitable expression of a sin-laden view of the world. In *Malcontent* the sinfulness is largely a dramatic device, an aunt-sally, for virtue to overthrow, and the atmosphere of corruption is generated as much by the satiric commentary of the hero and the gratuitous decadence of Maquerelle as by any compelling vision 'of what men were, and are. . .what men must be' (as the prologue to *Antonio's Revenge* puts it). Marston's retreat into sentimentality in *Malcontent* is an unfortunate result of Jonson's demand for overt moralizing – the play is dedicated to Jonson in fulsome terms and must be seen as the capitulatory and belated finale of the theatre war. No one, however, can deny the technical skill with which Marston handles both plot and structure of the play and its success won for it a transfer to the Globe, a little lightened by Webster (not the most jocund of dramatists) for the popular stage.

Middleton's *Phoenix* is technically a much less accomplished play than *Malcontent*, lacking the latter play's structural ingenuity and intensity of atmosphere. But in many ways it is closer to *Measure for Measure*, and in one respect – the use of the device of the ruler-in-disguise to reflect King

139

James's ideas and compliment the new King – it is so remarkably like *Measure for Measure* in its aims that it is difficult to believe that the two playwrights were not aware of each other's intentions. Almost certainly the two plays were being written about the same time, for there is convincing evidence that *Phoenix* was written from late 1603 to early 1604 and its most likely first date of performance was February 1604.[9] The first quarto (1607) says on its title page that the play was 'presented before his Maiestie' and the most likely date of that presentation was 20 February 1604.[10] This may mean, therefore, that Middleton's play was first performed earlier than *Measure for Measure*, whose first performance may have been the Court performance recorded for 26 December 1604. It is possible that *Phoenix* prompted Shakespeare's play, but it is not impossible that the two playwrights had hit on the same idea independently, the ruler-in-disguise in *Malcontent* suggesting to both that this would be an excellent formula to present before a king known to favour hole-in-corner methods. Both playwrights, along with anybody who was anybody,[11] had been reading their *Basilikon Doron* and there they would read James's advice to his son, Prince Henry:

> delite to haunt your Session, and spie carefully their proceedings;
> taking good heede, if any briberie may be tried among them, which
> cannot over severely be punished. . .let it be your owne craft, to take
> a sharp account of every man in his office.[12]

The King observed his own advice at the trial of the Jesuit, Father Henry Garnet, during which James was present behind a screen.[13] *Measure for Measure* seemingly alludes to another occasion whan James and Queen Anne attempted to appear incognito at the Royal Exchange on 15 March 1604.[14]

The structure of *Phoenix* is loose, harking back to earlier 'realist' plays like the *Knack* plays. It consists of a string of satirical episodes that are connected principally by the presence of Prince Phoenix as observer, intervener and (at times) *agent provocateur*. Prince Phoenix has been advised by his father, the reigning duke of Ferrara, to travel abroad to gain experience of the world. Knowing that his father is seriously ill and might die while he is away, Phoenix decides to remain at home amongst his future subjects, disguising himself to 'spie carefully their proceedings' (to repeat James I's words). Each encounter with the citizenry (who are unashamedly English and only nominally Ferrarese) illustrates some aspect of the disorder in the land caused (as in *Measure for Measure*) by the over-indulgence of a too merciful Duke:

> Forty-five years I've gently ruled this dukedom;
> Pray heaven it be no fault,
> For there's as much disease, though not to th'eye,

In too much pity as in tyranny.

(I, i, 7–10)

Here, as in *Measure for Measure*, the theme of the need to balance justice with mercy echoes James, who in *Basilikon Doron* recommends to his son the need to strike the right balance, at the same time confessing a tendency in himself towards excessive clemency:

> mixe Iustice with Mercie, punishing or sparing, as ye shall finde the crime to have bene wilfully or rashly committed, and according to the bypast behaviour of the committer. For if otherwise ye kyth your clemencie at the first, the offences would soone come to such heapes, and the contempt of you grow so great, that when ye would fall to punish, the number of them to be punished, would exceed the innocent. . ... But in this, my over-deare bought experience may serve you for a sufficient lesson: For I confesse, where I thought (by being gracious at the beginning) to win all mens hearts to a loving and willing obedience, I by the contrary found, the disorder of the countrie, and the losse of my thankes to be all my reward.[15]

The Dukes of both Shakespeare's and Middleton's plays show a similarly disarming ingenuousness, though while Shakespeare boldly associates the laxity with the character who most closely resembles King James, the Duke of Vienna himself, Middleton more timidly (and less appropriately, considering a subject of the satire is flattery, touched on by the play at V, i, 181 and by *Basilikon Doron*)[16] associates the laxity with the dying Duke, whose forty-five year reign (as has been pointed out)[17] alludes to the length of Queen Elizabeth's reign. In *Phoenix* King James is flatteringly represented in the young Prince Phoenix, whose name was frequently used as an honorific of James Stuart.[18] Prince Phoenix represents a more naïve, less subtle version of the good ruler than Shakespeare's Duke Vincentio. He is made to expound the doctrine of balanced judgement, without his father's confession, in commenting on the corrupt Justice Falso's undue severity:

> So, sir, extremes set off all actions thus;
> Either too tame or else too tyrannous.

(III, i, 198–9)

which recalls *Basilikon Doron*'s apothegm *nam in medio stat virtus*.[19] Fortunately for Middleton, James's son, Prince Henry, was still too young to be mistaken for Prince Phoenix; adulation of Prince Henry's 'perfection' later caused his father stirrings of jealousy.

The various satirical episodes of *Phoenix* are interwoven with considerable complexity, and are chosen principally to illustrate themes of special interest to King James. The only one of these episodes directly related to

141

the framing device of Phoenix's departure and return to the Court concerns
the evil Proditor, the machiavel of the play. Proditor ('traitor') has all the
qualities of Marston's Mendoza, though Middleton fails to develop his role
as the central threat to order. Early in the play we find him failing to
seduce the chaste Castiza and contemplating the assassination of Prince
Phoenix, but his principal role comes towards the end of the play in his
plotting to accuse Phoenix before the Duke of planning to assassinate his
own father and assume power. Phoenix, in disguise, receives this
information in advance of the attempt by pretending to ally himself with
the villain, and has no difficulty in exposing Proditor before his father in
the last scene of the play. The suggestion has been made that Proditor is
intended as a portrait of Sir Walter Raleigh,[20] but the character is so
obviously a stereotype of the stage machiavel that it is not easy to detect
much individuality in it.

Middleton is more at home with such grimly comic sketches as that of
the Sea-Captain, who, having committed the solecism of marriage, is in the
process of selling his wife so that he can accuse her of adultery and obtain a
divorce. Other successful satirical portraits are those of Tangle, the corrupt
lawyer, who comes to the Captain's aid, of the corrupt magistrate Falso and
of the Jeweller's Wife, who steals from her husband to keep her
impecunious lover in funds. The scarcely related episodes that centre on
these characters provide Middleton with the kind of sardonic comment on
man's rapacity and lustfulness that becomes the hallmark of the later
satirical comedies.

The episodes of the Sea-Captain are presented in the first two acts and
focus on two themes of particular concern to James: the sacredness of
marriage and the practical problem of discouraging privateering on the
high seas. The theme of matrimony is broached through the Captain's
disillusionment with his recent marriage to Castiza:

> What lustful passion came aboard of me that I should marry; was I
> drunk? Yet that cannot altogether hold, for it was four o'clock
> i'th'morning; had it been five, I would ha' sworn it. . ... Oh, that a
> captain should live to be married! Nay, I that have been such a
> gallant salt-thief should yet live to be married. What a fortunate
> elder brother is he, whose father being a rammish plowman, himself a
> perfumed gentleman spending the laboring reek from his father's
> nostrils in tobacco, the sweat of his father's body in monthly physic
> for his pretty, queasy harlot: he sows apace i'th'country; the tailor
> o'ertakes him i'th'city; so that oftentimes before the corn comes to
> earing, 'tis up to the ears in high collars, and so at every harvest the
> reapers take pains for the mercers: ha! why this is stirring happiness
> indeed. Would my father had held a plow so, and fed upon squeez'd
> curds and onions, that I might have bath'd in sensuality! But he was

142

too ruttish himself to let me thrive under him; consumed me before he got me; and that makes me so wretched now to be shackled with a wife, and not greatly rich, neither.

(I, ii, 40–3, 51–67)

Here is one of Middleton's favourite themes, the cupidity of man that drives him perpetually in cycles of getting and spending (in both the economic and sexual senses of the words) and it is expressed with the characteristic gusto that has all the vitality of real life. The ability to present satire in vividly realistic terms was one of Middleton's major contributions to Jacobean drama. It is not difficult to credit Brooks's argument that the Captain is a portrait of Middleton's own sea-captain stepfather, Thomas Harvey.[21] Here the fictional sea-captain sees marriage as a trap sprung by a combination of a man's lustfulness and cupidity, and his only escape is to go to sea. In consort with the lawyer Tangle he hits on the idea of selling his wife to Proditor, so combining profit with freedom.

The ubiquitous Phoenix gets wind of the Captain's blatant attempt to pervert the marriage laws and with the help of Castiza's son, Fidelio (reflecting Middleton's role in the dispute with Harvey) exposes the fraud and passes the 500 crowns of the bride price to the bride herself, while the captain is sent packing. The sacredness of marriage is asserted in a homily in which Phoenix both praises 'honourable matrimony' and attacks those who would undermine it:

> Reverend and honorable matrimony,
> Mother of lawful sweets, unshamed mornings,
> Dangerless pleasures, thou that mak'st the bed
> Both pleasant and legitimately fruitful;
> Without thee,
> All the whole world were soiled bastardy.
> Thou art the only and the greatest form
> That put'st a difference between our desires
> And the disordered appetites of beasts,
> Making their mates those that stand next their lusts.

(II, ii, 161–70)

This kind of explicitness is alien to Middleton's satiric method and is abandoned in the later comedies, in which the audience is required to realize for itself the positive implications of the satire. Such a radical departure from the Middletonian norm is usually explained by pointing out that this is an early work, though *Family of Love* generally eschews such explicitness. It is much more likely that in *Phoenix* Middleton wants to draw his audience's attention to themes that will emphasize the play's Jamesean affiliations. For King James had gone out of his way to advise his son at some length on the solemnity of marriage in *Basilikon Doron*, urging

143

on Prince Henry the sacredness of the institution, the importance of marital chastity and the horror of bastardy:

> First of all consider, that Mariage is the greatest earthly felicitie or miserie, that can come to a man, according as it pleaseth God to bless or curse the same. Since then without the blessing of God, yee cannot looke for a happie successe in Mariage, yee must bee carefull both in your preparation for it, and in the choice and usage of your wife, to procure the same. By your preparation, I meane, that yee must keepe your bodie cleane and unpolluted, till yee give it to your wife, whom-to onely it belongeth. . .. When yee are Maried, keepe inviolably your promise made to God in your Mariage; which standeth all in doing one thing, and abstayning from another: to treat her in all things as your wife, and the halfe of your selfe; and to make your body (which then is no more yours, but properly hers) common with none other. I trust I need not to insist here to disswade you from the filthy vice of adulterie: remember onely what solemne promise yee make to God at your Mariage. . .[22]

It is characteristic of James that he includes in his solemn admonitions such risqué jokes as the punning on the 'doing of one thing', a bawdy use of the verb 'do' that the Captain echoes when he asks 'when I'm abroad, what can I do at home?' (I, ii, 45–6).[23] The King's delight in strange combinations of the sublime and the ridiculous, and especially combining raucous bawdy with moral admonition is mentioned by David Mathew in his biography of James I. Remarking on the close relationship between the King and Bishop John Williams towards the end of the King's life, Mathew comments that Williams 'understood the king's wit, both the simplicity and the strain of bawdy'.[24]

The Captain is finally dispensed with at the end of the second scene of Act 2, when Prince Phoenix, having witnessed the Captain's attempt to sell his wife, reveals his true identity, after the thoroughly Jamesean aside 'Who scourgeth sin, let him do't dreadfully' (II, ii, 262). James liked nothing better than to 'scourge sin dreadfully' as on the occasion of his journey from Scotland at the beginning of his English reign, when at Newark he ordered the summary execution of a cutpurse who had been caught while travelling with the royal party.[25] There was often, too, a theatrical, even grotesque, side to this dreadful justice, as on the occasion when James ordered a last-minute stay of execution for three of those condemned for the so-called 'Main' plot as they stood on the scaffold. David Stevenson quotes a passage from the contemporary chronicle of Sir Richard Baker describing this occasion:

> this was the course that the king held in showing mercy. After the death of the three before named he signed three other warrants for the execution of the late Lord Cobham, the Lord Grey and Sir Griffin

144

Markeham, on a certain day then following; but before that day came he privately framed another warrant, written with his own hand to the Sheriffe. . .by which he countermanded the former Warrants: and that there might be no notice taken of it: he sent it by Mr John Gybbe. . .one utterly unknown to all the company, appointing him to deliver it so, that it might not take effect, till after their severall confessions, and at the very point of their Execution, which was accordingly performed; At which time, it was a wonderful thing to see how the Delinquents falling on their knees, lamented their misdoings, and most of all how they extolled the kings unspeakable mercy.[26]

'Unspeakable' (in a more modern sense) seems the right epithet for so fantastical a king of dark corners. Shakespeare, too, shows himself thoroughly aware of the theatrical side of his Sovereign's sense of justice in the similarly elaborate and grotesque deceptions that Duke Vincentio plays first on Claudio and then (even more grotesquely) on the drunken Barnadine. Middleton's sea-captain is dismissed to immediate exile at sea, where his venom 'may do least harm' (II, ii, 316). He has offended not only in his irreverent attitude towards marriage and chastity, but in his profession of privateer at a time when James was making an attempt to stamp out the practice.[27]

Equally acceptable to Middleton's royal audience would have been the emphasis the play gives to the importance of law and in its satire on legal corruption. The importance of the King's role in upholding justice is (inevitably) a central theme of *Basilikon Doron*, as it is in Shakespeare's *Measure for Measure*. James is concerned both with the role of king as law-giver and with the more abstract principles of justice in *Basilikon Doron*; and while Middleton is more concerned with legality in *Phoenix*, Shakespeare's play makes the discussion of the nature of justice a central issue. In the second part of *Basilikon Doron* James advises his son on the responsibilities of the king as law-maker in distinguishing between the good king and the tyrant. The good king concerns himself with 'the making and execution of good Lawes', whereas the tyrant perverts the law 'to serve only for his unrulie private affections'.[28] He goes on to warn his son to beware of allowing the law to be manipulated for private ends. Middleton's interest in law is evident, especially in the early plays (one of which, *Michaelmas Term*, gets its title from the law schools). This interest may be as much to do with Middleton's own experience with the tangled dispute with Thomas Harvey as with the legal interests of the Paul's audience. In *Phoenix* Middleton is principally concerned to satirize legal corruption and this satire revolves around the figures of the madly litigious Tangle, whom the Captain consults on the disposing of his wife, and the more macabre figure of the corrupt justice of the peace, Falso. Tangle is essentially a 'humours' character in the Jonsonian manner, a man preoccupied with his one obsession of litigation, who is driven completely mad when he loses two of his lawsuits and who is only finally purged of his complaint by having all his law terms bled out of him. The other character, Falso, is a more typical Middletonian rogue. Brooks suggests that the name may combine syllables from the names of Falstaff and Justice Shallow,[29] but while there is something of Falstaff's swagger about him, he is essentially a darker, more sinister figure. He is very much the corrupt magistrate and his function in the law satire is emphasized in a scene with Tangle in which they fire legal jargon at one another in a duelling parody (II, iii, 141–256). Falso, however, is no harmless fool; he connives with his own servants in robbing travellers and when Phoenix and Fidelio bring one of them (Furtivo) before him, he pretends to commit him (without acknowledging that he knows him) only to release him later. The examination of Furtivo is vintage Middleton in its ironic exploitation of multiple levels of perception. Phoenix and Fidelio, believing (as Phoenix says) that Falso is 'a maintainer of equal causes', take Falso's somewhat eccentric interrogation of the prisoner at its face value, while we in the audience have already heard Falso interviewing two of the servants who took part in the robbery, to whom he boasts of his own days as a highway thief:

> I ha' seen the day I could have told money out of other men's purses – mass, so I can do now – nor will I keep that fellow about me that dares not bid a man stand: for as long as drunkenness is a vice, stand is a virtue.
>
> (III, i, 50–4)

Middleton exploits this duplicity by having Furtivo's two companions in crime present (as Falso's servants) during the interrogation, adding their knowledgeable asides to Falso's. In the last act of the play Falso's duplicity is revealed before the Duke (V, i, 127–55). There is, however, a much more sinister side to Falso that removes him altogether from the ranks of such amiable rogues as Falstaff. For Falso has a wealthy niece, of whom he is the guardian. To get hold of her money he proposes an incestuous relationship with her that will bind her to him. That it is the money rather than the sexual pleasure that he is interested in, however, is suggested by his contentment when she declares her wish to leave his household and her money rather than suffer his conduct. Falso's character anticipates the arch-rogue Sir Bounteous Progress in *A Mad World, My Masters*, but whereas Sir Bounteous's sinfulness is symbolic of the mad world of sin that humanity is heir to, Falso remains essentially confined to a narrower role of satiric portrait of the corrupt magistrate. Middleton's characteristic linking of sex and money finds its fullest expression in the episodes concerning Falso's daughter, who steals from her husband to pay her lover and who calls her lover 'Pleasure', while with equal allegorical frankness he refers to her as 'Revenue'. Middleton's characteristic allegorical tendencies rarely reveal themselves quite so openly.

As with the satire on the abuse of marriage, the satire on law in *Phoenix* is complemented by panegyric, in this case on legality, again spoken by Prince Phoenix and again making explicit the moral affinities between the play's hero and the published views of King James. The panegyric is sparked off by Tangle's confession that he finances his own lawsuits by giving false legal advice to others (I, iv, 165) and in getting free legal representation by directing others to his own lawyer (I, iv, 179–80). Prince Phoenix responds by lamenting the corruption of the law and then in highly emblematic fashion describes its origins in the sacred authority of the King as chief magistrate:

> Admired Law,
> Thy upper parts must need be sacred, pure,
> And incorruptible; they're grave and wise;
> 'Tis but the dross beneath 'em, and the clouds
> That get between thy glory and their praise
> That make the visible and foul eclipse. . .
>
> (I, iv, 201–6)

This (as Brooks notes)[30] is flattering to the King, who saw himself (and was seen) as the highest source of justice in the land. It is a particularly interesting passage (if dramatically jejune) because it reveals that essentially symbolic habit of Middleton's mind, that gets so skilfully re-interpreted in naturalistic terms in the major comedies. Brooks, incidentally, illustrates close parallels to this speech in other works of Middleton. *Phoenix* points the way to Middleton's brilliant surface realism in his later plays, more especially in its lively portraits of the Captain and Falso. The dazzling irony of later comedies, where the nefarious work of this mad world goes on against an undercurrent of subtle allusions to the standards of the next, is only fitfully achieved in this play – most notably in the scene where Falso interrogates Furtivo, or in the splendidly grotesque irony of Falso's meditation on the terms of his brother's will:

> Well, he was too honest to live, and that made him die so soon. Now, I beshrew my heart, I am glad he's in heaven; he's left all his cares and troubles with me, and that great vexation of telling of money; yet I hope he had so much grace to turn his white money into gold. . .
>
> (I, vi, 79–84)

There is not, unfortunately, very much of such virtuosity. Middleton, in this play, prefers a heavy-handed explicitness to assert his orthodoxy before his Prince; but it holds out the promise of a brilliance that Middleton was later to redeem in such good measure.

Measure for Measure achieves its compliment to King James in not dissimilar ways, but with very different emphasis. Shakespeare, too, chooses the fashionable mode of naturalistic comedy, but his play eschews satire, except incidentally, and takes as central from *Basilikon Doron*, not the civil issues chosen by Middleton (though these are involved), but the moral and religious themes to which he rightly judged King James gave priority. Darryl Gless, in his book on Shakespeare's play, has pointed to the importance of the religious themes in *Basilikon Doron* and their influence on *Measure for Measure*.[31] The first of the three sections of James's work is devoted to the Christian basis of good government and takes as its theme 'A Kings Christian Duetie Towards God'.[32] James prided himself (to the confusion of his bishops) on his knowledge of theological matters and indeed saw himself as having an essentially religious role as God's anointed. It is highly appropriate that his surrogate is given a priestly role in *Measure for Measure*, albeit popish. Accordingly the play is more about salvation than legal judgement and the biblical text to which its title alludes (the Sermon on the Mount) is interpreted primarily as offering spiritual rather than political guidance. In this, Shakespeare's next public play, *King Lear*, is its complement, for *Lear* demonstrates the vanity of a world built on the sands of pagan assumptions.

The idea for the plot of the play probably came initially from Shakespeare's reading of Giraldi's *Hecatommithi*, already used for *Othello*. The story is the fifth novella of the eighth decade, a decade that is dedicated to the exploration of ingratitude – a theme Shakespeare largely ignores for *Measure for Measure* but the impact of which is merely postponed. His next two plays, *Timon* and *King Lear*, explore this theme; the latter at the profoundest levels. In the dedication of the eighth decade to Lucio Paganucci, the secretary to the Duke of Ferrara, Giraldi also makes it clear that this group of novelle will deal with government, and particularly the corrupt magistrate, for as he explains to Paganucci, 'there is nothing that shows more clearly what men are than those who find themselves either by luck or merit magistrates (magistrati). . .sometimes fate raises to the magistry (a magistrato) a soul who is unworthy of that honour'.[33] Several of the stories accordingly go on to illustrate this theme of the unjust magistrate, including the story Shakespeare chooses for *Measure for Measure*. The fifth novella is told by one of the women of the party, Fulvia, who in her introduction to the tale says she is going to tell a story concerning the ingratitude of an unjust minister named Juriste, who was appointed by the Emperor Massimiano. Juriste betrays his trust in the same way as Angelo in *Measure for Measure*. He offers to save the life of a young man accused of rape (Vico) if Vico's sister (Epitia) agrees to sleep with him; when she does so Juriste betrays his promise and has Vico beheaded. Epitia appeals to the Emperor and Juriste is arrested: he is forced to marry Epitia and is to be beheaded, but is saved by the earnest pleading of Epitia to spare him. In this story (says Fulvia) she will illustrate not only the monstrous sin of Juriste's ingratitude, but also how the goodness of a woman redeems a wicked man. This latter theme is of particular importance because Fulvia is deliberately answering the previous two novelle, which have both illustrated the wicked ingratitude of women. Of the three interwoven themes of Fulvia's story: ingratitude, woman's kindness and the unjust magistrate, Shakespeare chooses to concentrate on the single issue of the magistrate's abuse of power, which he uses to illustrate the wider theme at the centre of the play: the Calvinistic theme of the inevitability of human sinfulness.

Reading Giraldi's novelle must have reminded Shakespeare of an old play published some twenty-five years or more before, George Whetstone's *Promos and Cassandra*. The plot of this two-part play is in many ways similar to the Giraldi story, showing how a corrupt ruler (Promos) treacherously goes back on a promise to free a young man (Andrugio) accused of fornication, after Promos has persuaded Andrugio's sister (Cassandra) to sleep with him. Like Juriste and Angelo, Promos orders the execution of the young fornicator. But unlike the Giraldi story the young man is not executed; in *Promos and Cassandra* a compassionate jailor has a dead man's head substituted for Andrugio's and the young man is allowed to escape, eventually to be reunited with his sister. Like Epitia, Cassandra appeals to the supreme ruler for justice and Promos is brought to judgement, made to marry the woman whose chastity he violated and is saved from death by his wife's earnest plea for clemency. Both versions emphasize at the end the importance of clemency as well as strictness in a king. At the beginning of the sixth novella in *Hecatommithi* Giraldi remarks that he could not judge which pleased the ladies listening to the story more, 'the justice or the clemency of Massimiano':

> Here the most mature said that Clemency is a most worthy companion to Royal Justice, because it moderates punishments and thus one reads that it is very appropriate for princes. For it induces a certain temperance in their minds that makes them benevolent towards their subjects and they concluded that Massimiano was shown worthy of empire in both Justice and in Clemency.[34]

No better subject could be chosen to set before the King at Whitehall who confessed (as we have seen) to indulgence as a ruler and clearly secretly prided himself on it.

Promos and Cassandra did not only suggest such modifications to Giraldi's story as the substitution of the dead man's head and the happy outcome (a modification to the ending that, incidentally, Giraldi had himself made when he converted his novella into the play of *Epitia* towards the end of his life). More important than these details of the plotting is the influence the

149

old play had on Shakespeare's dramatic method. For *Promos and Cassandra* is one of those early examples of unromantic comedy concerned with the exposition of low life as well as corruption in high places. Whetstone's abilities as a dramatist are severely limited, or perhaps (more fairly) we ought to say that in 1578, when the play was published, there had not developed those extraordinarily supple dramatic techniques that in barely twenty years transformed the art of the theatre from college exercise or crude entertainment to the most sophisticated dramatic vehicle the theatre has ever known. For all its prosaic woodenness, however, *Promos and Cassandra* provided Shakespeare with a dramatic formula that suited the new fashion for unromantic comedy.

In the first part of *Promos and Cassandra* Whetstone alternates between the story of the unjust magistrate and scenes which show the effect of Promos's new legal severity on the lower orders. The low-life scenes centre on the prostitute and bawd Lamia and her largely successful attempts to subvert the new order by corrupting Promos's chief executive, Phallax. Phallax's cynicism makes him an easy target and contrasts with his master's puritanical austerity and agonized sense of guilt when he finds himself infatuated with Cassandra. The contrast between the two men is potentially an interesting one, but is presented in too facile a way to allow it much force. Whetstone's moral didacticism leads him to present Promos as a moral example, rather than as an individual struggling with his conscience (an approach that partly survives in Shakespeare's treatment of Angelo). We hear of Promos's agony over his deception of Cassandra, when he orders Andrugio to be executed, not directly through soliloquy (though soliloquy over-abounds in the play) but in a mocking speech addressed directly to the audience by Phallax in a reductive language that provides a complete barrier to the audience's sympathies:

> I marvell much what worketh so my Lord Promos' unrest.
> He fares as if a thousand Devils were gnawing in his brest:
> There is sure some worme of griefe, that doth his conscience nip,
> For since Andrugio lost his head he hath hung downe the lippe.
>
> (V, i, 1–4)[35]

This satiric caricature of Promos deliberately dehumanizes, so that – in the true manner of the morality tradition – the doctrinal message rings out clear by keeping emotional interest in the character at a minimum. It is interesting that Shakespeare adopts a mixed mode for his play, retaining some of this symbolic use of character, most notably in the role of the Duke, while in other cases he involves the audience's emotions empathically by infusing the characters with an intense individuality.

There is no better example of this latter than in the great scene between Isabella and her brother, where Claudio is pleading with her to save his life. Whetstone has a similar scene, which he treats as a debate between

150

brother and sister, presenting opposing views of the moral dilemma. In effect it is a debate between Charity and Chastity:

> *Andrugio*: Nay Cassandra, if thou thy selfe submyt,
> To save my life, to Promos fleashly wyll,
> Justice wyll say thou dost no cryme commit:
> For in forst faultes is no intent of yll.
> *Cassandra*: How so th'intent is construed in offence,
> The Proverbe saies, that tenne good turnes lye dead,
> And one yll deede, tenne tymes beyonde pretence,
> By envious tongues report abrode doth spread.
> Andrugio so my fame shall vallewed bee,
> Dispite wyll blase my crime, but not the cause. . .
>   (Part I, III, iv, 34–43)

There is no danger here of the audience wishing to take sides, because there are no personalities to identify with, we simply have a rehearsal of the moral issues involved. Shakespeare transforms this debate into an intensely personal conflict of wills between a young man desperately fearful of death and a young woman equally tormented by the prospect of losing her sexual honour and breaking her novitiate vows, without losing sight either of the obligations of their relationship or the moral dilemma that confronts them:

> *Isabella*:   Dost thou think, Claudio,
> If I would yield him my virginity
> Thou mightst be freed?
> *Claudio*:   Oh heavens, it cannot be!
> *Isabella*: Yes, he would give't thee, from this rank offence,
> So to offend him still. This night's the time
> That I should do what I abhor to name;
> Or else thou diest tomorrow.
> *Claudio*:   Thou shalt not do't.
> *Isabella*: O, were it but my life,
> I'd throw it down for your deliverance
> As frankly as a pin.
> *Claudio*:   Thanks, dear Isabel.
> *Isabella*: Be ready, Claudio, for your death tomorrow.
> *Claudio*: Yes. – Has he affections in him,
> That thus can make him bite the law by th'nose
> When he would force it? – Sure, it is no sin;
> Or of the deadly seven it is the least.
> *Isabella*: Which is the least?
> *Claudio*: If it were damnable, he being so wise,
> Why would he for the momentary trick
> Be perdurably fin'd? – O Isabel!

151

Isabella: What says my brother?
Claudio: Death is a fearful thing.
Isabella: And shamed life a hateful.
Claudio: Ay, but to die, and go we know not where;
   To lie in cold obstruction, and to rot;
   This sensible warm motion to become
   A kneaded clod. . .

(III, i, 96–120)[36]

and Claudio goes on to give that terrifying, pagan picture of the afterlife in which all man's hatred and fear of death seems to be summed up.

The yawning gap between Whetstone and Shakespeare here is not merely the gap between minor talent and supreme mastery, it is a wholly different way of treating the theatre. In place of Whetstone's intellectual debate, here we have the complex and contradictory movements of two perplexed minds trying to come to terms with an unresolvable dilemma. Claudio's first response – he is a decent man with a moral conscience not unlike his sister's – is to reject the idea of his sister's sacrifice of her virginity. But as the dialogue continues, the more pressing reality of a death unsupported by Christian conviction crowds in on him and he shifts ground. The debate is as much in himself as with his sister. For a morality drama all this would cloud the issue – and indeed no very clear resolution emerges from the dialogue; but that does not mean that Shakespeare has here abandoned concern with the doctrinal themes that inform the play. As we shall see, the dialogue has precise doctrinal implications; but now Shakespeare is uniting his power of creating personality with an equally secure use of characters as symbol. For the first time, perhaps, in the canon, Shakespeare is fusing with total success the affective and the symbolic and anticipating the more sustained triumph of this fusion in *Lear*, *Macbeth* and *Antony and Cleopatra*. One of the weaknesses of *Measure for Measure* is that this achievement is not wholly sustained throughout the play. Isabella's austere, if erroneous, dignity, for example, becomes compromised and distorted beyond the audience's reasonable tolerance at the level of personality by the requirements of the play's (and the King's) doctrine that the catholic 'superstition' of vowed celibacy should be repudiated. At the level of real psychology the exchange of sleeping partners (where Isabella's behaviour is not so very dissimilar from that of a high-class bawd) and the Anglican triumph of sex-in-marriage at the end lack complete credibility. In *All's Well that Ends Well* the bedroom substitution of Helena for Diana escapes censure because the primary mode of the play does not ask for psychological realism. Shakespeare fails to pull it off a second time because the later play more insistently asks us to respond to the characters as people. The effect of the doctrinal imperative in human terms in *Measure for Measure* is that Isabella is left at the end, a little incongruously, holding hands with a

Duke who is himself more convincing as personification than as personality.

Although the superb scene between Isabella and Claudio is wholly convincing in psychological and affective terms, it none the less asserts very accurately the doctrinal distinction James I makes in *Basilikon Doron* between two types of spiritual blindness, two opposing states of error he describes as the 'two diseases. . .Leaprosie, and Superstition; the former is the mother of Atheisme, the other of Heresies'. In these terms Claudio is clearly a spiritual leper, however venial his sin might appear in modern eyes (or most Jacobean eyes come to that). James describes the 'leprous conscience' as one that has lost the acute awareness of sin that is necessary to keep us humble before God (the analogy alludes to the fact that leprosy deprives the extremities of the body of all sense of feeling):

> By a leprouse conscience, I meane *a cauterized conscience*, as Paul calleth it, being become senseless of sinne, through sleeping in a carelesse securitie as King Davids was after his murther and adulterie, ever til he was wakened by the Prophet Nathans similitude.[37]

Claudio, like David in his adultery with Bathsheba, has shown himself blind to his own sinfulness, and he too is similarly sexually intemperate. The intense love of life Claudio shows in this scene and his fear of death are specifically singled out as characteristic of the moral leper:

> And therefore, I would not have you pray with the Papists, to be preserved from suddaine death, but that God would give you grace so to live, as ye may every houre of your life be ready for death: so shall ye attaine to the vertue of trew fortitude, never being afraid for the horrour of death, come when he list.[38]

This is the message Duke Vincentio conveys to Claudio in those splendid lines on the vanity of the world at the beginning of the scene (III, i, 5ff). It is a lesson that Claudio, in his impetuosity, says he understands, only to find his new resolution collapsing at the first temptation:

> To sue to live, I find I seek to die,
> And seeking death, find life. Let it come on.
> (III, i, 42–3)

The collapse of this short-lived calm is a sign both of his youthful intemperance and that he does not know himself. In contrast, the Duke is said (by Escalus) to be 'A gentleman of all temperance' (III, ii, 231) and one who 'above all other strifes, contended especially to know himself' (III, ii, 226–7). Both temperance and self-knowledge are singled out by James for special commendation:

Temperance, Queene of all the rest within you. . .that first

commaunding your selfe, shall as a Queene, command all the
affections and passions of your minde. . .[39]

In the passage on the 'leprous conscience' James exhorts his son to analyse
his conscience and learn to know himself as he really is:

let not your selfe be smoothed over with that flattering φλαυτία,
which is overkindly a sicknesse to all mankind: but censure your selfe
as sharply, as if ye were your owne enemie: *For if ye iudge your selfe, ye
shall not be iudged*, as the Apostle saith. . .[40]

It is no coincidence that when Claudio's Christian resolution does break
down, his vision of the afterlife is not that of the Christian, but of the
'atheist' (that is, in seventeenth-century terms, the non-Christian), for as
James has warned us, the 'leprous conscience. . .is the mother of atheisme':

> Ay, but to die, and go we know not where;
> To lie in cold obstruction, and to rot;
> This sensible warm motion to become
> A kneaded clod; and the delighted spirit
> To bath in fiery floods, or to reside
> In thrilling region of thick-ribbed ice;
> To be imprison'd in the viewless winds
> And blown with restless violence round about
> The pendent world: or to be worse than worst
> Of those that lawless and incertain thought
> Imagine howling, – 'tis too horrible.
>
> (III, i, 117–27)

The splendid imagery of these lines asks us – as we willingly do – to
engage ourselves in Claudio's vision of the horrors of death. His response is
surely the natural response. Shakespeare would have read the novella in the
Hecatommithi that follows the story of Epitia, about a handsome young man
from Corfu who feigns apostasy for fear of death 'which as you all know is
the most terrible of all things'.[41] Claudio's speech is itself apostasy from a
Christian (and specifically from a Protestant) point of view. Even Claudio
himself recognizes this in admitting that his vision of the howling souls is
heretical ('lawless') and dubious. He presents no consistent view of the
afterlife (hence the difficulty modern commentators have had in interpret-
ing it). Death is seen at first as mere negation, the cold dead body rotting
in the ground; in contrast to the warmth and movement of this life,
becoming a lump of clay. Claudio's sensuality revolts against the death of
all sensation, but the alternatives he conjures up are no more reassuring,
the pagan vision of the once delighted spirit (which is surely the
significance of 'delighted' here)[42] now bathed in fire, imprisoned in ice or,
like Lucretian atoms, blown about in the winds. Even these horrors may

not be as bad as the unknown world of death that thought conjures up. Clearly this is no Christian response to death and its very incoherence and eclecticism stresses what is most terrifying about death to the pagan, the uncertainty of what death may bring. This is exactly the kind of 'atheism' that results from the spiritual sloth of the 'leprous conscience', that failure constantly to keep in mind our soul's health and our need of God's grace. To avoid this sinful state of mind we must meditate on death and on our unfitness to meet God's judgement:

> As for a preservative against this Leaprosie, remember ever once in the foure and twentie houres, either in the night, or when yee are at greatest quiet, to call your selfe to account of all your last dayes actions, either wherein ye have committed things yee should not, or omitted the things ye should doe, either in your Christian or Kingly calling. . . . Remember therefore in all your actions, of the great account that yee are one day to make: in all the dayes of your life, ever learning to die, and living every day as it were your last.[43]

Much has been written concerning the veniality of Claudio's sin and its similarity to the 'sin' Angelo is led into with Mariana by the Duke and the saintly Isabella. But Shakespeare requires us to distinguish between the crime which Claudio commits and for which he is justly condemned to die and the sin of being attached to the things of this world, which has been evinced both by his sexual intemperance and his fear of death.

In his failure to be 'resolute for death', Claudio demonstrates the perilous state of his soul. The key scriptural passage for both *Basilikon Doron* and the play is the first epistle of St John, 2: 15–17 (I quote the Geneva version as one with which Shakespeare would be familiar, even if James himself disapproved of it):[44]

> Love not the worlde, nether the things that are in the worlde. If any man love the worlde, the love of the Father is not in him. For all that is in the worlde (as the luste of the flesh, the luste of the eyes, and the pride of life) is not of the Father, but is of the worlde. And the worlde passeth awaye, and the luste therof: but he that fulfilleth the wil of God, abideth ever.

Claudio sins in the lust of the flesh as he himself confesses in admitting that his plight arises from a surfeit of 'liberty' (I, ii, 117), but equally his state of mind shows him guilty of 'pride of life' in being too concerned with this life and not enough with the next. It is not the sleeping with Juliet before the completing of the marriage ceremony that matters so much in itself (in terms of sin as opposed to law) but the state of mind that is evinced when he is called to account legally for his behaviour, which confirms him as someone perilously fond of the things of this world. And just as Claudio is made to face up to his spiritual peril, by being made by the Duke to confront the death he fears, so Angelo by sleeping (as he thinks) with Isabella is made to confront his own spiritual turpitude in the revelation that he has committed a worse crime than that for which he has condemned Claudio. In both cases the Duke 'like power divine', leads the sinner to an understanding of his sinfulness, that 'right knowledge and fear of God' which, James tells his son, is the beginning of wisdom.[45]

The similarities between Angelo's spiritual condition and Claudio's help to emphasize that we are all guilty in the eyes of God. Indeed the play demonstrates this thesis in presenting each of the three main characters, Angelo, Claudio and Isabella, with a test of their virtue. In each case the initiate proves to be lacking in temperance and self-knowledge. All three show a pride that blinds them to the essential sinfulness of their own humanity. Angelo admits, in soliloquy, to the 'pride' he has taken in the image of sobriety he has cultivated:

> The state whereon I studied
> Is, like a good thing being often read,
> Grown sere and tedious; yea, my gravity,
> Wherein – let no man hear me – I take pride,
> Could I with boot change for an idle plume
> Which the air beats for vain.
>
> (II, iv, 7–12)

Angelo understands his own hypocrisy – he has, he says 'heaven in my mouth. . . and in my heart the strong and swelling evil/Of my conception' (II, iv, 4–6), where 'conception', incidentally, means 'the fact of being conceived'[46] as well as 'thought' and refers to original sin. He would hide his pride of life (defined in the Geneva gloss as 'ambition') from men, but fails to consider the more important relationship to God, paying, as he himself admits, mere lip-service to his religious duties. Here again then, is that 'pride of life' that ignores the central truth of human existence, that each of us is 'death's fool', as the Duke reminds Claudio. As with Claudio, this pride in life comes to express itself in sexual infatuation – in lust of the flesh. Ironically, Angelo, in his pride, comes to reject all comparison with Claudio in discussing the case with Escalus: 'When I that censure him do so offend,/Let mine own judgement pattern out my death' (II, i, 29–30). Isabella, with her spiritual hypersensitivity, understands that we are all alike subject to sin:

> If he had been as you, and you as he,
> You would have slipp'd like him. . .
>
> (II, ii, 64–5)

and that only God's grace saves us from damnation: 'He that might the vantage best have took/Found out the remedy' (II, ii, 74–5). All this, of

156

course, assumes an audience capable of making some nice theological distinctions. The finer points would not have been lost on the royal audience of December 1604, because they originate in James's own Calvinistic preoccupations with reprobation and conscience.

Just as Claudio illustrates James's view of one kind of spiritual malaise, the man who is insufficiently alive to his own state of sin, so Isabella illustrates the error James describes as the 'disease' of 'superstition'.[47] And just as Claudio's sin leads to 'atheisme', so Isabella's leads to 'heresies'. James defines superstition as 'when one restraines himselfe to any other rule in the service of God, then is warranted by the word, the only trew square of Gods service'.[48] Here James is entering into the field of sectarian controversy, for his definition is based on the Protestant insistence that (to quote the sixth of the Thirty-Nine Articles):

> Holy scripture containeth all things necessary to salvation, so that whatsoever is not read therein, nor may be proved thereby, is not to be required of any man, that it should be believed as an article of the Faith, or be thought requisite or necessary to salvation.

James is particularly insistent on this in *Basilikon Doron*:

> Remember also, that by the right knowledge, and feare of God. . .ye shall know all things necessarie for the discharge of your duetie, both as a Christian, and as a King; seeing in him, as in a mirrour, the course of all earthly things, whereof hee is the spring and onely moover. Now, the onely way to bring you to this knowledge, is diligently to read his word, and earnestly to pray for the right understanding thereof. *Search the Scriptures*, sayth Christ, *for they beare testimonie of me*: (John 5, 39) and, *the whole Scripture*, saith Paul, *is given by inspiration of God, and is profitable to teach, to convince, to correct, and to instruct in righteousnesse; that the man of God may be absolute, being made perfite unto all good workes.* (2 Tim.3, 16–17)[49]

He returns to this priority of Scripture in elaborating his definition of 'superstition':

> And for keeping your conscience sound from that sicknesse of superstition, yee must neither lay the safetie of your conscience upon the credit of your owne conceits, nor yet of other mens humors, how great doctors of Divinitie that ever they be; but yee must onely ground it upon the expresse Scripture: for conscience not grounded upon sure knowledge, is either an ignorant fantasie, or an arrogant vanitie. Beware therefore in this case with two extremities: the one, to beleeve with the Papists, the Churches authority, better then your owne knowledge; the other, to leane with the Anabaptists, to your owne conceits and dreamed revelations.[50]

Isabella, as a convent novice, is the victim of the 'arrogant vanity' of sworn celibacy, assumed through trusting the Catholic Church's authority rather than Scripture. Shakespeare emphasizes her 'superstition' in having her desire 'restraints. . .in the service of God' not warranted by Scripture, on the first occasion that we meet her:

> *Isabella*: And have you nuns no farther privileges?
> *Nun*: Are not these large enough?
> *Isabella*: Yes, truly; I speak not as desiring more,
>   But rather wishing a more strict restraint
>   Upon the sisters stood, the votarists of Saint Clare.

(I, iv, 1–5)

All of this to the Anglican James (and we must presume, to Shakespeare) was a heresy of Popish superstition and we need not be surprised that *Measure for Measure* was the one play the English Jesuits of Valladolid excised from their copy of the second folio.[51] Darryl Gless points out that the chief Protestant objection to the cloistered life was that it was spiritually self-indulgent, and quotes – among a host of Protestant authorities – the reference in *Venus and Adonis* to 'self-loving nuns'.[52] Gless also quotes *Basilikon Doron* to demonstrate that James was explicitly concerned to argue against the 'cloistered virtue' fostered by monasticism:

> For it is not ynough that ye have and retaine (as prisoners) within your selfe never so many good qualities and vertues, except ye employ them, and set them on worke, for the weale of them that are committed to your charge: *Virtutis enim laus omnis in actione consistit.*[53]

The Duke shares these views; for one of the reasons he gives for wanting Angelo to take over the reins of government, is so that Angelo's private virtues may be more publicly manifested:

> Heaven doth with us as we with torches do,
> Not light them for themselves; for if our virtues
> Did not go forth of us, 'twere all alike
> As if we had them not.

(I, i, 32–5)

Isabella is also 'self-loving' in her response to Claudio's appeal to her to save his life. 'Self-love', James points out in his comment on φιλαυτία 'is overkindly a sicknesse to all mankind';[54] it is the antithesis of charity, the love of our fellow-beings. Isabella's uncharity shows not only in her refusal to consider sacrificing herself for her brother, but in her increasingly hysterical response to his pleading, which reaches its height in the accusation that Claudio is an habitual lecher, with a suggestion in the imagery that he is nothing better than a male prostitute:

> Thy sin's not accidental, but a trade;
> Mercy to thee would prove itself a bawd;
> 'Tis best thou diest quickly.
>
> (III, i, 148–50)

This is an uncharitable traversty of Claudio's 'true contract' with Julietta and it is left to the 'gracious' Duke (acting as the channel of God's grace) to find a way to 'redeem your brother from the angry law' (III, i, 200–1). Isabella's conduct here is also in marked contrast with the 'reformed' Isabella of Act V, when (on her knees) she pleads for Angelo's life with the argument that 'A due sincerity govern'd his deeds' (V, i, 444) when he ordered Claudio's execution. Here Isabella has come to understand the 'protestant' emphasis that the fact must defer to the inner state of mind.

To see Isabella's role in this light is not to defend Claudio's appeal, for he, as we saw, is equally guilty of sin. Isabella's position is illogical, for she is 'superstitiously' defining sin in terms of effect rather than cause, committing the 'popish' error of substituting spiritual appearance for spiritual reality:

> Better it were a brother died at once,
> Than that a sister, by redeeming him,
> Should die for ever.
>
> (II, iv, 106–8)

Angelo points to Isabella's inconsistency here, for she has just been arguing that Angelo should moderate his absolute standards of justice to take into account that human frailty that Christ atoned for: 'How would you be/If He, which is the top of judgement, should/But judge you as you are?'(II, ii, 75–7). Indeed she misunderstands Angelo's paradoxical suggestion that the 'sin' of saving Claudio might be an act of charity, by agreeing to take on the burden of that sin:

> *Angelo*: I – now the voice of the recorded law –
>   Pronounce a sentence on your brother's life:
>   Might there not be a charity in sin
>   To save this brother's life?
> *Isabella*:   Please you to do't,
>   I'll take it as a peril to my soul;
>   It is no sin at all, but charity.
>
> (II, iv, 61–6)

Isabella believes Angelo to be offering to bend the law to save Claudio, which she is quite willing to accept as a charitable 'sin', and so shows herself fully able to distinguish between fact and intent. When she realizes that the subject at issue is not bending Angelo's principles but her own, she appeals to that letter of the law that she had earlier repudiated, as

159

Angelo is swift to point out:

> *Isabella*:　　lawful mercy
> 　Is nothing kin to foul redemption.
> *Angelo*: You seem'd of late to make the law a tyrant. . .
>
> 　　　　　　　　　　　　　　　　(II, iv, 112–4)

Shakespeare had earlier shown the ambivalence of Isabella's position in her ambiguous reply to Angelo's first suggestion that she should give her virginity for Claudio's life:

> 　　　　　Sir, believe this:
> 　　I had rather give my body than my soul.
> 　　　　　　　　　　(II, iv, 55–6)

The thread that leads out of this labyrinth of paradox, of sin that is charity, redemption that is damnation, is to be found in the sectarian conflict between the Protestant stress on the soul's relation to God and the 'papist' stress (as Protestants understood it) on outward forms. Isabella in these terms is in error in confusing spiritual form with spiritual substance: the 'body' she would preserve in its virginity, with the 'soul' of her charity towards her brother. Angelo (speaking 'scripture') defines the problem with clarity even while he himself fails to benefit from the wisdom:

> 　　O place, O form,
> 　How often dost thou with thy case, thy habit,
> 　Wrench awe from fools, and tie the wiser souls
> 　To thy false seeming!
> 　　　　　　　　　　(II, iv, 12–15)

Angelo's is very much a case like St Paul's: 'I alowe not that which I do: for what I wolde, that do I not' (Romans 7: 15). Isabella is no fool, but one of those 'wiser souls' tied to 'false-seeming'. She too has to be saved from her spiritual error through suffering the consequences of Claudio's supposed death. She must be brought to a more charitable viewpoint, marked first by her willingness to help Mariana to a husband and finally by abandoning the false idol of virginity in her acceptance of the Duke's hand in marriage. The Duke recognizes Isabella's essential goodness at the same time as he recognizes her 'superstitious' confusion between form and substance:

> The hand that hath made you fair hath made you good. The goodness
> that is cheap in beauty makes beauty brief in goodness; but grace,
> being the soul of your complexion, shall keep the body of it ever
> fair. . .
>
> 　　　　　　　　　　　　　　　　(III, i, 179–83)

Here the force of 'shall' (must) makes the Duke's utterance one of admonition rather than statement, for he is reminding her that what gives the body beauty is the grace of God, that makes it an expression of spiritual truth. It is not anything we do, but what God gives us, that makes us virtuous. It was a Protestant complaint that there were Pelagian tendencies in Rome's teaching. Isabella's journey from 'superstitious ignorance' to spiritual understanding, is, suitably, not to be expressed so much in doctrine as in the actual processes of living. In the course of the play she moves away from vain 'forms' towards active witness. Having to participate in the deception of Angelo as an accessory to a deed similar to that for which Claudio has been condemned to die, is a step away from the rigidity of 'popish' forms towards an active participation in good works. It is therefore highly suitable that her act of charity towards Mariana should take a similar form to that of her brother's sinful act; Isabella is learning to tell form from substance. And because ultimately the 'arrogant vanity' of 'popish' forms is a kind of pride, Isabella must experience public humiliation before arriving at spiritual truth. Calvin had insisted in the *Institutes* that Christian wisdom must be founded on humility[55] and Isabella is duly humbled at the end of the play when the Duke pretends to disbelieve her accusations against Angelo and sends her to prison. By now, however, Isabella has learnt not to trust in outward forms and leaves it to God to reveal in His good time the truth of her accusation:

> And this is all?
> Then, O you blessed ministers above,
> Keep me in patience, and with ripen'd time
> Unfold the evil which is here wrapt up
> In countenance!
>
> (V, i, 117–21)

When she returns it is in the same spirit of patience that Juliet has evinced early in the play in accepting the punishment for her transgression. Isabella asks pardon of the Duke (V, i, 384) and accepts patiently the supposed death of her brother (V, i, 397). Finally she is able to join Mariana on her knees (the emblem of humility on the Jacobean stage) to plead for Angelo's life. Even now, however, Isabella's habitual preference for outer forms over inner truths shows her not yet totally wedded to the Duke's spirituality:

> For Angelo,
> His act did not o'ertake his bad intent,
> And must be buried but as an intent
> That perish'd by the way.
>
> (V, i, 448–51)

The Duke (understandably) rejects this appeal until Angelo has expressed true penitence (473) and Claudio can be revealed.

Measure for Measure has as often been interpreted as allegory as in terms of realistic comedy. It is not quite either (or both), and this, in spite of its superb strengths, is where its weakness lies. Shakespeare has chosen a mode

161

of realistic comedy then coming back into fashion, that allows him to present his theological theme in terms of real people in a particular dilemma, a mode congenial to Shakespeare because of his unique powers of affective characterization. But these very powers presented an old temptation we have met before and that here again Shakespeare does not entirely resist; a temptation to humanize his characters in ways that tend to distort his theme. This happens in two ways in *Measure for Measure*: first it encourages an emotional response in the audience that identifies us too closely with particular characters (in this case Claudio and Isabella most obviously, but also to a lesser extent Lucio) and so clouds their thematic function, and second it creates unwanted incongruities between those characters that can be treated realistically and those (notably the Duke) whose function is predominantly thematic and the mode of whose presentation is predominantly allegorical. It is interesting to compare Shakespeare's dramaturgical handling of these problems in this play with Middleton's in *Phoenix* and the slightly later comedies, where he chooses a similar mixed mode. Middleton's ironic distancing, in his earlier comedies at least, avoids arousing his audience's emotions. In *Phoenix* an amusing character like the Sea-Captain, presented with considerable realistic detail, as we saw, and possibly portrayed from life, functions as an ironic specimen in the catalogue of aberrant types. It is typical of Middleton's technique that he does not give his Sea-Captain a personal name; we are not to get too close to him as a personality. The pervading ironic tone prevents close emotional contact with the audience, even with such sympathetic characters as Fidelio and the long-suffering wife. Prince Phoenix himself fits well into this scheme of detached observation by being the detached observer, the directing lens through which the audience is made to focus its attention. Of course Middleton can avoid the temptations to which Shakespeare partly succumbs because his talent is so much narrower. Middleton's language mostly lacks that amazing Shakespearean resonance that can conjure up the deepest emotions in a few lines. Middleton's very limitations of language and characterization aid him in achieving consistency, while the wealth of Shakespeare's genius tempts him towards inconsistency of mode. It is not that mixed modes are necessarily unsatisfactory, for the morality tradition had encouraged such combinations, but even when Middleton introduces (rarely for him) a wholly allegorical figure, as in the introduction of the succuba to *A Mad World, My Masters*, the transition between realism and surrealism is easily effected because the distinction is kept clear and the imaginative response required precisely signalled. In *Measure for Measure*, on the contrary, the Duke's allegorical presence as 'judicious ruler' and 'power divine' runs over into human participant in the affective action. His role as father confessor to the distraught Claudio, for instance, at the beginning of Act III, conjures up strong feelings of sympathy for Duke Vincentio as the helper of the hero in distress. Claudio's emotional appeal to us as a young

162

man about to die on a technical point of law is so strong that it attracts towards it all those figures who participate in the drama, making the Duke as sympathetic to us for his good intentions as Angelo is found repellent for causing the dilemma. Yet the Duke's actions also create emotional distress; for the audience knows that he has the power to end the misery when he wishes and there is – at the affective level – a kind of cruel perversity in the Duke's refusal to do so. Allegorically, of course, the Duke's behaviour is perfectly justified, not only as the spiritual guide, who must chastise and cause to suffer in order to be kind, but as the idealized image of King James judiciously weighing mercy with justice. The Duke's character uncomfortably and, at bottom, unsuccessfully, straddles two dramaturgical modes without achieving the necessary synthesis of symbol and symbolized. It has thus been possible for criticism to run the whole gamut of response to the Duke from seeing him as Christ figure (Wilson Knight)[56] to condemning him outright in Lucio's terms as a 'fantastical duke of dark corners'.[57]

The Duke has not been alone in inspiring opposing responses in different critics; indeed all the major characters seem to have generated opposing views, not in isolated cases but repeatedly. Isabella is particularly subject to these contrasting interpretations that also, inevitably, reflect differences in estimating her brother. To Una Ellis-Fermor, for instance, Isabella is a 'divided mind. . .unaware of its own division', an unpleasant combination of hypocrisy and sexual frigidity in an unpleasant play;[58] at the other extreme some nineteenth-century responses (like that of Mrs Anna Jameson) see her as an exemplar of 'moral grandeur, a saintly grace, something of vestal dignity and purity'.[59] These differences are partly to be explained by the value the critic places on virginal purity, but the controversy stems more from Shakespeare's mode of presentation than from what is presented. If it were a question (as E. M. Pope argues)[60] of adjusting ourselves to the high price of virginity in Jacobean England, we could make the necessary allowance, as we do for many other examples on the Jacobean stage where chastity is being given rather more value than most twentieth-century readers are inclined to give it. The problem here is to adjust this observation to the affective impact of the drama itself. Isabella's palpable distress at both her brother's plight and the preservation of her solemn vows, as she understands them, is too real and too strong to allow the kind of theoretical detachment needed to fulfil whatever estimate is assigned to her (whether as the equivalent of Angelo in frigidity and hypocrisy or as 'a thing enskied and sainted'). Shakespeare's tendency to fill out his allegorical forms ends by arousing vivid emotions but obscuring thematic issues. Take, for example, that extraordinary passage in the second interview between Isabella and Angelo, where he is struggling to make clear to her what he is demanding to save her brother's life, by putting the sacrifice of her virginity to her as a hypothetical question. Her response is to reject

such a suggestion out of hand, but in curious terms that seem to demand
levels of interpretation that undercut the literal meaning:

> were I under the terms of death,
> Th'impression of keen whips I'd wear as rubies,
> And strip myself to death as to a bed
> That longing have been sick for, ere I'd yield
> My body up to shame.
>
> (II, iv, 100–4)

Not surprisingly commentators have found these lines charged with sexual
meaning (the Arden editor quotes Kenneth Muir and comments on the
imagery, 'its occurrence here is psychologically revealing'). Certainly, if
these were the words of a real person one would suspect a strong libido
desperately seeking its freedom. Isabella's thematic role in the play is not in
itself incompatible with this impression of strong latent sexuality, for her
spiritual progress will require her to recognize her sexuality as God-given
and to be used (like Helena's in *All's Well*) for God's purposes. Yet the
imagery itself, which links sexuality with cruelty and death, is disturbingly
emphatic, suggesting sexual malaise (which is surely not appropriate to any
plausible interpretation of the 'good' Isabella) rather than theological
miscalculation. In these lines the audience has every right to link Isabella's
sexual frustration with the uncontrollable pressure that causes Angelo to
say: 'And now I give my sensual race the rein' (II, iv, 159). To link Isabella
and Angelo in this way, however, is to distort the theme of the play quite
seriously, for it confuses the distinction between Angelo's wilful depravity
and Isabella's quite different state of mistaken, but honest, piety.
Shakespeare has succumbed to his old temptation of enriching the real
psychology of his character at the cost of thematic confusion. It is not all
that surprising, then, that some critics see Isabella as Angelo's *alter ego*,
while others see her as his antithesis.

The differences over Claudio are not as acute as this, because there is no
essential discrepancy between his personality and his thematic role. There is
not much doubt that Shakespeare wants us to regard him as sinful – he
himself admits his error and no one denies it. That his sentence is unduly
harsh is not only the usual critical reaction, but also the Duke's, and
therefore the play's. Disagreement chiefly arises over his 'unmanliness' in
pressing, in the face of death, for his sister's sacrifice of her virginity. Our
response to this will naturally depend on our own ideological response to
the heroic, but thematically the play makes it clear that such a fervent
attachment to life is un-Christian, and to accept this point of view tends to
heighten the tragic dilemma of a young man whose healthy appetites
conflict with the moral laws of his society.

If there is any conflict of interpretation here it stems from the general
presentation of human exuberance in the play rather than from Claudio's

own particular case. Law and order must triumph in a play addressing the kingly fount of law and order, but Shakespeare's natural sympathy for humanity as it is rather than as it ought to be leads to some feelings of uncertainty. The rogues, pimps and whores that people the play's underworld are not so easily to be put down as the laws of Vienna require (which may, of course be a point that Shakespeare is consciously or unconsciously making). Clearly Viennese society suffers from sexual malaise, but it also exhibits a perky resilience that arouses almost as much admiration as condemnation. This is most obviously the case in Shakespeare's portrait of Lucio, who, as slanderer of the Duke, must eventually be repudiated (James is particularly severe on the traducer of princes in *Basilikon Doron*). Yet his kindly sympathy for Isabella and his friend Claudio, and even his own sexual exuberance, make it difficult to accept the thematic judgement entirely. The Middletonian solution of having Lucio marry the prostitute he has used and who has borne his child (just though it is in all equity) is less easy to accept in practice without the habitual Middletonian ironic detachment. Lucio, too, is a somewhat contradictory character, especially if we are to believe Mistress Overdone's accusation that he combines sexual irresponsibility with acting as police informer (III, ii, 192–7); but the overall impression is surely one of irrepressible liveliness, of Shakespeare enjoying his cakes, ale and ginger. This general uncertainty about where our sympathies are meant to centre is further compounded by the attitude of the Provost, whose humanity makes the tortuous clemency of the Duke look like cruelty. It is the Provost who describes Claudio as 'a young man/More fit to do another such offence,/Than die for this' (II, iii, 13–15) – a sentiment that seems closer to Lucio's attitudes than to the Duke's. One suspects some conflict between Shakespeare's head and Shakespeare's heart running through the play. It is noticeable that the most Middletonian of all Shakespeare's characters in *Measure for Measure* runs the least risk of engaging our sympathy. The splendid grotsque of Barnadine, who is too busy recovering from a hangover to be willing to agree to his own execution, catches that sardonic spirit that is at the heart of Middleton's comic vision.

Shakespeare lacked the narrow Calvinistic vision of either Middleton or his Sovereign, and in attempting to revive the old comedy of satiric realism to meet the new fashions, he found himself diverted from the confined thematic paths he chose in this play, by his customary humanity. The result in *Measure for Measure* is a splendid but flawed play, where the complex analysis of sin and judgement does not fully integrate with the picture of humanity it presents. It is not accidental that it is in the attitude to sexuality in particular that this discrepancy is most obvious. Both Claudio's and Lucio's sins are essentially that they are more warm-blooded than their author's monarch and his surrogate in the play, the Duke Vincentio. Shakespeare finds it impossible to repress his preference for human warmth over kingly righteousness.

6

ANGER'S PRIVILEGE: *TIMON OF ATHENS* AND *KING LEAR*

TIMON OF ATHENS

Nothing can prepare us adequately for *King Lear*. It stands out from its predecessors so massively, its dramatic power is so intense, that no circumstances can fully explain how the 40-year-old playwright came to conceive it and carry it through to its almost flawless execution. Neither *Measure for Measure* nor *Othello* prepare us for it, though dramaturgically *Lear* continues the use of techniques first attempted in *Othello*, nor does the radically different *Macbeth* of the following year throw much light on it. How, then, did Shakespeare come to choose the old romantic play, the *True Chronicle History of King Leir*, for rewriting, sometime late in 1604 (perhaps) or early 1605? And what sparked off that colossal imaginative restructuring that must have overwhelmed its Globe and royal audience (in which order?) during 1605, with Richard Burbage memorably playing 'kind Lear', as we know from commemoratory verses written to mark Burbage's funeral in 1618?[1] It is right to start with a mystery, for the play remains, however clear its impact, ultimately inexplicable, its independence an indication that Shakespeare is now conscious that he has once again outdistanced his rivals.

This does not mean, however, that we cannot learn a good deal about the play and define its impact more accurately by seeing it in its contemporary context. The play has been much misunderstood, in spite of the general agreement on its power; much controversy has arisen over its interpretation and this partly because it has not been read in the context of its creation in so far as we can glimpse at it. The first solid evidence we have of the play's performance is the reference in the Stationers' Register dated 26 November 1607 to a performance of 'Mr William Shakespeare his historye of Kynge Lear as yt was played before the kings maiestie at Whitehall uppon St Stephans night at Christmas Last by his maiesties servants playing usually at the Globe on the Banksyde'. This entry is confirmed by the title-page of the first quarto (1608), which advertises it 'As it was played before the Kings Majestie at Whitehall upon S. Stephans night in Christmas

166

Hollidayes. By his Maiesties servants playing usually at the Globe on the Bancke-side.' It is unlikely that this performance before the King in December 1606 was the first performance, because the scholarly consensus (though there are dissentients) places the writing of the play in the previous year.[2] The fact that the play turns romantic material into tragedy perhaps suggests it was written specifically for the Globe audience. None the less *Lear*, like *Measure for Measure* before it and *Macbeth* after, is strongly influenced by James's views and personality, and the fact that it was first performed at the Globe (if it was) would certainly not preclude its having been written with an eye to James's approval. Apart from more detailed matters of royal concern, the play deals more centrally with kingship and more especially kingliness – the qualities of a king – and kingliness, moreover, with a peculiarly Stuart emphasis, than any of the other major tragedies, singling out Lear's royal title in its own.

Although *Measure for Measure* shares its interest in kingship and kingliness with *Lear* and (as I suggested in the previous chapter) the tragedy complements the theme of the Christian basis of good government in the earlier play by predicating a world without Christian comfort, nevertheless an immense artistic gulf separates the two works, which it is not easy to bridge. This is not just a question of dramatic power, nor to be explained as simply a change from comedy to tragedy; it is rather that nothing in *Measure for Measure* (or *Othello* come to that) prepares us for the scale of the dramatic experience provided by *King Lear*, nor the abrupt change of mode from 'realistic' city comedy to legendary and symbolic history. There is little in the contemporary drama of the kind we saw in earlier examples of Shakespeare's sudden changes of direction (*Troilus* and *All's Well* for example), to explain this new departure. Indeed *Lear* remains somewhat isolated as a revival of the genre of legendary history at the height of the fashion for city comedy. Again it would be easier to understand the situation out of which *Lear* arose if we could have a more precise knowledge of stage events at this time. If, for instance, Beaumont and Fletcher's *Cupid's Revenge* at Blackfriars, which is also legendary history and like *Lear* uses Sidney's *Arcadia* as a source, predates *Lear* (as it might) we may have another example of Shakespeare responding to a new trend that had begun to influence the playhouses, a trend which brought Beaumont and his partner to the forefront of theatrical attention and which Shakespeare was to follow in *Cymbeline*, *Pericles* and *Winter's Tale*.

It would be easier to understand how *Lear* came to be written if we could fit *Timon of Athens* into the gap between *Measure for Measure* and *Lear*, for in many ways *Timon* looks like a false start for *Lear* and it has long been acknowledged that the two plays have much in common. *Timon*, however, is often placed after, rather than before *Lear*. As *Timon* was (it seems) never finished and therefore never acted in Shakespeare's lifetime, there is little to go on in dating it except its affinities with other plays of Shakespeare.

Coleridge describes *Timon* as 'an after vibration' of the greater work[3] and the Arden editor specifically rejects the idea of *Timon* being a first stab at the Lear theme[4]. The two main arguments for placing *Lear* first are that the language of *Timon* is closer to later plays and that a principal source, North's *Plutarch*, is used for the plays after *Lear*: *Antony and Cleopatra* and *Coriolanus*. Neither are strong arguments. The text of *Timon* is generally agreed to be in an uncompleted state, the language often unrevised, so that judgements about its intended final form must be hazardous. Plutarch was probably not a major direct source for *Timon*, but in any case Shakespeare had used North's *Plutarch* for *Julius Caesar* and it is characteristic of him to turn back after a period to earlier source material, as we have seen in previous chapters. Shakespeare's reading was nothing if not economical; it had to be, given his multifarious activities. It seems to me much more likely that Shakespeare abandoned the completion of *Timon* at the last moment with the realization that he could achieve a much more satisfactory working of its main theme in a new play, than that having achieved his greatest play he would want to go over similar ground again, only to find he'd made a mess of it. All our knowledge of Shakespeare suggests a bold imagination attempting radically new directions (usually set off by others), not repeating earlier formulae, especially at this period.

There is a compelling reason for linking *Timon of Athens* and *Lear* in their use of a common source. This is in Shakespeare's very improbable, but now I think indisputable, use of a comedy on Timon that was not published for the first time until 1842, when it was printed for the Shakespeare Society. Muriel Bradbrook has established beyond doubt that the text of MS 52 in the Dyce collection of the Victoria and Albert Museum was the basis for an Inns of Court performance.[5] She dated the play after Shakespeare's *Timon*, however, accounting for the resemblance between the two by arguing that the Inns of Court play borrowed from Shakespeare. This seems highly unlikely seeing that *Timon of Athens* was not published until 1623. The MS play makes allusions to several of Jonson's 'comicall satyres' (the latest being *Poetaster*) and J. C. Bulman has argued convincingly that this and other evidence points overwhelmingly to a date in 1601 or 1602 for its production, when Jonson's topical plays would be fresh in the minds of London playgoers.[6] In another article Bulman has also established beyond reasonable doubt that Shakespeare made extensive use of the earlier play in writing *Timon of Athens*.[7] This case had been argued earlier by (among others) R. H. Goldsmith. In an article in *Shakespeare Quarterly* in 1958, 'Did Shakespeare use the old Timon comedy?'[8] Goldsmith presents a number of parallel passages not only between the comic *Timon* and *Timon of Athens* but also with *Lear*, and argues that the character of Laches in the comedy not only resembles the good Steward of Shakespeare's play but also Kent in *Lear*. A further point that Goldsmith does not make, but which strengthens his case, is that the derivation of Kent from the servant Laches helps to explain why the aristocratic Kent is presented so convincingly throughout *Lear* in the role of a servant.

Both Bulman and Goldsmith illustrate their arguments fully and there is no need to do more than summarize them here. Goldsmith's examples show how extraordinarily close *Lear* and *Timon* are in conception and how ideas are transferred from the *Timon* comedy to both plays.[9] Timon's appeal to the gods to witness his undeserved suffering, for instance, found in the comedy (IV, iii) is echoed in *Lear* (III, ii, 49ff), while all three plays have passages in which the protagonist curses mankind and the ingratitude of men (MS *Timon* V, ii, 55ff and IV, i, 41ff; *Timon of Athens* IV, i, 21ff; *Lear* III, ii, 1ff). There are times when the sounds of *Lear* seem to be reverberating in the earlier play, as for instance, in the curse that Timon delivers on all mankind at the end of Act V, scene ii in the comedy:

> All plagues fall on this generacion
> And never cease, heare me, o heare me Iove. . .
> Lett *Atlas* burthen from his shoulders slide
> And the whole ffabrick of the heavens fall downe
> While Timon lyves, yea now while Timon prayes
> Returne Earth into thy former Chaos. . .
> Such a Revenge, best fitts such wickednesse.
> (V, ii, 2240–1, 2243–6, 2250)[10]

It is not that there are any very precise verbal echoes of this in *Lear* – Shakespeare's highly verbal imagination nearly always transmutes the language of his sources – but rather that the lines have a convincing dynamic that opens up the possibilities that Shakespeare came to realize, first hesitantly in his own *Timon* and then in the *Lear* of:

> And thou all shaking thunder, smite flat
> The thicke Rotunditie of the world, cracke natures
> Mold, all Germains spill at once that make
> Ingrateful man.
> (III, ii, 6–9)[11]

or in the last great outburst of angry grief:

> Had I your tongues and eyes, I would use them so,
> That heavens vault should cracke.
> (V, iii, 258–9)

or again in the great curse on Goneril:

> harke Nature, heare, deere Goddesse, suspend thy purpose, if thou did'st intend to make this creature fruitful. . .
> (I, iv, 296–8)

The power and energy of Shakespeare's lines are inimitable and anything put beside them must pale into comparative insignificance. Yet the lines of the *Timon* comedy are not those of any ordinary amateur, they have a vigour that might well have prompted Shakespeare to explore again the rhetoric of anger.

The theme of ingratitude is central to all three plays, whereas in other versions of the Timon legend the emphasis is more single-mindedly on Timon's misanthropy, though Lucian mentions ingratitude as its cause. Accordingly only the *Timon* comedy among Shakespeare's sources (as Bulman notes)[12] devotes as much attention to Timon before his fall from prosperity as after it. Both plays show Timon's extreme generosity and so highlight the ingratitude of the friends he has helped. Both *Timon* plays and *Lear* adapt the material to the *de casibus* pattern, so that, again as Bulman points out, the structure of both Shakespearean plays is close to that of the MS *Timon*. One further possible influence of the comic *Timon* on *Lear* is in Shakespeare's decision to make Lear's madness a central feature of his play (there is nothing equivalent in the direct sources). In the comedy Timon's anger boils over into madness, as for instance when he pelts his guests with stones painted as artichokes (IV, v) and he is several times, and with reason, referred to as mad (e.g. 1652–4, 1967) in an action that becomes increasingly farcical. One clear inference is that *Timon of Athens* must precede *King Lear*, for it is unlikely that Shakespeare, having first used the *Timon* comedy obliquely for the unrelated story of King Lear, would have afterwards used it literally to retell the Timon story. Everything points to a first attempt to convert the *Timon* comedy into a viable satiric tragedy (as with *Lear* he attempted the rewriting of the old comedy of *King Leir*) and – when that proved unsatisfactory – to rethink the material that had so obviously caught his imagination at a more subtle and complex level in *King Lear*.

The initial impulse to use the Timon story may have come from his reading of Painter's *Palace of Pleasure* from which he had taken the story of *All's Well* (novel 38). Painter tells Timon's story in novel 28, emphasizing his misanthropy and unreason. Timon was known in the Renaissance as the archetypal satirist of mankind[13] and it would be perfectly comprehensible if, after the failure of the earlier comical satire of *Troilus and Cressida*, Shakespeare decided to accept the challenge of re-attempting dramatic satire, but in non-comic terms, in the year that was to see Jonson's greatest stage triumph in the tragicomic satire of *Volpone*,[14] with Middleton in the ascendant and Marston's satire still filling Blackfriars. The MS *Timon*, with its emphasis on ingratitude, would also lead to a connection with the reading Shakespeare had done in preparing *Measure for Measure*, for, as we have seen, the central theme of the eighth decade of Geraldi's *Hecatommithi* was ingratitude, and this connection with Giraldi comes to have particular force in the rewriting of the theme in *King Lear*. *Timon of Athens* also has much in common with *Measure for Measure*, which often skirts on satire, in its tone of disillusionment (though *Timon* is more extreme) and in its depiction of a society at the point of disintegration. *Lear, on the other hand, brilliantly synthesizes a central concern with the hero as an individual with a much wider concern for social order.* One obstacle in the way of accepting that Shakespeare had made use of an unpublished student play has been the difficulty of explaining how he could have got hold of it. This is in a sense not a critical problem, for the only thing that matters to the interpreter of the two tragedies is not how he came by the MS play, but that he did in fact use it. Yet one line of transmission might be guessed at that *has* a bearing on the critical interpretation of the text, for it again helps to reinforce a date for *Timon of Athens* between *Measure for Measure* and *King Lear*. This stems from the Middleton connection.

That there is a direct Middleton connection with *Timon of Athens* was first mooted by William Wells in 1920[15] and Dugdale Sykes in 1924,[16] and subsequently given impressive, if not conclusive, support by, among others, David Lake in his book on the Middleton canon.[17] This seems to point to Middleton's hand in Act III largely (but also at I, ii; IV, ii, iii) and may imply either that Shakespeare took up a play Middleton had abandoned or (more likely) that the play started as a joint venture. As Shakespeare got older such a combined effort obviously had its attractions, as we can see in the later collaborations with Fletcher. This again would be consistent with the period between *Measure for Measure* (where, as we saw, there are remarkable similarities with Middleton's *Phoenix* that may suggest some sort of collusion)[18] and *Lear*, for during 1605 Middleton seems to have been working with the King's Men in their staging of his *Revenger's Tragedy*, conceivably with Shakespeare in the cast. Interestingly, F. G. Fleay in his *Shakespeare Manual* (1876) argued for the strong resemblance between the language of *Timon of Athens* and *Revenger's Tragedy*, but on the false assumption that the latter was by Cyril Tourneur.[19] The possibility that Middleton and Shakespeare were writing in association at this time might help solve the mystery surrounding *Timon of Athens*'s connection with the MS play of *Timon*. Middleton's connection with the law has never been formally established, though it is not at all unlikely that, like Marston, he would have proceeded from his Oxford College round about 1600 to one of the Inns of Court. His plays show a marked interest in law and a knowledge of legal terminology that may point to some formal training. The information contained in a legal document that in February 1601 he was 'here in London daylie accompaninge the players' implies that he was not yet considered to be more than a hanger-on. Be that as it may, Bulman has suggested, in his introduction to the Malone Society edition of the play, that Middleton may have had a hand in writing the MS *Timon*.[20] The evidence he gives is admittedly slender (the appearance of the rare Middleton spelling 'Ex'lent' twice in the MS)[21] and a cursory examination of the text for Middletonian 'markers' does not confirm the attribution. As the anonymous playwright indulges in considerable stylistic parody and what may best be described as stylistic horseplay, this may not in itself be conclusive. One curious and very unusual feature of the MS is an extreme volatility in the use of the apostrophe, producing such forms as *ti's*, *byt'h*, *Tha'ts*, *pla'cd*, *H'ees*, *sp'rite*, *accur'sd* and many others, in spite of attempts by the copyists to correct them here and there.[22] This kind of irregularity would tend to get corrected in the process of type setting, but remains a feature of Middleton's texts. The contributions to *Timon of Athens* attributed to Middleton, for instance, as published in the 1623 folio,[23] produce (in Act III) such forms as 'deny'de' (lines 993, 995, 1082) as well as the more orthodox 'denied', and such eccentric forms as *'mong'st* (1096) and *If't'twill* (1188). Such volatility is also suggested by Lake's analysis of Middleton's spelling.[24] Confirmation of this peculiarity is also obtained from Middleton's own MS version of the late play *Game at Chess*, which turns up a variety of misplaced apostrophes, some of which it shares with the MS *Timon*.[25] Clearly a more detailed examination of the MS *Timon* is called for before the probabilities can be properly assessed.

Whatever Middleton's role, if any, in the conception and execution of *Timon of Athens*, the play has undoubted Middletonian qualities. Its grim view of human nature, more relentlessly insisted upon here than in any other Shakespeare play (though not consistently illustrated) reflects Middletonian assumptions concerning the depravity of man as they appear in his plays around this time. Timon's early optimism is shown to be foolish and his later tirades against human nature are not (it seems) repudiated – Alcibiades' valedictory speech refers to 'noble Timon' (V, iv, 80). He clearly retains the respect of those in the play who command respect, notably the faithful steward, Flavius, and indeed most of his servants, to judge by their comments on his fall into misfortune:

First Servant:　　Such a house broke?
　So noble a master fall'n, all gone, and not
　One friend to take his fortune by the arm,
　And go along with him.
Second Servant:　　As we do turn our backs
　From our companion thrown into his grave,
　So his familiars to his buried fortunes
　Slink all away, leave their false vows with him,
　Like empty purses pick'd; and his poor self,
　A dedicated beggar to the air,
　With his disease of all-shunn'd poverty,
　Walks like contempt, alone. More of our fellows.
　[*Enter other Servants*]
Steward: All broken implements of a ruin'd house.

Third Servant: Yet do our hearts wear Timon's livery,
   That see I by our faces. . .

(IV, ii, 5–18)

If the Wells/Sykes view of Middleton's contribution to the play is correct, these are Shakespeare's lines[26] and certainly they show Shakespeare's customary optimism concerning the decency of ordinary folk. The scene ends, however, with lines ascribed to Middleton, in which the Steward turns from this expression of fellow-feeling to comment satirically on the hypocrisy and ingratitude of Timon's erstwhile friends, using their example to tar humanity in general with the same brush:

> Poor honest lord, brought low by his own heart,
> Undone by goodness; strange, unusual blood,
> When man's worst sin is he does too much good!
> Who then dares to be half so kind again?
> For bounty, that makes gods, do still mar men. . .

(IV, ii, 37–41)

This sentiment is strangely at odds with the first part of the scene where we have seen Timon's bounty to his servants rewarded by their sympathy and loyalty; but it would be thoroughly characteristic of Middleton both in its sweeping condemnation of mankind's depravity, and equally in the sardonic irony with which it is expressed.[27] The language itself reflects the change; changing from the rich complexity of Shakespearean English to the thinner, more cerebral, analytical medium that is a concomitant of Middleton's disdain of human nature. Middleton delights in showing the variety of ways in which men pervert the good, and makes splendid comic capital out of it. There is that piquant moment, for instance, in *Chaste Maid in Cheapside* when Mrs Allwit responds to Whorehound's conversion to virtue with the comment: 'He is lost for ever' (V, i, 54), or the earlier scene in the same play where the guests who gather for a solemn celebration of a christening, spend their time backbiting and grabbing as much food on offer as they can get their hands on. The Middletonian irony is heard again in a later *Timon* scene attributed to him, when the Steward makes a general comment on the depravity of the world:

> How rarely does it meet with this time's guise,
> When man was wish'd to love his enemies!

(IV, iii, 468–9)

Here the writer's sardonic Christianity has momentarily caused him to forget he is contributing to a play about pre-Christian Athens. Shakespeare is very careful to avoid such mistakes in the pagan Britain of *King Lear*. Such sententiousness, thoughts for the day, habitually break into Middleton's satiric comedies, as in Whorehound's sudden conversion,

173

already mentioned, or the equally sententious moment when Penitent Brothel acknowledges the folly of his ways in *A Mad World, My Masters*:

> Where were thy nobler meditations busied
> That they durst trust this body with itself,
> This natural drunkard that undoes us all
> And makes our shame apparent in our fall?
>
> (IV, i, 7–10)

Middleton likes to take the opportunity of the moment to hammer home his view on the universal depravity of mankind.

Shakespeare needed a harsher satiric voice than he habitually possessed to make a success of scourging satire. Thersites, for instance, succeeds as Ajax's fool, but not as satiric spokesman. In *Lear* the problem is brilliantly solved by giving the satiric role to the kindly Fool; but then *Lear* is tragedy, not satire. One way the Jacobean playwrights found round the problem of limitation of range was to combine complementary talents. There are clear examples of a division of labour along these lines in Middleton's collaborations. In the first part of *Honest Whore*, for instance, Dekker's humane (and rather sentimental) attitudes are balanced and complemented by Middleton's sardonic voice. In *Roaring Girl* the same two collaborators play off each other's strengths, though in a somewhat more complex manner, and something very similar is achieved in *Changeling* in giving the cheerful Rowley responsibility for a humane sub-plot that acts as a contrast and commentary on Middleton's merciless exposure of depravity in the story of Beatrice-Joanna.

In *Timon* the third act (attributed to Middleton) presents the downturn into disaster, in which we see Timon's friends and acquaintances one by one refusing him aid. In scene iv we see Timon's creditors gather to insist on payment as Timon's fortunes flounder. Middleton delights in scenes showing the hypocrisy and rapacity of men. In the almost contemporaneous *Trick to Catch the Old One*, for instance, he gives us two scenes between the hero, Witgood, and his creditors. In the first of these (III, i) we find them obsequiously pressing money on him in the belief that he is shortly to marry a rich widow, and in the second (IV, iii), having been disabused, they gather round like vultures to pick what they can of his bones: 'we must have either money or carcass' (IV, iii, 57). Another characteristic of Middleton's plays around this time is in the intimate link seen between human greed for money and sexual appetite,[28] illustrating Calvin's view 'that the whole man is in himself nothing else than concupiscence'.[29] The link is particularly forcefully made, too, in the comic *Timon* where Timon falls in love with the beautiful Callimela. Her father, Philargurus ('lover of silver'), decides she should accept Timon in preference to her other suitor, Gelasimus, simply because Timon is the richer. Callimela, very much the daughter of her father, is quite content to obey him, remarking:

> Who doth possesse most golde shall mee possesse,
> Let womans love bee never permanent.
>
> (III, ii, 1263–4)

The same intimate relationship between money and sex recurs in *Timon of Athens*, as Kenneth Muir remarks in his book on Shakespeare's tragedies.[30] When Shakespeare's Timon stumbles on a hoard of gold (IV, i) he launches into a powerful invective on its corrupting power:

> This yellow slave
> Will knit and break religions, bless th'accurs'd,
> Make the hoar leprosy ador'd, place thieves,
> And give them title, knee and approbation
> With senators on the bench. This it is
> That makes the wappen'd widow wed again:
> She whom the spital-house and ulcerous sores
> Would cast the gorge at, this embalms and spices
> To th'April day again.
>
> (IV, iii, 34–42)

This theme of the commercializing of sex is reasserted in the curious scene that follows immediately after when Alcibiades enters with 'a brace of harlots' (IV, iii, 81). Timon, now defining himself as misanthropy itself ('I am Misanthropos and hate mankind', IV, iii, 54), offers gold, first to Alcibiades to aid him in putting Athens to the sword and then to the harlots, so that they can attract more partners and spread their venereal disease more widely (IV, iii, 135). The scene is powerfully Middletonian as the whores in chorus clamour for more and more of the gold: 'Well, more gold. What then?/Believe't that we'll do anything for gold' (IV, iii, 152–3). The theme is introduced somewhat arbitrarily, indeed it is somewhat implausible that Alcibiades, presented otherwise as a stern military man, should have these two harpies in attendance while on military service (he enters 'with drum and fife, in warlike manner'). But clearly Shakespeare is overwhelmingly interested in the emblematic impact of the scene here in order to focus on his theme of the corrupting power of money. For the scene is (in spite of its Middletonian pedigree) almost certainly Shakespeare's in execution (the richness of imagery in the presentation of the 'wappen'd', i.e. 'fucked', widow made April again is beyond the range of Middleton, though the cant word 'wap' occurs in a Dekker passage of *Roaring Girl*).[31] An interesting feature of the scenes in which Timon discovers gold in both *Timon of Athens* and the comic *Timon* is the change made in the classical source. In Lucian's dialogue *Timon the Misanthrope* the gold has been deliberately planted in the ground on the order of Jove because Timon has been 'sufficiently punished'.[32] Shakespeare follows the MS play in excluding the gods from the action in both *Timon of Athens* and,

175

even more conspicuously, in *Lear*, in both plays the gods are obstinately deaf.

One problem with *Timon of Athens*, a problem difficult to overcome in the collaboration of two playwrights, is that the two voices have not been fully integrated – as we saw from Act IV, scene ii. Shakespeare, not surprisingly, given the force and range of his genius, does not seem to have made a successful collaborator. The discrepancies between his approach and Fletcher's in *Two Noble Kinsmen* border (unintentionally) on the ludicrous, as I have argued elsewhere.[33] But the problems of *Timon of Athens* go much further than that. Even in Shakespeare's unaided sections there is a fundamental uncertainty at the heart of the play. This centres on Timon himself, whose function falls somewhere between tragic hero and satiric scourge, and fails to convince as either. In the beginning he is presented as both noble and generous and as a gullible fool; and while this combination is not impossible either in real life or on the stage (both James I and Othello might be cited as examples) it is difficult to accept the Timon we actually see, whom in Acts 1 and 2 we watch entertaining on a lavish scale that he (and we) are warned cannot last. At the beginning of Act 2 one of Timon's creditors, a senator, decides he must recover the money he has lent while Timon still has some:

> And late, five thousand; to Varro and to Isidore
> He owes nine thousand, besides my former sum,
> Which makes it five and twenty. Still in motion
> Of raging waste? It cannot hold, it will not.
> If I want gold, steal but a beggar's dog
> And give it Timon – why, the dog coins gold;
> If I would sell my horse and buy twenty moe
> Better than he – why give my horse to Timon;
> Ask nothing, give it him, it foals me straight
> And able horses. No porter at his gate,
> But rather one that smiles and still invites
> All that pass by. It cannot hold; no reason
> Can sound his state in safety.

> (II, i, 1–13)

However much we try to make allowance for the Elizabethan approval of conspicuous expenditure in high places[34] and however compromised the observer is here by his desperate concern to get back his money, we find it difficult not to endorse the senator's description of Timon's behaviour as 'raging waste', essentially irrational and doomed to shipwreck ('no reason/Can sound his state'). The senator himself may be responding hysterically, but the hysteria belongs to Timon as well, producing those strange grotesque, images of dogs coining and horses foaling riches. We are already here in a world where the abnormal, the grotesque prevails, and Timon is part of it.

The same picture is given, if a little less frenetically, by the good steward, Flavius, who comments on his master's 'riot' of expenditure:

> No care, no stop; so senseless of expense,
> That he will neither know how to maintain it,
> Nor cease his flow of riot. Takes no accompt
> How things go from him, nor resumes no care
> Of what is to continue. Never mind
> Was to be so unwise, to be so kind.
>
> (II, ii, 1–6)

The paradox here of a kind foolishness or a foolish kindness might suggest the classic foolish wisdom of the Christian, were it not that the Steward's 'foolish' loyalty so much better fits such an ideal than does Timon's 'riot'. Lear's Fool repeats similar criticisms of his master ('thou had'st little wit in thy bald crowne, when thou gavest thy golden one away', *Lear*, I, iv, 177–8), but Lear's Fool is, unlike Flavius, a weaker, sillier thing than his master and rather tends to heighten our sense of the grandeur of Lear's gesture of renunciation than suggest the embodiment of wisdom. In *Lear* the old King is indeed the representative of a higher foolishness, like Timon's steward, and also Kent. In *Timon of Athens* on the contrary, Timon is the fool, Flavius the man of wider sympathies. It is Flavius' decency that proves an uncomfortable commentary on Timon's foolish extravagance, detracting from that dignity without which no hero can be fully tragic. Timon (as Flavius says) behaves more like a 'humour', a man unbalanced by some irrational obsession, a man we might rather laugh at than sympathise with:

> There is no crossing him in's humour,
> Else I should tell him well, i'faith, I should,
> When all's spent, he'd be cross'd then, and he could.
>
> (I, ii, 156–8)

If this scene (as Sykes thinks)[35] is by Middleton, it might be another example of faulty co-ordination, but the impression of Timon's foolishness is not different in kind (if perhaps in degree) in the later scenes.

A further barrier to our response to *Timon* as tragedy is the tendency throughout the play to treat the action emblematically, which has the inevitable effect of distancing emotional involvement by the audience. This tendency is noticeable from the opening scene where we meet a poet, painter and jeweller jockeying for Timon's patronage. All three are in the process of prostituting art, and so illustrate the central theme of man's subordination to Mammon. The poet himself takes up this theme in his poem, where he describes in an allegory of fortune the desertion of an erstwhile rich man by his shallow friends. The poem's argument is a vignette of the play's action and helps not only to suggest that the symbolic mode is to prevail, but also that the action is less important in itself than in its moral significance. The play tends to work consistently at this emblematic level, so that Timon is seen first as an example of fortune's fickleness who becomes a byword for misanthropy and only secondarily as a personality in his own right. There is, for example a lack of clarity in Timon's social position: early in the play we get the impression that he is a private citizen, perhaps a merchant prince; only later in the play are there hints of political and military status (IV, iii, 93–6; V, i, 158–62). Of all Shakespeare's tragic heroes Timon is the least open to psychological interpretation, which is perhaps why commentators have had, more than usually, to resort to Shakespeare's 'mythical sorrows' to provide a psychological explanation. The other characters of the play similarly are given a symbolic role at the expense of individual personalities. We are presented with a series of types: the good steward (designated as 'steward' throughout), the group of faithful retainers, the hypocritical friends, the unnamed prostitute artists, the cynical Apemantus, who represents the voice of destructive satire. This depersonalization makes it much harder for the audience to sympathize with Timon's plight or relate his world to its own. There is too, a certain insubstantiality in the other characters of the play, none of whom, with the exception of Alcibiades, stands out as an interesting person in his own right, so that Timon's encounters often appear as a kind of shadow boxing. Alcibiades' comparative solidity only helps emphasize the weightlessness of the rest. This tendency to think in types is thoroughly un-Shakespearean, but characteristic of Middleton (especially at this time) whose thought, for all the 'realism' of his techniques, remains essentially wedded to allegory. The nomenclature of *Timon of Athens* shows an incongruous mixture of Middleton type-casting and Shakespearean individualization. Something of this tendency to use character as emblem survives in *Lear*, but combined with a powerful and convincing real psychology that weds symbol and symbolized with total conviction.

Timon comes into his own as raging satirist after his fall in Act III, but Apemantus, who is Shakespeare's own creation (there is no equivalent in the comic *Timon*) represents the voice of satire from his first appearance in the play. Apemantus is a late experiment in the Jonsonian satirical commentator, showing the bitterness and satirical violence, but also the truthfulness, of figures like Macilente in Jonson's *Every Man Out of his Humour*. Macilente receives specific (if oblique) reference in the comic *Timon* (III, iv, 1403). A characteristic of the raging satirist is excess. Like Thersites, Apemantus lays about him, hurling abuse at whoever crosses his path and expressing contempt for all mankind. There is (as in Shakespeare's Troy) much to condemn in Athens, but Apemantus' viewpoint is essentially unbalanced and therefore unacceptable as a view of the world. The main purpose of creating these satirical commentators in Jonson's and

Marston's comedies is to create a tone of denigration that will further the playwright's satirical intention, a tone of disillusionment and distrust that permits the author to reveal aspects of human nature that normal decencies require should be kept concealed. The effect on the audience is inevitably and intentionally to alienate feeling; we enter a world where we can identify neither with the satiric commentator nor with his victim, but are stimulated to critical judgement of the human qualities exposed. The satiric commentator is therefore essentially a comic device, exploiting incongruity, asking us to measure aberration from an implied norm that we ourselves supply.

When Timon, after his fall, becomes as disillusioned with mankind as Apemantus, Shakespeare attempts to counter the alienating effect of extreme satire by setting up a contrast between the two figures. This is the principal purpose of the encounter between the two misanthropists in Act IV, scene iii, when Apemantus comes to congratulate Timon on his new-found disillusionment, only to be rejected as someone who attacks mankind out of the poverty of his spirit and experience:

> Thou art a slave, whom Fortune's tender arm
> With favour never clasp'd, but bred a dog.
>
> (IV, iii, 252–3)

Timon, on the other hand, sees himself as expressing views earned from hard-won experience. Apemantus turns this contrast round by claiming to represent a disinterested, impartial view in contrast to Timon's expressions of personal pique:

> If thou didst put this sour, cold habit on
> To castigate thy pride 'twere well; but thou
> Dost it enforcedly. Thou'dst courtier be again
> Wert thou not beggar. Willing misery
> Outlives incertain pomp, is crown'd before;
> The one is filling still, never complete,
> The other, at high wish. Best state, contentless,
> Hath a distracted and most wretched being,
> Worse than the worst, content.
>
> (IV, iii, 241–9)

Apemantus complains that his impoverished misanthropy is a kind of contentment, for it accepts the nature of things without illusion, whereas Timon's misanthropy is a kind of pride stemming from his own disappointment. The distinction would seem to be establishing a more human and therefore more sympathetic view of Timon's reaction to his misfortune, compared to the largely gratuitous satire of Apemantus. Whatever the contrast sought here, however, the effect is different, for dramatically the debate between the two misanthropists has the effect of associating them together. The violent language they use against each other makes them indistinguishable:

> *Timon*: . . .I had rather be a beggar's dog than Apemantus.
> *Apemantus*: Thou art the cap of all the fools alive.
> *Timon*: Would thou wert clean enough to spit upon!
> *Apemantus*: A plague on thee, thou art too bad to curse.
> *Timon*: All villains that do stand by thee are pure.
> *Apemantus*: There is no leprosy but what thou speak'st.
> *Timon*: If I name thee.
>   I'll beat thee, but I should infect my hands.
> *Apemantus*: I would my tongue could rot them off!
>
> (IV, iii, 358–67)

This is childish and absurd, a comedy of anger that precludes any sympathy for the speakers and twins them as similar grotesques; all tragic dignity has fled. Middleton makes splendid comic capital out of anger in an early scene of *A Trick to Catch the Old One* where the two misers Hoard and Lucre (note the names) show their fatuity in a not dissimilar billingsgate:

> *Hoard*: Doost scoffe at my just anger? oh that I had as much power as usury ha's over thee.
> *Lucre*: Then thou wouldst have as much power as the devill ha's over thee.
> *Hoard*: Toade!
> *Lucre*: Aspick.
> *Hoard*: Serpent.
> *Lucre*: Viper.
> *Spichcock*: Nay, Gentlemen, then we must divide you perforce.
>
> (I, iii, 60–9)[36]

Spichcock's intervention brings in normality to highlight the childishness and absurdity of these two old men, whom the play suitably repudiates and mocks.

When in *King Lear* Shakespeare brings his hero to the breaking-point of sanity, as the anger mounts, he transforms this *Timon* scene into one of the finest achievements of his imagination. In Act III, scene iv, Lear, having suffered humiliation after humiliation at the hands of all too credible daughters, reaches a peak of anger that is at the point of developing into a Timon-like misanthropy:

>   this tempest in my mind
> Doth from my senses take all feeling else
> Save what beates there – filiall ingratitude,
> Is it not as this mouth should teare this hand
> For lifting food to't, but I will punish sure,

No I will weepe no more, in such a night as this!
O Regan, Gonorill, your old kind father
Whose franke heart gave you all, O that way madness lies,
Let me shun that, no more of that.

(III, iv, 12–21)

Here Shakespeare converts the external conflict in _Timon_ between anger as a comment on a vicious world and anger as personal indulgence into a conflict within Lear's mind, a conflict whose intensity expresses itself as temporary insanity. This not only makes Lear an infinitely more sympathetic figure as he struggles with the all-too-human problem of distinguishing between reality and feeling, but also succeeds in presenting him more successfully as an emblem of human suffering and so highlights the enormity of the conduct of his daughters. Instead of having the hero, as in _Timon_, compete in extravagance with the grotesque figure of the raging satirist, Lear's anger plays itself out against a background of Kent's humane concern. When the grotesque voice of Edgar's Tom o'Bedlam is added it is as external counterpoint to Lear's internal disorder, not in competition with it. By reconstructing the scene in human rather than emblematic terms, Shakespeare achieves a total transformation of the dramatic effect, but one suspects that the achievement of _Lear_ would not have been possible without first experiencing the mistakes of _Timon_.

Shakespeare, at any rate, was apparently not satisfied with _Timon_ and it is not too difficult to see why: it works neither as satire nor tragedy and for related reasons. Timon is not a satisfactory tragic hero, his early extravagance is naïve and foolish, while his reaction to adversity shows a similar extravagance of response; it is difficult not to agree with Apemantus' comment: 'The middle of humanity thou never knewest, but the extremity of both ends' (IV, iii, 301–2).[37] Apemantus' comment reveals another central problem for the play: where is sanity to be found? Apemantus is as much an extremist as Timon, and while this fits both characters for the role of scourging satirist, the lack of alternative values presents satire without clear terms of reference. Neither the enigmatic figure of Alcibiades nor the stereotype figure of the good steward provide us with sufficient anchorage, so there is no way of telling how much we are expected to accept Timon's misanthropy as fair comment and how much is the result of Timon's incontinence. The dramatic insubstantiality of Timon's opponents make the job of assessment even more hazardous. Given these problems, as much inherent in the material as in Shakespeare's treatment of it, it is surprising that he persisted with it for so long and that the play got so near completion. James I's notorious extravagance and generosity would make the Timon story topical as a warning for princes. But Shakespeare's persistence suggests a strong imaginative compulsion to explore the theme of ingratitude and the rhetoric of anger. _Lear_ similarly witnesses to that compulsion, making use of material that is far more capable of complex presentation of the theme. Lear's anger is both more justly motivated and more subtly displayed in psychological terms. More important still, the anger that in Timon remains an expression of personal disillusionment, in Lear reaches out to become a powerful indictment of the inhumanity to man of both man and the gods.

KING LEAR

Geoffrey Bullough includes among the possible sources of *King Lear* a contemporary account of a Kentish gentleman, Bryan Annesley, whose three daughters were in dispute about his state of mind. The third daughter, whose name was Cordell, defended her father from attempts by the eldest to have their father declared insane and his estate distrained. On Annesley's death in July 1604, Cordell erected a monument to her father 'against the ingratefull nature of oblivious time'.[38] There was a tenuous Shakespeare connection in that Sir William Harvey (the Countess of Southampton's third husband) was an executor of Annesley's will and later married Cordell Annesley.[39] Such a contemporary event might well have reminded Shakespeare of the old play of *Leir*, which dates from fifteen or so years earlier but was published in 1605, possibly (as Bullough conjectures)[40] as an attempt to profit by the current scandal.

Certainly if he was searching for material to explore the theme of ingratitude in high places, especially filial ingratitude, his mind must have gone back to those stories in Giraldi's *Hecatommithi* that had inspired *Othello* and *Measure for Measure*, and in particular to the third story of the eighth decade almost immediately preceding the story of Epitia (story 5) which he had used for *Measure for Measure*. Discussion of sources usually concentrates on narrative similarities, but thematic parallels are at least as important and perhaps more so in explaining how a writer manipulates his narrative material. The central theme of the eighth decade of *Hecatommithi* is ingratitude and each of the ten stories illustrates ingratitude in some form. As the stories continue, certain sub-themes develop which link the stories into smaller groups: we have already met the sub-theme of the corrupt magistrate in discussing *Measure for Measure*. The opening story of the eighth decade tells of the ingratitude of a boy who betrays his master and this leads the next story-teller, Don Lucio, to comment that his story will in turn illustrate a worse case of ingratitude because it involves the ingratitude of son to father: 'how much more binding is the tie of blood and Nature, and the obligation of son to father is greater than any other that one can imagine'.[41] The theme of filial ingratitude is developed further when one of the ladies of the group, Fulvia, comments that Don Lucio's story shows how much greater a daughter's love (pietà) is than a son's. To this one of the men, Don Flaminio, replies that however much kinder women are than men by nature, there are worse examples of female ingratitude than the son's ingratitude of the previous tale.[42] This theme is then taken up by the teller of the next tale, Don Aulo, who introduces his narrative with the comment:

It is true that women are very loving towards their fathers and mothers, not just because of the greater need they have for love than men, but also because they are soft and most kind by nature. But if it happens that any one of them should turn their minds to evil ways, they so improve on the evil of men that they may truly be called infernal furies in human shape and the story I am preparing to tell you will perhaps make that clearer than should be needed.[43]

Don Aulo's story introduces us into a world of intrigue and cruelty in high places that powerfully suggests the collapse of all order and decency and is centred, moreover, on the inhuman treatment of a king 'almost eighty years old' (presso a gli ottanta anni).[44]

The king of Scythia, Apesio, now nearing 80, has two daughters, Omosia and Agatia. Apesio is anxious that these should marry the sons of the previous king, Olbio, on whose death the low-born general Apesio had been elected king. He accordingly arranges that the wild (cruda) daughter, Omosia, should marry the mild Eumonio, while the proud Anemero, his brother, is to be mated with the 'pleasantness' (piacevolezza) of Agatia, in the hope that such a union might calm him down. Agatia, we are told, is 'gentle and courteous, as women ought naturally to be'.[45] Apesio's intentions of settling the succession (compare Lear's 'that future strife/May be prevented now')[46] go suddenly awry, because Anemero has been smarting for forty years under the rule of the plebeian Apesio and proposes to his wife that the time has come to depose him. Agatia naturally refuses, more especially because the old King has been particularly generous to his son-in-law: 'having in particular given to him all his patrimony without keeping back the smallest part of it, as well as giving him considerable authority in the kingdom'.[47] The King's intention is that his sons-in-law should inherit the kingdom between them. The other daughter, Omosia, has similar thoughts to her brother-in-law, Anemero, plotting the death of her father so that she can become Queen. Seeing that her father is in robust health in spite of his age, she proposes to her mild husband that they should assassinate the old man. Eumonio refuses, reminding her of the ties of nature:

that she held in such contempt reasons of consanguinity (le ragioni del sangue) and the laws of nature, which constrain even wild beasts to love the one who has begotten them.[48]

His wife considers he is mean-spirited (di animo vile) and humbler than a

183

man should be (e humile più che ad huomo non si conviene), and turns to seek an alliance with Anemero:

> knowing you to be a man of spirit and it seeming to me that you desire royal greatness not less than I myself desire it, I have decided to reveal to you these my masculine thoughts.[49]

Anemero agrees that they should kill their respective spouses, marry and take over the kingdom, but (like Goneril) she warns that they need to act 'i'th'heat': 'because thinking about great things is nothing if it leads to nothing'.[50] Like Goneril (and Lady Macbeth)[51] Omosia is a woman of awesome immorality. The kindly spouses are duly dispatched and the old King is confronted in the Senate by Anemero, who, failing to get support, drags his father-in-law (now described as old and weak) from his throne and hurls him down a flight of steps.[52] Omosia, not to be outdone, proclaims her husband king, reproving him, however, for not having killed the old man outright. At the end of the tale there is some sort of justice, for Omosia dies in childbirth, while Anemero's reign lasts scarcely a year before he is ousted, his sons killed in front of him and he himself sent into exile, where he dies after a long and painful illness: 'whence you see manifestly that the evil deed for good ends finally leads the evil-doers and the wicked to a miserable end'.[53]

   I have presented Giraldi's tale in some detail because it seems to me that alone of Shakespeare's possible sources, this story gives the very atmosphere of aggressive evil that is so marked a feature of *King Lear*. As in *Lear* the central theme is the evil of filial ingratitude and this is specifically and powerfully associated with women. Nowhere else in Shakespeare are women presented as capable of generating so much violent and independent cruelty. Goneril not only instigates the evil, but stays in charge of the action, while her husband, Albany, like Giraldi's Eumonio, is presented as an essentially kindly man. Goneril's eventual 'marriage' to Edmund also resembles the transfer from good to bad husband in Giraldi's story. The destructive force of femininity becomes a central thematic concern as the world of the patriarchal Lear tumbles. This reveals itself tellingly in that strange, and apparently irrelevant nausea with feminine sexuality that Lear displays in his madness:

> down from the wast tha're centaures, though women all above, but to the girdle doe the gods inherit, beneath is all the fiends, ther's hell, ther's darknesse, ther's the sulphury pit, burning, scalding, stench, consumation, fie, fie, fie, pah, pah, Give mee an ounce of civet, good Apothocarie, to sweeten my imagination. . .
>
> (IV, vi, 124–31)

Another aspect of Giraldi's story that seems to be reflected in *King Lear* is the regal authority of the protagonist, and it is just this insistence on regality that distinguishes *Lear* from the private catastrophe of Timon. Leir, in the old play, is of course a king, but he is a king enfeebled by age and presented as in his dotage. When his Gonorill comes to express her love for him in accordance with his request, she does so in the most absurdly flattering terms that would fool no one but a fool:

> I prize my love to you at such a rate,
> I thinke my life inferiour to my love.
> Should you injoyne me for to tye a milstone
> About my neck, and leape into the Sea,
> At your commaund I willingly would doe it:
> Yea, for to doe you good, I would ascend
> The highest Turret in all Brittany,
> And from the top leape headlong to the ground. . .
>
> (Leir, I, iii, 240–7)[54]

Shakespeare transforms this into a passage of courtly decorum which the Jacobean audience would recognize immediately (*pace* Bradley)[55] as appropriately deferential to a great king and to a father:

> Sir, I do love you more then words can weild the matter,
> Dearer then eye-sight, space or libertie,
> Beyond what can be valued rich or rare,
> No lesse then life; with grace, health, beautie, honour,
> As much as child ere loved, or father found. . .
>
> (Lear, I, i, 56–60)[56]

This is fulsome, of course, but certainly not more so than the language habitually served up for royalty in Jacobean England. A translation of Jean Bede's *Right and Prerogative of Kings* made by Robert Sherwood in 1612 makes the point:

> God will have us love [the King] more than our own blood, it sufficeth the King that we render unto him the service that children own to their most dear parents seeing that the honour due unto them is comprehended in the name of father and mother.[57]

Shakespeare has changed Gonorill's speech in the old text both to emphasize the deference owed to the great King and to exonerate him from failing to realize he is being hypocritically flattered. Conversely Shakespeare changes the deferential words of Cordella's refusal to express her love in the terms Leir demands in the old play to the startling rudeness of Cordelia's economically truthful reply 'Nothing my Lord'. Cordelia's blatant defiance of propriety serves to excuse the King's explosive reaction, whereas Cordella's gentle words turn away wrath and make Leir's response again unreasonable and foolish, a sign of his dotage. Shakespeare echoes the opening line of Cordella's response in Goneril's 'I do love you more then

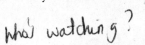

who's watching?

words can weild the matter':

> I cannot paynt my duty forth in words,
> I hope my deeds shall make report for me:
> But looke what love the child doth owe the father,
> The same to you I beare, my gracious Lord.
>
> (Leir, I, iii, 277–80)

Cordella's reply is as carefully decorous in manner as it is firm in its refusal to flatter.

The sense of Lear's greatness, his extraordinary vigour in his old age (like Apesio he is around 80, yet we see him returning from hunting during the first Act), the impression given that he has been a king for many years and is in absolute control of his kingdom, that he is (as Kent tells him, I, iv, 32) the image of authority, his deep sense of political responsibility in arranging for the succession: 'that future strife/May be prevented now' (I, i, 44–5),[58] the generous willingness to relinquish power to ensure a satisfactory succession, he shares with Giraldi's Apesio. King Apesio has been on his throne for forty years, he is a warrior king approaching eighty and anxious to settle the succession, having, too, what James I calls (in *Basilikon Doron*)[59] the 'curse' of female heirs. Shakespeare's care in emphasizing Lear's regal stature has been oddly misunderstood in the democratic twentieth century, but it is crucial in understanding the transformation of the *Timon* theme of ingratitude. For by making Lear a king and emphasizing his outstanding kingly qualities, Shakespeare transforms a case of private (and not entirely undeserved) misfortune in *Timon* to a study of the breakdown of order in society, and by freeing Lear from the silliness that equally afflicts Timon and the old Leir he transforms stories of foolish weakness into a drama of classical proportions in which dark and destructive forces overwhelm a man who (to use Aristotelian terms) is 'better than average'.

Perhaps it is not so surprising in an age when kings have been either outlawed or emasculated and the authority of fathers questioned, that Shakespeare's presentation of his great King has been so misunderstood. His very act of wisdom and generosity in giving up power while he is still able to manage an orderly succession has been described (by those duly taking their pensions at 65) as political irresponsibility. His failure to detect flattery in the voice of decorum and love in the voice of rudeness has been condemned by an age as suspicious of politeness as it is approving of the kind of personal integrity that discounts the feelings of others. Lear's imperiousness, his aggressive authority, today associated with tyranny and selfishness, would to his early audiences appear as certain signs of greatness in a king. We can be certain of this because we have James I's opinion on the matter and Lear is every inch a Jamesean king.

One of the most obvious defects of *Timon* is that, uniquely in

186

Shakespearean tragedy, the tragic protagonist lacks greatness, both in the sense that he has no clear status in his society and in the Aristotelian sense that he lacks 'magnanimity', greatness of soul. *Lear* sets out to remedy this lack, and what better way than by reflecting James's ideas of kingly greatness. It is the primary function of the opening scene to establish Lear's pre-eminence. This is done at the beginning of the scene by deliberate contrast. The disreputable Gloucester and his son Edmund, got 'tween unlawful sheets, are presented in a short dialogue with Kent (owing nothing to the *Leir* source material) whose purpose is to emphasize the illegitimate origins of Edmund and his father's sense of guilt and shame in begetting him: 'I have so often blusht to acknowledge him, that now I am braz'd to it' (I, i, 9–11). Gloucester's sin is truly being visited on the children as we learn that Edmund, away from court for nine years, is to be bustled away again to hide his father's shame. Bastardy, even in our own day, has carried a totally irrational stigma and was the subject of particular vituperation among the Elizabethans.[60] James explicitly warns his son of the evils consequent upon illegitimacy in a passage of *Basilikon Doron* that is relevant to the opening of *King Lear*:

> I trust I need not to insist here to disswade you from the filthy vice of adulterie: remember onely what solemne promise yee make to God at your Mariage: and since it is onely by the force of that promise that your children succeed to you, which otherwayes they could not doe; aequitie and reason would, ye should keepe your part thereof. God is ever a severe avenger of all periuries; and it is no oath made in iest, that giveth power to children to succeed to great kingdomes. Have the King my grand-fathers example before your eyes, who by his adulterie, bred the wracke of his lawfull daughter and heire; in begetting that bastard, who unnaturally rebelled, and procured the ruine of his owne Soverane and sister. . . . Keepe praecisely then your promise made at Mariage, as ye would wish to be partaker of the blessing therein.[61]

The morality of *King Lear* as a whole is not quite as straighforward as this, for while the consequences of Gloucester's adultery are duly spelt out in the action, Lear's licit fatherhood gets no reward. In *King Lear* we are in a pagan world without the comforts of Christian hope. Shakespeare has designed a neo-classical tragedy where is shown (in Fulke Greville's words) 'the disastrous miseries of man's life, where orders, laws, doctrine and authority are unable to protect innocency from the exhorbitant wickedness of power'.[62] The contrast between Gloucester and Lear in this, as in other ways, is to stress Lear's righteousness and the undeserved nature of his suffering.

Criticism has been taught by Bradley to see the morality of Gloucester's suffering as an exact parallel to Lear's.[63] In the quarto version of the play, however, Shakespeare spells out the contrast between them unequivocally in giving Edgar a short soliloquy at the end of Act III, scene vi whose dramatic purpose is to highlight Lear's undeserved suffering:

> How light and portable my paine seemes now,
> When that which makes me bend, makes the King bow.
> He childed as I fathered. . .

(III, vi, 115–17)

The contrast is clear: the innocent child (Edgar) has been made to suffer for the sins of the guilty father (Gloucester): in contrast, the innocent father (Lear) suffers for the sins of his children. The two fathers are being contrasted, not compared.

It is a paradox of Shakespeare's handling of his material that the Christian play of *Leir* is given a pagan reading, while the pagan material taken from Sidney's *Arcadia* for the sub-plot is made to reflect a pattern of Christian morality. This is all the more notable because Sidney takes pains to reflect a pagan world in his romance. So Edgar asserts a confidence in divine justice as he contemplates his dying brother:

> The Gods are just, and of our pleasant vices[64]
> Make instruments to scourge us. The darke and vitious
> Place where thee he gotte, cost him his eies.

(V, iii, 171–3)

The Arden editor finds echoes of both the *Book of Wisdom* and the old play of *Leir* in these lines. Edgar's complaisant morality here, however, is challenged by the ending of the main plot where 'innocency' suffers equally with the guilty. Albany, like Edgar, finds a coherent pattern in the events that bring about the deaths of Goneril and Regan: 'This Iustice of the heavens that makes us tremble,/Touches us not with pity' (V, iii, 230–1). For Albany there is no Aristotelean pattern here. But the full irony of Albany's optimism appears at the end of the play when, having pronounced a somewhat facile intention of seeing wrongs righted: 'all friends shall tast the wages of their vertue, and al foes the cup of their deservings' (V, iii, 302–4), his attention is distracted by the dying King lamenting over the murdered corpse of Cordelia. Albany's shocked response is to renounce his right to the throne, so great in this play is the gap between hope and fulfilment. Kent's enigmatic question when he sees Cordelia dead in Lear's arms is the appropriate one for the play as a whole: 'Is this the promis'd end?' (V, iii, 263). Aristotelean pity is duly reasserted.

Just as James stresses the terrible consequences of breaking the marriage vows, so in both *Basilikon Doron* and *The Trew Law of Free Monarchies* (1598) he spells out the obligations and sacred bonds of parents to children and children to parents. He links this, especially in the latter tract, to the obligations of subjects to their king. The extended metaphors of king as

188

father and father as king dominate *King Lear*. James also links this metaphor upwards to the king's filial relationship to God. This relationship is notably lacking in the world of *King Lear*, which shows, no doubt to the approval of King James, that secular government cannot hold, since (to quote the King), 'Monarchie is the trew paterne of Divinitie'.[65] Again *Basilikon Doron* can provide a commentary:

> Foster trew Humilitie, in bannishing pride, not onely towards God (considering yee differ not in stuffe, but in use, and that onely by his ordinance, from the basest of your people) but also towards your Parents. And if it fall out that my Wife shall out-live me, as ever ye thinke to purchase my blessing, honour your mother: set Beersheba in a throne on your right hand: offend her for nothing, much lesse wrong her: remember her
>
> *Quae longa decem tulerit fastidia menses*;
>
> and that your flesh and blood is made of hers: and beginne not, like the young lordes and lairdes, your first warres upon your Mother; but presse earnestly to deserve her blessing. Neither deceive your selfe with many that say, they care not for their Parents curse, so they deserve it not. O invert not the order of nature, by iudging your superiours, chiefly in your owne particular! But assure your selfe, the blessing or curse of the Parents, hath almost ever a Propheticke power ioyned with it: and if there were no more, honour your Parents, for the lengthning of your owne dayes, as God in his Law promiseth.[66]

How well James would have understood the import of Lear's great curse on Goneril at that performance in December 1606, how full of sympathy he must have felt at seeing the old king denied that deference to rank and paternity that was not just his due, but that God demands as a tribute to His orderliness. Equally acceptable would have been the illustration in the play of the vulnerability of kings. And notice that James specifically tells the young Prince Henry that after he has become king, his Mother must sit at his right hand as his 'superior'. How totally have modern commentators (like George Orwell and Freud) misunderstood the Jacobean mentality in suggesting that Lear should have known better than to expect deference once he had relinquished power. What impact those scenes must have had on the King as he watched first Goneril and then Regan defying God's ordinances in brutally denying their father the symbols of his rank and status as their father, inverting the order of nature:

Lear: When were you wont to be so full of songs sirra?
Foole: I have us'd it nuncle, ever since thou mad'st thy daughters thy mother, for when thou gavest them the rod, and put'st downe thine own breeches, then they for sudden ioy did weep, and I for sorrow

sung, that such a King should play bo-peepe, and goe the fooles among. . .

(I, iv, 185–93)

The Fool, wise after the event, blames Lear for giving his daughters the opportunity for their wickedness, but this is to turn morality on its head and joins the paradoxes of daughters as mothers, of weeping for joy and singing for sorrow. Lear's blindness was not a moral blindness – indeed his motives for forgoing power are clearly entirely moral and honourable – but an error of judgement caused by a lack of knowledge (exactly that quality of *hamartia* Aristotle describes as the proper basis for tragedy in the *Poetics*).

Dramaturgically *King Lear* continues that exploration of neo-classical concepts of tragedy begun in *Othello* and culminating in *Coriolanus*. As in *Othello*, Shakespeare is more concerned with the aesthetic than with the moral effect of the action. The sub-plot (strictly breaking the 'rule' which prescribed unity of action) is primarily concerned not to assert a Christian morality, but to act as foil and contrast to the main. *Lear*, even more than *Othello*, fulfils Fulke Greville's description of pagan tragedy (already quoted) where Greville goes on to explain the effect of showing innocent suffering: 'so out of that melancholy vision, [to] stir up horror or murmur against Divine Providence'.[67] This is the Christian moralist's view of ancient tragedy. Shakespeare's more aesthetic approach requires us to contemplate the 'horror' of a world before Christ's act of redemption. *Lear*, more than any other of Shakespeare's tragedies, achieves that catharsis of feeling through pity for the suffering of the powerless and fear for man's vulnerability. In doing so it manifests an attitude to character similar to that of *Othello*. There is a certain remoteness about Lear, as there is about Othello. This is partly a result of Lear's eminence, his status as king, and partly a result of the Lear rhetoric which, like Othello's, has a public, formal quality, and a quality of self-dramatization that befits a public figure, but also acts as a barrier to intimate acquaintance. We only begin to enter into Lear's mind when, in his madness, it becomes public. There are none of the self-revelatory soliloquies in *Lear* like those of *Hamlet* or Macbeth's soliloquy of self-doubt before the murder of Duncan. Instead, soliloquy is used (as it is with *Hamlet*'s rivals) to define Edmund's role as villain, or to inform the audience of Edgar's change of function. The audience are not encouraged in this play to adopt too close an identification with the hero; again the stress is on sympathy rather than empathy. As with *Othello*, however, sympathy requires a measure of identification and in *Lear* Shakespeare provides us with an extraordinarily convincing portrait of an old man, as much in his terrible vulnerability as in the obstinacy of ways entrenched over eighty years. Goethe's response is apt: 'Ein alter mann ist stets ein König Lear'.[68] Unlike *Othello*, however, *King Lear* also works equally powerfully on a mythic level. Commenting on the exceptional power of the play, Freud relates the pattern of the conflict between father and daughters to myths of the goddess of death.[69] Lear's struggle to remain himself as he is slowly torn to pieces by feminine forces against which he is doomed, re-enacts those ancient dionysiac rituals of the dismemberment of the king (or god) that Frazer recounts in *The Golden Bough*. If the play were merely about the redemption of King Lear (to use Bradley's famous phrase)[70] it could not have the universal power it so obviously has. To explain the power, Lear's suffering and death has to be understood as a sacrifice to unknown gods.

Lear, then, enters on to the stage in pointed contrast to Gloucester's shady privacy. The 1608 quarto stage direction marks a royal entry: 'Sound a sennet, Enter one bearing a Coronet, then Lear, then the Dukes of Albany, and Cornwell, next Goneril, Regan, Cordelia, with followers'; hierarchy is strictly preserved here, with the women taking second place as required by God (or the gods) and by Nature. Lear's first words are words of command and like the successful warrior king he is and has been over many years ('I have seene the day,/With my good biting Fauchon/I would have made them skippe', V, iii, 276–7), he immediately turns to the practical matter in hand, the arrangement of the succession: 'that future strife/May be prevented now'. James, in the audience, would have been uneasy at this point, for Lear's political settlement involves the division of the kingdom into three parts and James himself was emphatic and tireless in urging on his subjects the advantages of unity and in particular of union with Scotland. In *Basilikon Doron* he specifically warns his son to avoid the partitioning of his kingdom, quoting ancient British history on the danger:

make your eldest sonne *Isaac*, leaving him all your kingdomes; and provide the rest with private possessions: Otherwayes by deviding your kingdomes, yee shall leave the seed of division and discord among your posteritie; as befell to this Ile, by the division and assignement thereof, to the three sonnes of *Brutus*, *Locrine*, *Albanact*, and *Camber*.[71]

Lear does, however, have the special circumstance of the 'curse' of female succession to contend with.[72] From Shakespeare's point of view this difference between the monarch on stage and the monarch in the audience must have been useful, for the last thing he would want is to incur the danger of having the audience identify the one king with the other. Shakespeare ignores the connections with Scotland he would have found in his sources.[73] Lear is no more James than Duke Vincentio is James, but (like the Duke) he is presented as a monarch acceptable to James's notion of what a king should be. It is noticeable that Shakespeare does not allow the play to dwell on the division of the kingdoms; it is not central to the play's agenda and the later trouble is caused not by the division itself – on the contrary the inheriting Dukes align themselves against the invading army of France – but by the malign nature of the inheritors. Tragedy would hardly have been averted if Goneril had been made the sole heiress.

If the division in itself, then, is not important, except in allowing Shakespeare welcome opportunity to distance Lear from James, Lear's handling of the division is crucial. Like the division itself, the request to each of the daughters in turn for expressions of their love, is a *donné* of the source material. Shakespeare retains it not only because it is convenient to the plot, but because it is essential to the characterization. Again modern commentators have often blamed Lear for asking such a silly question of his daughters, but James would hardly have seen it like that. Spenser, telling the same story in the *Faerie Queene*, writes of Lear's question as 'sage':

> and with speeches sage
> Inquyrd, which of them most did love her parentage?
> (II, x, 27)

Milton, similarly, pauses in his *History of Britain* to comment that Lear's question was a 'trial [of love] that might have made him, had he known as wisely how to try, as he seem'd to know how much the trying behoov'd him'.[74] The question was eminently sensible, but not the reaction to the answers. James would almost certainly have approved the request, not only because it seems to echo Christ's request to his disciples when they complain of the woman anointing His feet with ointment: 'which of them, therefore, tell me, will love him most' (Luke 7: 42) – and Shakespeare's wording is much closer to the Geneva wording than to the old play of *Leir* – but because James himself was obsessed with the need for declarations of love, as appears from his surviving correspondence.[75] It is surely one of the more bizarre products of public school reticence that sees anything perverse in a father asking his daughters how much they love him. Shakespeare's purpose throughout this first scene is clearly to stress the old King's need of love – the word itself appears insistently throughout this scene – and it is not only a mark of Lear's affectionate nature that he should think love so important, but psychologically it is exactly what we would expect of an old man, until now all-powerful, giving himself into the power of his daughters. Who would not want reassurance at such a moment?

There is nothing exceptional in either Goneril's or Regan's answer to their father's request: their answers are exercises in courtly hyperbole demanded by the occasion. Cordelia's reply, on the other hand, is shocking, and is intended to shock (the folio text actually tries to make it even more shocking – but fails – in having Cordelia repeat her 'Nothing'). James would, of course, be as outraged as Lear at such a breach of decorum, but would he have approved of Lear's response? The guidance James gives us on the subject of both anger and flattery is a great help in focusing on this problem, though it doesn't solve it.

That flattery was an occupational hazard of the powerful was a commonplace of Renaissance political commentary.[76] Marston makes it a central theme of his play *The Fawn*, which appeared about 1604. In it Duke Hercules of Ferrara adopts disguise only to hear truths about himself that flattery had kept from him – disguise was, as we have seen, one of the devices favoured by James to overcome flattery's hazards. Hercules, hearing for the first time what people really think of him, meditates on the perils of flattery:

> By Him by Whom we are, I think a prince
> Whose tender sufferance never felt a gust
> Of bolder breathings, but still liv'd gently fann'd
> With the soft gales of his own flatterers' lips,
> Shall never know his own complexion. . .
> Thou grateful poison, sleek mischief, flattery,
> Thou dreamful slumber (that doth fall on kings
> As soft and soon as their first holy oil),
> Be thou forever damn'd. I now repent
> Severe indictions to some sharp styles;
> Freeness, so't grow not to licentiousness,
> Is grateful to just states.
>
> (I, ii, 306–10, 313–19)[77]

That James himself was much preoccupied with this problem we can see from a passage in *Basilikon Doron*:

> Choose then for all these Offices, men of knowen wisedome, honestie, and good conscience; well practised in the points of the craft, that yee ordaine them for, and free of all factions and partialities; but specially free of that filthie vice of Flatterie, the pest of all Princes, and wracke of Republicks: For since in the first part of this Treatise, I fore-warned you to be at warre with your owne inward flatterer φιλαυτία, how much more should ye be at war with outward flatterers, who are nothing so sib to you, as your selfe is; by the selling of such counterfeit wares, only preassing to ground their greatnesse upon your ruines.[78]

The difficulty, of course, is recognizing a flatterer when you see one, hence the need to move among your subjects incognito. Kings were in a notoriously difficult position, especially those who, like Lear, had been long in power, for it was in everybody's interest to tell them only what they wanted to hear. In spite of his acute awareness of the problem, James was himself highly susceptible to flattery.[79]

In accepting his two daughters' assurances of their love, therefore, Lear is in no position to judge their truthfulness. His isolated position as ruler would inevitably preclude an intimate relationship with his daughters. The decorum with which they express themselves would make his task all the more difficult. Lear's error of judgement, therefore, is based on ignorance born of his isolation as king and the fault of the tragic kind Aristotle describes as most suitable for the hero of tragedy,

> whose fall into misery is not due to vice and depravity, but rather to some error, a man who enjoys prosperity and a high reputation, like Oedipus. . .[80]

Lear commits an error of judgement that, like Oedipus, he was in no position to avoid. One of the earliest critical comments on the play to have survived, that of Lewis Theobald, rightly sums up the play in Aristotelian (if somewhat moralized) terms. The play calls both for pity for an over-generous father and fear of the evil consequences of human ingratitude:

> the first a caution against unwary bounty; the second against the base Returns and Ingratitude of children in an aged parent. The error of the first is to be painted in such colours as are adapted to Compassion; the baseness of the latter set out in such a light as is proper to Detestation.[81]

Theobald's emphasis on Lear's bountifulness reminds us again of Lear's Jamesean affinities (we earlier heard James confessing to being over-generous).

The problem of Lear's anger is more difficult to resolve, though it is very different from what most commentators have assumed. His first response to Cordelia's 'Nothing, my Lord' is one of shocked disbelief, as he asks her twice to reconsider her reply. Her reformulations only make matters worse as she enters into a somewhat cheeseparing view of love: 'I love your Maiestie according to my bond, nor more nor lesse.' It is not just that 'bond' here is ambiguous (Shylock insists on his bond in the judgement scene of *Merchant of Venice*), but that the language of 'nor more nor lesse' seems to reinforce the commercial connotations of the term. Antony's reply to Cleopatra's 'If it be love, indeed, tell me how much', puts Cordelia's reply into uncomfortable perspective: 'There's beggary in the love that can be reckon'd'.[82] This is not how most modern commentators have seen it, because modern values place individual integrity higher than filial duty. To James, however, in the audience, as to Lear on stage, Cordelia's language must have sounded perverse in both manner and matter and Lear's explosion of anger would have been felt to be appropriate enough. In a speech to Parliament on 21 March 1610 James declared: 'Kings are justly called Gods, for that they exercise a manner or resemblance of Divine power upon earth.'[83] This absolute authority he later in the same speech applies by analogy to fathers over their children, in a passage that gives us more than a hint of how he might have responded to this opening scene of *Lear*:

Now a Father may dispose of his Inheritance to his children, at his pleasure: yea, even disinherite the eldest upon iust occasions, and preferre the youngest, according to his liking; make them beggars, or rich at his pleasure; restraine, or banish out of his presence, as hee findes them give cause of offence, or restore them in favour againe with the penitent sinner: So may the King deale with his Subjects.[84]

What appears to modern audiences as arbitrary self-indulgence in Lear, would to James have been Lear's rightful exercise of his prerogative as king and father. It was, moreover, as James himself pointed out to his son, the duty of a king to know when and how to get angry:

And so, where ye finde a notable iniurie, spare not to give course to the torrents of your wrath. *The wrath of a King, is like to the roaring of a Lyon.* (Proverbs 20).[85]

This begs the question whether Cordelia's reply could be regarded legitimately as a 'notable injury' and King James's views on the virtue of anger in a king are hedged about with qualifications. In the *Trew Law of Free Monarchies* he again draws his favourite analogy between the king and subject on the one hand and father and child on the other, in insisting on the propriety of anger as a means of correction:

As the kindly father ought to foresee all inconvenients and dangers that may arise towards his children, and though with the hazard of his owne person presse to prevent the same; so ought the King towards his people. As the fathers wrath and correction upon any of his children that offendeth, ought to be by a fatherly chastisement seasoned with pitie, as long as there is any hope of amendment in them; so ought the King towards any of his Lieges that offend in that measure.[86]

Clearly Lear seeks the 'amendment' of Cordelia before his anger is given full reign: 'Goe to, goe to, mend your speech a little.' Even when this warning is followed by another provocative insistence on packaging her love between father and husband, Lear's patience still holds: 'But goes this with thy heart?' Cordelia's insistence on the letter of her own moral law finally and inevitably leads to Lear's royal and paternal response to such open defiance:

Lear: But goes this with thy heart?
Cordelia: I good my Lord.
Lear: So yong and so untender.
Cordelia: So yong my Lord and true.
Lear: Well let it be so, thy truth then be thy dower. . .

(I, i, 106–10)

There is nothing equivalent to this repeated attempt of the King to understand his daughter in the old play. In that, not only is Cordella careful to remain decorous and polite throughout, but she also makes clear that her stand is in opposition to her sisters' blatant and absurd flattery:

> I hope my deeds shall make report for me. . .
> My toung was never usde to flattery.
>
> (I, iii, 278, 302)

Cordelia and Lear engage in a dialogue of the deaf in which Lear's emphasis on rightful ceremony and social hierarchy fail to find a common language with Cordelia's insistence on personal integrity and truthfulness. Shakespeare is not asking us to apportion blame (since deafness is not blameworthy) but showing us how Lear's error of judgement stems from a clash of values.

James, writing about anger in *Basilikon Doron*, insists that care should be taken to weigh up the appropriateness of the response:

> But forget not to digest ever your passion, before ye determine upon anything, since *Ira furor brevis est*:[87] uttering onely your anger according to the Apostles rule, *Irascimini, sed ne peccetis*. . .[88]

It would be interesting to know whether in December 1606 James considered Lear had sufficiently digested his passion before his royal anger breaks out in the denunciation of Cordelia, and whether on this occasion anger truly (as Kent later puts it) 'has a priviledge' (II, ii, 76). Certainly the provocations are great; Cordelia's flouting of all decorum to king and father in full court and on such a formal occasion was no light misdemeanour. An assessment of Lear's conduct at this point requires the nice judgement that James liked to bring to bear on such matters. At least the King would have appreciated the King's difficulty – which is more than can be said of most modern commentators.

Far outweighing any consideration of the appropriateness or otherwise of Lear's judgement in this scene is the impression given of his authority. Even the fault (if fault it is) is the royal fault of peremptoriness. For Shakespeare is not primarily asking for moral judgement here, but asking us to experience the dramatic impact of the King's greatness in preparation for his fall and the collapse of his orderly world. Kent's intervention in attempting to persuade Lear to revoke his decision against Cordelia not only increases the dramatic intensity of the scene but reinforces the impression of Lear's greatness. For at first Kent couches his intervention in the most deferential terms, witnessing at the same time to the affection as well as the awe that the great King has inspired:

> *Kent*:   Royall Lear,
> Whom I have ever honor'd as my King,
> Loved as my Father, as my maister followed,

> As my great patron thought on in my prayers.
> *Lear*: The bow is bent and drawen make from the shaft.

(I, i, 141–5)

That Lear has inspired love as well as required love has been often ignored. The moment on the heath when he notices the fool shivering with cold has been regarded as the awakening of a new humanity in the old man, the beginning of the redemption of King Lear. The description of Lear in Burbage's funeral elegy as 'kind Lear', however, is the right one, as even Goneril concedes. 'Hee alwaies loved our sister most' (I, i, 293), whatever else it implies, confirms Lear as someone to whom love matters. Indeed his angry reaction to Cordelia surely witnesses to this. The play is not about the redemption of King Lear, but about his damnation; damned not because of any sin he has committed, but, like the good pagans of Dante's *Inferno*, condemned because he lives before Merlin (and Christ).

Structurally *King Lear* is not patterned on the old morality plays (as *Macbeth* is), there is no pattern of spiritual development in the play. The pattern derives from its *de casibus* theme and is closely similar to that of *Timon of Athens*, a threefold pattern in which the hero begins in prosperity, then suffers rejection through the ingratitude of men (in Lear's case, women) and finally collapses into despair and death in a hostile world where supernatural aid is not forthcoming. While this essential structure remains intact, however, the proportions are radically altered. The period of prosperity in *Lear* is drastically reduced to the opening scene (in *Timon* it is the first two acts). This allows a much greater concentration on the tragic part of the action and is therefore more appropriate for tragedy, permitting a much more detailed and convincing presentation of the process of disintegration. Almost two acts (I, ii-II, iv) are devoted to the depiction of Lear's fall, brought about by his daughters' unkindness, in place of the single, sketchy third act of *Timon*. The change has immense advantages dramatically. By concentrating on the two figures of Goneril and Regan in sequence, in place of the scarcely differentiated creditors who refuse to help Timon, Shakespeare humanizes the action and so makes it more affecting and more terrible. Moreover the tormentors are next of kin, *unkind* in the Elizabethan sense as well as in our own. The repetition of Lear's humiliation, first with Goneril then with Regan, like the parallels established in the sub-plot, establish a pattern of brutality that prevents our comforting ourselves with the thought that Goneril is a rare aberration. Such repetition occurs in *Timon*, but without the same affective impact. *Lear* eschews all comic suggestion, except for the Fool's all too impotent asides, in engaging us emotionally in the events. One of the terrifying aspects of the scenes with the two daughters is the plausibility of the case that Goneril and Regan present – we remember Granville-Barker's opinion that Goneril's request that Lear should 'disquantity' his retinue is

197

'reasonable'.[89] The process in which the King is successively humiliated by his daughters is all too terrifyingly human. The thought of the hundred unruly knights ruining polite carpets no doubt inspired the lady in the Stratford audience to remark that Lear must have been a very tiresome old man to have about the house.

James, as he watched his December entertainment, would have had a different perspective. In an age when large retinues were regarded, not just as permitted, but required of people of high rank (the Earl of Pembroke in 1598 boasted he could produce 210 serving men in defence of his Queen)[90] Lear's wish to retain his hundred knights is modest. By abdicating he has not, of course, ceased to be of exalted rank. Gervase Markham, in a book published in 1598, is insistent on the obligation of the gentry to keep as large a retinue as their rank permits, both for the employment it affords and because an orderly society depends on a proper assertion of rank. A true gentleman, says Markham, should be:

> garded gallantly with a sort of seemly servants, alwayes well appoynted as well as to shew his power, as to grace his person.[91]

Markham laments that the gentry nowadays neglect their duty and cut down on their retinues so that they can selfishly indulge themselves with the saving. G. B. Harrison notes the shock with which contemporaries received the news of the Earl of Essex's punishment, when the Queen ordered the dismissal of his retinue:

> Tomorrow the Earl's household, being 160, are dispersed, and every man to seek a new fortune; some few are retained to attend him where it be her Majesty's will to send him. This is the greatest downfall we have seen in our days, making us to see the vanity of the world.[92]

Goneril explains precisely why she is engaged in this process: she seeks a confrontation with her father; in doing so she destroys the very fabric of the relationships on which her own authority rests:

> And let his Knights have colder looks among you, what growes of it no matter, advise your fellows so. I would breed from hence occasions, and I shall, that I may speake, ile write straight to my sister to hould my very course, goe prepare for dinner.

> (I, iii, 22–6)

The attack on Lear's retinue, as she admits here, has been planned in advance of any trouble they might cause. At the end of the first scene we hear Goneril and Regan planning their Father's humiliation almost as soon as he has handed power over to them:

> pray lets hit together, if our Father cary authority with such dispositions as he beares, this last surrender of his, will but offend us.

> (I, i, 307–10)

Goneril has just been describing the 'dispositions' to which she refers as a rashness and lack of self-knowledge that has always characterized him and is now exacerbated by old age. If this view of Lear is correct, that he 'hath ever but slenderly knowne himselfe', he clearly would be a difficult man to deal with. The view that the two daughters give of their Father, however, is clearly in contradiction to Kent's attitude to his sovereign and indeed hardly credible in a man who has successfully wielded power for so long. It is one of the ironies of much modern *Lear* criticism that this partial account of Lear has been treated as if it were incontrovertible testimony. Kenneth Muir tells us baldly: 'Goneril's diagnosis is near the truth.'[93]

When we are in any position to test the evidence, the attitude of Goneril and Regan is found to be false. In ordering Oswald to disobey the King, Goneril makes as her principal excuse the unruliness of the behaviour of both Lear and his retinue:

> By day and night he wrongs me,
> Every houre he flashes into one grosse crime or other
> That sets us all at ods, ile not indure it,
> His Knights grow ryotous, and himselfe obrayds us,
> On every trifell when he returnes from hunting,
> I will not speake with him. . .
>
> (I, iii, 3–8)

'Grosse crime', even reading crime as 'offence',[94] sounds improbable and the actual appearance of the 'unruly' knights, far from corroborating Goneril's accusation, show them (as we would expect of the retinue of so imperious a King) to be particularly concerned with ceremony and order:

> My Lord, I know not what the matter is, but to my iudgement, your highnes is not entertained with that ceremonious affection as you were wont, ther's a great abatement of kindness[95] apeers as well in the generall dependants, as in the Duke himselfe also, and your daughter.
>
> (I, iv, 61–8)

The gentleman's words here not only bear evidence to that 'ceremonious affection' in which Lear has been habitually held, but in his own language and attitude he exhibits those qualities of courtly decorum that show a proper respect for rank and order. This is certainly not the language of a riotous knight, indeed his complaint centres on Goneril's flagrant impropriety. His respect for the King surely amply reinforces Kent's admiration for and deference to his master. Similarly when one of Lear's retinue reports to Kent the plight of the old King at the beginning of Act III the tone is one of humane and respectful sympathy, not of disorderly roughness. Lear's response to the servant's accusations of neglect is equally revealing:

I have perceived a most faint neglect of late, which I have rather blamed as mine owne ielous curiositie, then as a very pretence and purport of unkindnesse. . .

(I, iv, 72–6)

Far from showing arrogance or vanity, such extreme sensitivity and reticence as can make an old man consider whether his impressions have been due to his own vanity is surely remarkable here, and is on a level with his initial hesitations in responding to Cordelia's rudeness. The absurdity of the accusations aimed at Lear and his retinue is finally confirmed at the end of Act II, when Regan, as an excuse for locking her Father out of her castle, informs us: 'He is attended with a desperate traine' (II, iv, 308). When we next see him he is alone on the heath with the Fool. Any close attention to the text, therefore, suggests we are to dismiss Goneril's accusations that the knights indulge in 'epicurism and lust', turning the palace into a 'brothel' (I, iv, 267) as nonsense, and accept Lear's emphatic defence of them:

> Detested kite, thou liest.
> My train are men of choice and rarest parts,
> That all particulars of duty know,
> And in the most exact regard support
> The worships of their name.

(I, iv, 271–5)[96]

Once again it is worth noting the nature of Lear's defence, with its precise emphasis on the courtly virtues of duty, honour and decorum.

With such evidence from the text, how then has the impression gained such firm hold that the daughters' objections are 'reasonable', for few productions of *Lear* fail to provide their quota of riotous knights? The combination of Lear's imperiousness and his penchant for hunting, his peremptoriness as he commands 'Let me not stay a iot for dinner' (I, iv, 8) makes Goneril's view of him plausible to a modern audience. This behaviour, however, is simply a reflection of his royal nature and would remind a Jacobean audience yet again of his innate authority. It is the kind of imperious behaviour they expected (and got) from their own monarch. The hunting is stressed to show that the charge that her father is in his dotage (I, iii, 16–20) is as baseless as the other charges. Shakespeare needed to emphasize Lear's strength and robust health in order to make the fall tragic rather than merely pathetic, as it is in the old play of *Leir*. But the emphasis on hunting also has a special significance in relation to the play's royal audience, for James was inordinately fond of hunting. Indeed about this time he was coming in for considerable criticism for spending too much time on the hunting field and too little in the council chamber. Raymond Burns, in his recent edition of Day's *Isle of Gulls*, quotes from the Calendar of State papers for July 1603:

200

the new king. . .seems to have almost forgotten that he is a King except in his kingly pursuit of the stags, to which he is quite foolishly devoted, and leaves them [his council] with such absolute authority that beyond a doubt they are far more powerful than ever they were before. . .[97]

Again Burns quotes a letter of the Archbishop of York to Lord Cecil, 23 December 1604, in the same strain: 'I wish less wasting of the Treasure of the Realm, and more Moderation of the lawfull Exercise of Hunting, both that the poor Mens Corn may be less spoiled, and other his Majestie's Subjects more spared.' Similarly Sir Francis Osborne's *Traditional Memoirs* are quoted:

he dedicated. . .faire [weather] to his hounds. . .which was, through the whole series of his government, more acceptable, then any profit or conveniency might accrue to his people.[98]

These are hostile comments, but the reference in the first passage to the 'kingly pursuit' of hunting rightly acknowledges that this was regarded as the royal sport *par excellence*. Shakespeare is concerned with reinforcing the kingly image, and in a way peculiarly acceptable to James, not criticizing his hero, for Lear is not neglecting state business. In the drama of the period it is neglect of the hunt by rulers that often suggests unmanliness and unfitness to govern, as in the sudden cancellation of the hunt by Duke Alphonso in Chapman's *Gentleman Usher*.

The two great and terrible scenes in which first Goneril and then Regan attack the very basis of social order – that respect for forms and ceremonies which holds human wildness in check – expose man's feebleness and vulnerability in a demonstration that is all the more telling for being exemplified in such an imposing figure as Lear. His first response is, understandably, to call on divine aid (the goddess of Nature) to counter Goneril's impiety. When this fails to elicit a response and he is confronted by Regan in an identical situation, his doubts begin to grow that the universe may not guarantee the orderly world his reign has created:

You heavens give me that patience, patience I need,
You see me here (you Gods) a poore old man,[99]
As full of greefe as age, wretched in both,
If it be you that stirres these daughters hearts
Against their Father, foole me not to much,
To beare it lamely, touch me with noble anger. . .

(II, iv, 274–9)

Lear is still king enough to claim anger's privilege. The scene reaches its climax in the first sign of Lear's despair at the prospect of a disorderly universe, as the two sisters complete their auction of his status and dignity.

In the equivalent scenes of *Timon* (in Act III) our primary response is that Timon's extravagance is meeting its sardonic rewards; here, on the other hand, the beleaguered King is a truly tragic figure of undeserved calamity. On both the human and the symbolic level the Timon situation is powerfully transformed, for as well as the pathos of an old man treated by his children with cruelty, Lear himself sees his plight as a comment on the fragility of man's claim to rational sovereignty:

> O reason not the need, our basest beggars,
> Are in the poorest thing superfluous,
> Allow not nature more then nature needes,
> Man's life's as cheape as beasts. Thou art a lady;
> If onely to goe warme were gorgeous,
> Why nature needes not, what thou gorgeous wearest
> Which scarcely keepes thee warme. . .
>
> (II, iv, 267–73)[100]

This is an eloquent statement of that need for human ceremony and custom that modern anthropology and semiotics have been busy rediscovering. Without the complex signals of our interrelationships, human individuality has no meaning. In these lines the full power of the play's mythic force is revealed, for we see Lear as the defender of human meaningfulness in a world of disintegrating meaning. The patriarchal centre cannot hold. An abyss/abbesse of de(con)struction looms and weaves round him, the three sisters begin to reveal their identity as the harsh spinners, the Moirae. Not only Lear himself, but the whole of the society over which he has presided has been centred on a belief in an orderliness inherent in the world, which man can re-express in himself and in his society. The solidity is at the point of dissolution – the male certainties of fatherhood and kingship as a hierarchical model collapsing into a maelstrom of feeling uncontrolled and uncontrollable under the relentless force of his daughters' hostility. Behind the play (as Freud shrewdly hints)[101] lies the peculiarly male fear of undifferentiation, of loss of potency and, worse still, of being re-absorbed into the primal matter of mother earth. The father-daughter confrontation was perhaps suggested originally by Giraldi, whose Don Aulo, it is worth remembering, refers to evil women (and by implication his heroine) as 'infernal furies in human shape' (furie infernali in corpo humano). Male phallic rigidity in conflict with the fluidity and resilience of the feminine is the powerful psychological and mythic pattern underpinning the play. In *Lear* the long dialectical debate on the female/male dichotomy, which Shakespeare had conducted from *Hamlet* onwards, reaches its negative climax. The synthesis was to await *Antony and Cleopatra*.

Ostensibly Shakespeare leaves no doubt in the play about which side of the deconstruction debate he is on. The evil individualism of Goneril, Regan and Edmund and the benign individualism of Cordelia lead to the same sterile isolation, a world where dialogue is no longer possible, where men are islands. Of necessity this negative world collapses through its own incoherence. The deaths of Goneril and Regan and even of Cordelia are the logical outcome of this negativity. Lear's tragedy is that the forms and ceremonies of his civilized world are inadequate to reflect the divine will, for Lear inherits the just punishment of Adam's fall, not yet redeemed. Yet the power with which he endows the feminine and, even more, the brief glimpse we get of a world of love unstructured by authority in the scenes between Lear and Cordelia at the end, suggest an imaginative grasp of a different kind of order: what Holinshed describes (with different intention) as the 'gunarchie of Queen Cordeilla'. Again it is *Antony and Cleopatra* where this glimpse will become a vision.

The final vision of the play, developed over the last three acts, explores the full significance of a world without hope as, layer by layer, Lear is divested of his illusions. Patriarchy is unfrocked. In the last two acts of *Timon*, Timon's misfortunes convert him into the stereotype of the raging satirist as he sees the perversity of mankind in terms of other people. Lear's response is to look inward, to attempt to adjust to the vision of disorder his experience of suffering has presented:

> they flattered mee like a dogge, and tould me I had white haires in my beard, ere the black ones were there, to say I and no, to every thing I saide, I and no too, was no good divinitie, when the raine came to wet me once, and the winde to make mee chatter, when the thunder would not peace at my bidding, there I found them, there I smelt them out, goe to, they are not men of their words, they told mee I was every thing, tis a lye, I am not ague-proofe.
>
> (IV, vi, 97–107)[102]

The attempt to understand the horror of this revelation that the world does not conform to the patterns men try to impose on it, at first proves too much for him. His mind loses its hold on reality and his mad fantasies take just those forms of blind condemnation of mankind that Timon asks us to accept as a vision of reality. Lear's incoherent and apparently irrelevant attacks on human justice and human sexuality are the mind of the humanist adjusting to a Calvinistic vision of the general depravity of human nature:

> thou rascall beadle hold thy bloudy hand, why dost thou lash that whore, strip thine owne backe, thy bloud hotly lusts to use her in that kind for which thou whipst her, the usurer hangs the cozener, through tattered raggs, smal vices do appeare, robes and furd-gownes hides all. . .
>
> (IV, vi, 164–9)[103]

What in Timon is mere railing out of personal pique, here becomes a desperate and moving attempt to establish new bearings in a world undergoing sea-change. Lear attempts to take refuge in a stoical patience that exchanges power for sanity, accepting impotence as a condition of holding on to meaning, but this too is a vanity, for the very ties of love are subject to the laws of destruction.

For a brief moment, in meeting again with his younger daughter, love seems to triumph – as it did in *All's Well* and was again to do in the late plays. The demand for love which Cordelia failed to meet adequately in the first scene is now amply satisfied as she abandons the strict apportionment of feeling for an outpouring of affection that meets Lear's in generosity. It is ironic that modern commentators have frequently seen the fundamental change here as coming only from Lear, but it is equally Cordelia's puritanical rigidity that has given way in these late scenes, freeing her to accept her father's unbounded love. It is true that Lear himself sees Cordelia as 'a soul in bliss', while he is wracked in hell on a wheel of fire, but it is from his new sense of his own littleness in a hostile world that he derives this perception. The ending of the play destroys this vision of love triumphant. The Christian-like moment is shown to be illusory in a world before the birth of the God of love.

When Lear is fully restored to his sanity it is to meet yet again with defeat and he sees the possibility of happiness in an evil world only in terms of escape from it, 'like birds i'th'cage'. If it is to be happiness, then it will be a happiness in despite of the gods:

> have I caught thee?
> He that parts us shall bring a brand from heaven,
> And fire us hence like Foxes, wipe thine eyes,
> The good years[104] shall devoure em, flesh and fell,
> Ere they shall make us weepe, we'll see 'em starve first.
>
> (V, iii, 21–5)

It is uncertain whether this is prophecy or defiance, but in either case it assumes the hostility of gods towards men. It is Lear and Cordelia that the gods will or must persecute by driving them out of the sanctuary of their love for one another. There is indeed no refuge for Lear and shortly we see him confirming the malice of the gods with Cordelia dead in his arms. One of his last acts, an act of extraordinary and tragic resilience, is to kill the man that hanged her. In the end we are left with a world without hope, with the three principal survivors, Albany, Edgar and Kent seemingly attempting to shuffle off responsibility for the future. This negativity is emphasized in the quarto text by having the final lines spoken by Albany just after he has attempted to hand over power to Kent and Edgar, to be met by Kent's refusal and Edgar's silence. The pessimism of the play reflects the orthodox Christian view of the pagan world.

In *King Lear* Shakespeare transcends the drama of his time in creating a play of classical intensity that yet retains his characteristic subtlety of detailed psychological realism. It is both a drama of personality, of the kind we see in *Othello*, and a masterly presentation of myth: a myth of man's attempt and failure to build a coherent structure of meaning from a hostile universe. Yet however much it transcends the theatre out of which it arose, it also has inescapable links with that theatre. As an exercise in the *de casibus* theme, on the fall of princes, it repeats the pattern of earlier plays like *Richard II*, but now explored, like *Timon*, in a pagan world. Like *Measure for Measure* before it, it uses James's view on kingship and kingliness to explore the nature of authority in a fallen world, here divorced from divine sanction, and so doomed – as Duke Vincentio's was not – to failure. As an exercise, like *Timon*, in the anatomy of anger as a response to a wicked world, it absorbs the role of the satirist into the tragic vision of man's helpless vulnerability. It remains unique to its time and yet of its time. The great tragedies that were to follow show Shakespeare's power still at its height, yet none of them quite reproduces the overwhelming dramatic impact of *King Lear*.

* * *

We have now traced Shakespeare's response to a crisis brought about by the appearance of a new wave of mostly younger dramatists at the mid-point of his career. The brilliant experimentation of Marston, Jonson and Chapman for their sophisticated audiences in the 'private' theatres, the newly reopened Paul's Boys and Blackfriars, challenged Shakespeare's supremacy just at the point where he had achieved a mastery of a drama of personality, in which the audience were invited to identify emotionally with the central character or characters by entering vicariously into their magic or tragic worlds.[105] *Hamlet* proved to be Shakespeare's most daring and convincing exploration in this mode, before the onslaught of the new drama forced him to rethink his dramaturgy. We cannot, at this distance in time, be certain exactly what motivated the marked changes from *Troilus and Cressida* to *Timon of Athens* and *King Lear*, as he started on a series of dramatic experiments that took him into dramatic satire, both comic and non-comic, and into mythic comedy, but it cannot be a coincidence that his rivals were cultivating these fields in advance of him. A direct connection cannot be proved and must therefore remain, like most critical assumptions, conjectural; but that Shakespeare felt the impact of the new theatre we can be certain, for he tells us so in a passage in *Hamlet* describing the effect of the boy players' success on the adult companies. What concerned Shakespeare most, I believe, was not any financial loss, for the tiny audiences of the covered theatres were not likely to divert substantial sums of money from Shakespeare's company, but fear of lost prestige if the gentry defected. Shakespeare's response to this challenge led him into new satirical territory, for which his genius was not always entirely suited. It also led him towards a new kind of comedy that bore fruit not only in the splendid, but much misunderstood, *All's Well that Ends Well*, but in the late romances. His greatest achievement, *King Lear*, as we have seen, was built on the ruins of the scourging satire of *Timon*, which, even with Middleton's help, was beyond the range of Shakespeare's humane vision. *King Lear* finally saw the rivals outdistanced, but we have to thank the stimulus provided by these other major figures of our drama for the extraordinary outburst of artistic energy with which he met their challenge. They have had less than their due; and to that extent Shakespeare's own achievement has remained inadequately understood.

NOTES

INTRODUCTION

1 F. Bowers (ed.), *Satiromastix*, V, ii, 298–307, in *Dramatic Works of Thomas Dekker*, Cambridge, Cambridge University Press, 1953, vol.1, p. 382.
2 A. Dyce (ed.), 'Master Francis Beaumont's Letter to Ben Jonson', in *The Works of Beaumont and Fletcher*, London, Edward Moxon, 1843–6, vol.11, pp. 501–2.
3 F. L. Lucas (ed.), *The Duchess of Malfi*, in *The Complete Works of John Webster*, London, Chatto & Windus, 1927, vol.2, p. 34.
4 J. B. Leishman (ed.), *The Second Part of the Return from Parnassus* (IV, iii, 1772–3), in *The Three Parnassus Plays 1598–1601*, London, Nicolson & Watson, 1949, p. 337.
5 The epithet is Jonson's, 'To the Memory of my Beloved Mr William Shakespeare', line 55, *Ben Jonson*, edited C. H. Herford and P. E. Simpson, Oxford, Clarendon Press, vol. VIII, p. 392.
6 O. L. Dick (ed.), *Aubrey's Brief Lives*, Harmondsworth, Penguin Books, 1962 (originally published Secker & Warburg, 1949), p. 128.
7 A. Barton, *Ben Jonson, Dramatist*, Cambridge, Cambridge University Press, 1984, p. 94.
8 A. Nicoll, 'The dramatic portrait of George Chapman', *PQ*, XLI (1962), pp. 215–28.
9 F. P. Wilson, *Marlowe and the Early Shakespeare*, Oxford, Clarendon Press, 1953.
10 F. Cioffi, 'Intention and interpretation in literature', in D. Newton-De Molina (ed.), *On Literary Intention*, Edinburgh, Edinburgh University Press, 1976, p. 69.
11 R. W. Dent, *John Webster's Borrowing*, Berkeley and Los Angeles, University of California Press, 1960.

1 *HAMLET* AND THE LITTLE EYASES

1 *Hamlet, First Quarto, 1603* (facsimile), Menston, Scolar Press, 1972, Sig. E3ʳ.
2 W. Reavely Gair, *The Children of Paul's*. Cambridge, Cambridge University Press, 1982, p. 133.
3 References to the folio text are to C. Hinman (ed.), *The Norton Facsimile*, the First Folio of Shakespeare, New York, W.W.Norton, 1968.
4 Gair, op. cit., p. 133; I. Smith, *Shakespeare's Blackfriars Playhouse*, London, Peter Owen, 1966, p. 180.
5 C. T. Onions, *A Shakespeare Glossary*, enlarged and revised by R. D. Eagleson, Oxford, Clarendon Press, 1986, 'Innovation'. See also H. Child and J. Dover Wilson (eds), *Hamlet*, Cambridge, Cambridge University Press (reprinted) 1954, note to II, ii, 335–6.
6 H. Jenkins (ed.), *Hamlet* (Arden edition), London, Methuen, 1982, note to II, ii, 330–1. Quotations will be from this edition unless otherwise indicated.

7 Child and Wilson, ed. cit., note to II, ii, 335–6.

8 ibid., note to II, ii, 332.

9 ibid., note to II, ii, 339.

10 A. Harbage, *Shakespeare and the Rival Traditions*, New York, Macmillan, 1952, p. 44.

11 ibid., p. 45.

12 Jenkins, ed. cit., p. 13.

13 ibid., p. 1.

14 Child and Wilson, ed. cit., p. ix.

15 V. F. Stern, *Gabriel Harvey, His Life, Marginalia and Library*, Oxford, Clarendon Press, 1979, p. 127.

16 R. A. Foakes and R. T. Rickert (eds), *Henslowe's Diary*, Cambridge, Cambridge University Press, 1961, p. 55.

17 A. Harbage, *Shakespeare's Audience*, New York, Columbia University Press, 1941, Appendix IV, p. 178.

18 Foakes and Rickert, ed. cit., p. 203.

19 Harbage, *Shakespeare's Audience*, p. 178.

20 C. Hoy, *Introductions, Notes and Commentaries to Texts in The Dramatic Works of Thomas Dekker, edited by Fredson Bowers*, Cambridge, Cambridge University Press, 1980, vol.4, pp. 70–1.

21 C. H. Herford and P. and E. Simpson (eds), *Bartholomew Fair*, Induction, 106–7, in *Ben Jonson*, Oxford, Clarendon Press, 1938, vol.6, p. 16.

22 F. Bowers (ed.), *Dramatic Works of Thomas Dekker*, Cambridge, Cambridge University Press, 1953, vol.4, p. 182.

23 J. D. Jowett (ed.), *Henry Chettle, The Tragedy of Hoffman*, Nottingham, Nottingham University Press, 1983, line 1406.

24 G. K. Hunter (ed.), *Marston, Antonio's Revenge*, London, Edward Arnold, 1966, p. xviii. See also Jenkins (ed.), *Hamlet*, pp. 7–13.

25 G. Bullough (ed.), *Narrative and Dramatic Sources of Shakespeare*, London, Routledge & Kegan Paul, 1966, vol.7, pp. 16–17. (Referred to as *NDSS* hereafter).

26 W. Reavely Gair (ed.), *Marston, Antonio's Revenge*, Manchester, Manchester University Press, 1978, p. 15. Quotations are from this edition.

27 The story was first recorded in Rowe's 1709 edition of Shakespeare: 'She was so well pleas'd with the admirable Character of Falstaff in the two Parts of *Henry* the Fourth, that she commanded him to continue it for one Play more, and to shew him in Love.' Quoted in *The Merry Wives of Windsor*, edited H. J. Oliver (Arden edition), London, Methuen, 1971, p. xlv.

28 Jenkins, ed. cit., p. 10.

29 Gair, ed. cit., I, iii, 22, 24–6; II, i, 49–50, 52; III, iv, 25–6, 41–3.

30 E. Prosser, *Hamlet and Revenge*, Stanford, Stanford University Press, 2nd edn, 1971, pp. 221–7. Also L. L. Martz, *The Poetry of Meditation*, New Haven, Yale University Press, 1954, pp. 137–8.

31 Martz, op. cit., p. 14, quotes from a Jacobean translation of Luis de Granada: 'praier is also taken in another more large sense; to wit: for every lifting up of our heart to God. . .both meditation and contemplation, and every other good thought may also be called a Prayer.'

32 P. R. Horne, *The Tragedies of Gianbattista Cinthio*, London, Oxford University Press, 1962, pp. 51–2.

33 See my account of Giraldi's *Orbecche* and *Arrenopia* in D. L. Farley-Hills, *Jacobean Drama*, London, Macmillan, 1988, pp. 50–6.

34 W. Haller (ed.), 'Areopagitica', in *The Works of John Milton*, New York, Columbia University Press, 1931, vol.4, p. 311.

35 Jenkins, ed. cit., note to I, ii, 72.

36 Farley-Hills, op.cit. p. 55.

37 Jenkins, ed.cit., long note to I, ii, 1 (p. 433).

38 W. Ralegh (ed.), *Johnson on Shakespeare*, London, Oxford University Press, 1908, reprinted 1929, p. 193.

39 Jenkins, ed. cit., long note to III, iii, 89–95 (pp. 513–15).

40 ibid., note to III, iv, 29.

41 For an amusing example of this see L. Bohannon, 'Shakespeare in the Bush', *Natural History*, vol.75 (1966).

42 Jenkins, ed. cit., note to I, i, 82 and long note to I, iv, 12–13 (p. 447).

43 J. Dover Wilson, *What Happens in Hamlet*, Cambridge, Cambridge University Press, 1935, p. 101.

44 A. C. Bradley, *Shakespearean Tragedy*, London, Macmillan, 1905, 2nd edn reprinted 1926, pp. 153ff.

45 Bullough, *NDSS*, vol.7, p. 52.

46 Jenkins, ed. cit., p. 149.

47 ibid., p. 149.

48 Bullough, *NDSS*, vol.7, pp. 51–2.

49 cf. for instance I, v, 47–57 (the Ghost) with III, iv, 91–4, 183–9 (Hamlet).

50 Dover Wilson explicitly counters these assumptions. See M. Weitz, *Hamlet and the Philosophy of Literary Criticism*, London, Faber & Faber, 1972, originally published by Chicago University Press, 1964, pp.25–6.

51 R. Brown (ed.), *Merchant of Venice*, (Arden edition), London, Methuen, 1959, reprinted 1961, I, iii, 93.

52 K. Muir (ed.), *Macbeth*, (Arden edition), London, Methuen, 1959, reprinted 1961, I, iii, 123–4.

53 Bradley, op. cit., p. 97.

54 Prosser, op. cit., p. 180.

55 Jenkins, ed. cit., p. 155.

56 T. S. Eliot, 'Hamlet', *Selected Essays*, London, Faber & Faber, 1934.

57 Jenkins, ed. cit., pp.136–40.

58 ibid., long note to V, i, 139–57, (p. 551).

59 A. Holaday (ed.), 'Dedication of *Revenge of Bussy D'Ambois*', in *The Plays of George Chapman, The Tragedies*, Bury St Edmunds, St Edmundsbury Press, 1987, p. 442.

2 PORTRAITS OF THE IRON AGE: *TROILUS AND CRESSIDA*

1 R. A. Foakes and R. T. Rickert (eds), *Henslowe's Diary*, Cambridge, Cambridge University Press, 1961, pp. 47, 106–7, 121.

2 A. W. Weiner (ed.), *Thomas Heywood's The Iron Age*, New York and London, Garland Publishing, 1979. Quotations are from this edition. For detailed discussion of the dating see pp.xix-xxxv.

3 ibid., p.xxiii.

4 ibid., pp.xxv–xxxiii.

5 Geoffrey Bullough (following J. S. P. Tatlock) attempts a reconstruction of the plot of what he takes to be this play on the basis of a plot fragment extant in the British Museum Library. *Narrative and Dramatic Sources of Shakespeare*, London, Routledge & Kegan Paul, 1973, vol.6, pp. 98–9.

6 A. W. Weiner, ed. cit., p.xxxiii.

7 K. Palmer (ed.), *Troilus and Cressida* (Arden edition), London, Methuen, 1982, p. 19. Quotations are from this edition.

8 ibid., note to Prologue 28.

9 Bullough, *NDSS*, vol.6, pp. 220–1.

10 Weiner, ed. cit., p.[lxvii*].

11 ibid., pp. 167–8 (notes).

12 Quotations from Part 2 are from the edition of R. H. Shepherd, *Dramatic Works of Thomas Heywood*, 1874, reprinted New York, Russell & Russell, 1964, vol.3, pp. 430–1. I make some minor changes in punctuation.

13 Weiner, op. cit., p.xxxv.

14 ibid., p.xxii.

15 ibid., pp.xvi–xviii.

16 e.g. *Coriolanus*, II, i, 234, 'Nor, shewing, as the manner is, his wounds/To the people, beg their stinking breaths'; *Tempest*, Epilogue 11, 'But release me from my bands/With the help of your good hands:/Gentle breath of yours my sails/Must fill, or else my project fails.'

17 Palmer, ed. cit., Appendix, p. 309.

18 Kenneth Muir makes this suggestion in the note on 'clapper-claw' in his edition of *Troilus and Cressida*, Oxford, Clarendon Press, 1982, p. 193, n.2.

19 C. T. Onions, *A Shakespeare Glossary*, enlarged and revised by R. D. Eagleson, Oxford, Clarendon Press, 1986, 'clapper-claw'.

20 Palmer, ed. cit., pp. 21–2.

21 R. Kimbrough, *Shakespeare's Troilus and Cressida and its Setting*, Cambridge, Mass., Harvard University Press, 1964, p. 21.

22 Palmer, ed. cit., Appendix I, p. 306.

23 G. Taylor, '*Troilus and Cressida*: bibliography, performance and interpretation', in *Shakespeare Studies*, xv, 1982.

24 Foakes and Rickert, ed. cit., Introduction, pp.xxx–xxxi. See also J.C.Maxwell's discussion in his edition of *Titus Andronicus* (Arden edition), London, Methuen, 3rd edn, 1961, pp.xxii–xxiii.

25 Palmer, ed. cit., Appendix II, p. 309.

26 ibid., Appendix I, p. 306 and Appendix II, p. 307, n.2.

27 J. B. Leishman (ed.), *The Second Part of the Return from Parnassus* (IV, iii, 1770–3), in *The Three Parnassus Plays 1598–1601*, London, Ivor Nicolson & Watson, 1949, p. 337.

28 F. N. Robinson (ed.), *Troilus and Criseyde*, in *Complete Works of Geoffrey Chaucer*, London, Oxford University Press, 2nd edn, 1957, V, 1814–25.

29 H. Bergson (ed.), *Lydgate's Troy Book*, EETS, n.s.97, 1906, Millwood, New York, Kraus reprint, 1978, vol.1, II, 1–11.

30 ibid., vol.3, V, 3546–7, 3567–83.

31 The suggestion is made by L. Hotson, *The First Night of Twelfth Night*, London, Hart-Davis, 1964, pp. 94ff.

32 M. R. Wooodhead (ed.), *Marston, What You Will*, Nottingham, Nottingham University Press, 1980. Quotations are from this edition.

33 *Faerie Queene*, I, vii stanzas 2–11.

34 For the meaning of 'sore' as 'vagina' see *Love's Labours Lost*, IV, ii, 60, and H. A. Ellis's comment in *Shakespeare's Lusty Punning in Love's Labours Lost*, The Hague and Paris, Mouton, 1973; also M. Green, *The Labyrinth of Shakespeare's Sonnets*, London, Charles Skilton, 1974, pp. 4–5. For 'wound' see E. Partridge, *Shakespeare's Bawdy*, London, Routledge & Kegan Paul, revised and enlarged, 1968.

35 Palmer, ed. cit., note to II, ii, 189–90.

3 'THE WORD. . .WILL BRING ON SUMMER': *ALL'S WELL THAT ENDS WELL* AND CHAPMAN'S MYTHIC COMEDY

1 A. Harbage, *Shakespeare's Audience*, New York, Columbia University Press, 1941, Appendix IV.

2 D. Farley-Hills, *Jacobean Drama*, London, Macmillan, 1988, p. 79.

3 M. Wise (ed.), *Marston, The Malcontent*, London.Edward Arnold, 1965, Induction, 51–5.

4 A. B. Grosart (ed.), *Non-Dramatic Works of Thomas Dekker*, n.p., Huth Library, 1884, vol.1, p. 116.

5 G. L. Kittredge, 'Notes on Elizabethan plays', *JEGP*, II (1898), pp. 10–13.

6 R. J. C. Wait, *The Background to Shakespeare's Sonnets*, London, Chatto & Windus, 1972. pp. 69–86, 106–9.

7 T. M. Parrott (ed.), *The Plays of George Chapman, The Comedies*, London, Routledge & Kegan Paul, reprinted New York, Russell & Russell, 1961, vol.2, p. 906, note to *Gentleman Usher* IV, iii, 58–60. The reference (as Parrott notes) is to *The Complaint of Rosamond*, lines 141–4.

8 Parrott, ed. cit, vol.2, p. 655.

9 For this interpretation of the role of Zephyr in *The Allegory of the Seasons*, see E. Wind, *Pagan Mysteries of the Renaissance*, enlarged and revised edition, Harmondsworth, Penguin Books, 1967, pp. 124–5. Reference to Spenser is to *Faerie Queene*, III, vi, st.xxix–lii.

10 Parrott, ed. cit., vol.2, p. 892. Both Parrott and Hoy (op. cit., notes to *Satiromastix*) suggest that both plays refer to an actual Lady Furnivall, but no suitable candidate has been forthcoming.

11 Parrott, ed. cit., vol.2, p. 892, pp. 755–6.

12 G. K. Hunter (ed.), *All's Well that Ends Well* (Arden edition), London, Methuen, 1959, reprinted 1985, p. xxv. Quotations are from this edition.

13 G. K. Hunter, ed. cit., p. xxiv.

14 For Helena's 'Marian' role see R.G.Hunter, *Shakespeare's Comedy of Forgiveness*, New York and London, Columbia University Press, 1965, pp. 129–30.

15 G. Sandys, *Ovid's Metamorphosis Englished, Mythologiz'd and Represented in Figures*, Oxford, J. Lichfield, 1632, p. 335.

16 ibid., p. 367.

17 J. H. Smith (ed.), *Chapman, The Gentleman Usher*, London, Edward Arnold, 1970. Quotations are from this edition.

18 See Wind's discussion of Botticelli's 'Birth of Venus' in *Pagan Mysteries of the Renaissance*, pp. 138–40. See also the discussion of the distinction in Spenser's *Faerie Queene*, III, in C. S. Lewis, *Images of Life*, Cambridge, Cambridge University Press, 1967, ch. 3, and T. P. Roche, *The Kindly Flame*, Princeton, Princeton University Press, 1964, ch. 2. Roche quotes Ficino: 'There are, then, two Venuses: one is that intelligence, which we have identified with the Angelic Mind, the other is the power of generation attributed to the Soul of the World. Both are accompanied by Love, through which the first contemplates the beauty of God, and the second creates divine beauty in earthly forms' (p. 101). That the popular dramatists and their audiences were familiar with the distinction between the two Venuses is clear from a reference in Middleton's *Family of Love* (ed. S. Shepherd, Nottingham Drama Texts, Nottingham, Nottingham University Press, 1979, IV, ii, 1341–3).

19 P. B. Bartlett (ed.), *The Poems of George Chapman*, Modern Language Association of America, 1941, reprinted New York, Russell & Russell, 1962, p. 328, lines 71–3.

20 See my *Jacobean Drama*, pp. 92–3.

21 Smith, ed. cit., pp. xvi–xxi, the text is given in Appendix A, pp. 126–8.

22 P. O. Kristeller, *The Philosophy of Marsilio Ficino*, New York, Columbia University Press, 1943, reprinted 1964, p. 239.

23 ibid., p. 300.

24 ibid., p. 210.

25 ibid. p. 356.

26 J. Jacquot, *George Chapman, sa vie, sa poésie, son théâtre, sa pensée*, Annales de l'Université de Lyon, Paris, 1951, p. 95.

27 *Faerie Queene*, III, vi, st.xxviii.
28 Smith, ed. cit., note to IV, ii, 156–7.
29 J. G. Price, *Shakespeare's Unfortunate Comedy*, Liverpool, Liverpool University Press, 1968.
30 Mark Van Doren points out that one of Helena's favourite words is 'nature', *Shakespeare*, New York, Doubleday, 1939, p. 184.
31 See Wind, *Pagan Mysteries*, ch. 5.
32 Smith, ed. cit., note to V, iii, 33.
33 H. B. Charlton, *Shakespearean Comedy*, London, Methuen, 1938, p. 217.
34 A feature noted by R. G. Hunter, *Shakespeare and the Comedy of Forgiveness*, p. 106.
35 W. W. Lawrence, *Shakespeare's Problem Comedies*, New York, Macmillan, 1931, p. 68, writes: 'In *All's Well that Ends Well* – supremely cynical title – Shakespeare seems deliberately to take revenge on his own idealism of love.'
36 G. K. Hunter, ed. cit., note to I, i, 163–6.
37 *Faerie Queene*, III, iv, st.xxvi.
38 ibid., III, vi, st xlvii. It is worth noting that Time is a central figure in Spenser's Garden of Adonis.
39 I have adopted the folio punctuation, which makes the meaning clear. (As also at I, i, 61.)
40 Onions, *Glossary* (revised Eagleson), 'word', 6; and see *Oxford English Dictionary*, 'word', 11a.
41 G. K. Hunter, ed. cit. note to I, ii, 65–7.
42 For 'canary' in a bawdy context see *Merry Wives of Windsor*, II, ii, 62, 65, and for 'motion' cf. 'motion unregenerative', *Measure for Measure*, III, ii, 119.
43 For a similar use of 'pen' cf.*Merchant of Venice*, V, i, 237, and compare 'Pompey the Great', *Measure for Measure*, II, i, 215 and *Love's Labours Lost*, V, i, 121. See also R.G.Hunter, op. cit. p. 115 and note p. 253.
44 *Faerie Queene*, III, vi, st.48.
45 See Wind, op. cit., pp. 115–17.
46 A notable exception is R. G. Hunter, op. cit. ch. 5.
47 See Wind, op. cit., ch. 14 'The concealed God'.
48 E. Partridge, *Shakespeare's Bawdy*, revised and enlarged, London, Routledge & Kegan Paul, 1968, 'stable'.
49 G. K. Hunter, ed. cit., head-note to I, iii.
50 E. M. W. Tillyard, *Shakespeare's Problem Plays*, London, Chatto & Windus, 1950, p. 91.See also G. Bullough (ed.), *Narrative and Dramatic Sources of Shakespeare*, London, Routledge & Kegan Paul, 1958, vol. 2, p. 375.
51 Wind, op. cit., p. 234.

4: OTHELLO: A MAN KILLED WITH KINDNESS

1 E. Jones, '*Othello*, Lepanto and the Cyprus Wars', *Shakespeare Survey*, 21 (1970) pp. 47–52.
2 F. E. Halliday, *The Life of Shakespeare*, London, Duckworth, 1961, p. 181.
3 Some support is given for this assumption by Leonard Digges's verses prefixed to *Shakespeare's Poems*, 1640, where he contrasts the audience's preference for *Othello* over *Sejanus* (which we know was a Globe play). See B. Vickers (ed.), *Shakespeare, the Critical Heritage*, London, Routledge & Kegan Paul, 1974, vol.1, p. 28.
4 R. W. Van Fossen (ed.), *A Woman Killed with Kindness, by Thomas Heywood*, London, Methuen, 1961, p. lix. Quotations are from this edition.
5 See, for instance, the introduction to G. K. Hunter's edition of *All's Well That Ends Well*, pp. xxiii, xxv.
6 M. R. Ridley (ed.), *Othello*, (Arden edition), London, Methuen, 1962. Quotations are

from this edition.

7 G. Bullough (ed.), *Narrative and Dramatic Sources of Shakespeare*, London, Routledge & Kegan Paul, 1975, vol.7, p.239. Bullough's translation is of the second edition of *Gli Hecatommithi*, Venice, 1566, which opens: 'Gli Hecatommithi nella quale si dimostra, che solo, fra gli amori humani e quiete in quello, il quale e fra marito e moglie e che ne dishonesti non puo essere riposo' (p. 13)

8 Bullough, *NDSS*, vol.7, p. 239.

9 ibid., vol.7, p. 240.

10 F. T. Bowers (ed.), *Patient Grissil*, in *Dramatic Works of Thomas Dekker*, Cambridge, Cambridge University Press, 1953, vol.1. Quotations are from this edition.

11 C. Hoy, *Introductions, Notes and Commentaries to Texts in The Dramatic Works of Thomas Dekker edited by Fredson Bowers*, Cambridge, Cambridge University Press, 1980, vol.1, p. 130.

12 ibid., vol.1, p. 146.

13 The force of the paradox of a good black man can be illustrated from a contemporary sermon (Robert Wilkinson's *Lot's Wife*, preached at St Paul's Cross, 1607, p. 42): 'Thus the accursed seed of Cham, the Egyptians, Moors and Ethiopians, had for a stamp of their father's sin the colour of their faces.'

14 *Hecatommithi*, ed. cit., p. 21. A quotation from Menander that Iago may be recalling in describing Michael Cassio as 'A fellow almost damned in a fair wife' (I, i, 21).

15 cf.also *King Lear*, IV, vi, 129. A pictorial example from the twelfth-century Winchester Psalter is illustrated in M.Dames, *The Silbury Treasure*, London, Thames & Hudson, 1976, p. 111.

16 See, for example, the splendid example in Seracino's painting of 'Mars and Venus' recently shown in the *Times* exhibition of paintings in the Thyssen- Bornemisza Collection.

17 J. C. Trewin, *Shakespeare on the English Stage 1900–1964*, London, Barrie & Rockliff, 1964, p. 175. See also R. Rogers, 'Endopsychic drama in *Othello*', *Shakespeare Quarterly*, xx (1969), pp. 205–15.

18 Partridge, *Shakespeare's Bawdy*, 'corner', 'thing', 'use'.

19 ibid., 'occupation'.

20 T. S. Eliot, 'Shakespeare and the Stoicism of Seneca', *Selected Essays*, London, Faber & Faber, 1934, p. 130; F. R. Leavis, 'Diabolical Intellect and the Noble Hero', *The Common Pursuit*, London, Chatto and Windus, 1952; G. Wilson Knight, 'The Othello music', *The Wheel of Fire*, London, Oxford University Press, 1930 revised and enlarged 1949, London, Methuen.

21 Aristotle, 'On the Art of Poetry', in *Classical Literary Criticism*, translated with an introduction by T. S. Dorsch, Harmondsworth, Penguin Books, 1965, p. 50.

22 ibid.p. 50.

23 C. A. Zimansky (ed.), *The Critical Works of Thomas Rymer*, London, Oxford University Press, 1956, p. 132.

24 H. B. Charlton, *Castelvetro's Theory of Poetry*, Manchester, Manchester University Press, 1913, p. 105.

25 Vickers, *Critical Heritage*, vol.1, p. 28.

26 C. H. Herford and P. and E. Simpson (eds), *Ben Jonson*, Oxford, Clarendon Press, 1932, vol.11, p. 317. Quotations are from this edition.

27 ibid., vol.9, p. 191.

28 ibid. vol 4, p. 351 (line 45).

29 Halliday, *Life*, p. 235.

30 Herford and Simpson, ed. cit., vol.1, p. 141.

31 ibid., vol.5, p. 20, line 116.

32 ibid., vol.4, p. 350, line 18–20.

33 Quoted in J. W. Cunliffe (ed.), *Early English Classical Tragedy*, 1912, p. lxvii.

34 Herford and Simpson, ed. cit., vol.4, p. 351, line 43–8.

35 ibid., vol.2, p. 3. (The diarist is Manningham).

36 J. D. Duff (ed.) *Juvenal Satires*, Cambridge, Cambridge University Press, 1970, I, iv, 70–1.

37 Herford and Simpson, ed. cit., vol.1, p. 141, lines 326–7.

38 ibid. vol.11, p. 309, lines 31–2.

39 ibid., vol.5, p. 24, line 32.

40 E. K. Chambers, *The Elizabethan Stage*, Oxford, Clarendon Press, 1923, vol. 3, p. 359.

5: ROYAL MEASURES: *MEASURE FOR MEASURE* AND MIDDLETON'S COMEDY OF DISILLUSIONMENT

1 F. E. Halliday, *The Life of Shakespeare*, London, Duckworth, 1961, p. 181.

2 E. K. Chambers, *The Elizabethan Stage*, Oxford, Clarendon Press, 1923, vol. 1, pp. 218, 339; vol.2, pp. 209–10.

3 Halliday, *Life*, pp. 176–8.

4 D. Mathew, *James I*, London, Eyre & Spottiswoode, 1976, p. 127.

5 C. H. McIlwain (ed.), *The Political Works of James I*, Cambridge, Mass., Harvard University Press, 1918, reissued New York, Russell & Russell, 1965, p. 27.

6 The influence of *Basilikon Doron* on the play has been much debated, but is not now, I think, in serious doubt. For a summary of the evidence see D. L.Stevenson, *The Achievement of Shakespeare's Measure for Measure*, New York, 1966, pp. 144–55 and J. Bennett, *Measure for Measure as Royal Entertainment*, New York, Columbia University Press, 1966, pp. 81–104. Richard Levin has recently attempted to deny the influence on the grounds that some bad arguments have been used to defend it and that the influence cannot be proved (*New Readings vs Old Plays*, Chicago and London, University of Chicago Press, 1979, pp. 171–93). It is not clear what would constitute 'proof' in such cases (there is no 'proof', for instance, that Shakespeare used the old play of *King Leir* in writing *Lear*). It is illogical to argue that a hypothesis must be ignored because it is not susceptible of absolute proof. Such cases must rest on their overall plausibility and I hope to have added something to the plausibility of the hypothesis in the following pages of this chapter. The crucial point for my argument is not that Shakespeare is actually quoting from *Basilikon Doron*, but that he is reflecting attitudes in *Measure for Measure* publicly known to be favoured by James I.

7 J. Bennett, op. cit., p. 81: 'The whole character of Duke Vincentio was created, not to represent, but to please and flatter the king.' See also E. Schanzer, *The Problem Plays of Shakespeare*, London, Routledge & Kegan Paul, 1963, pp. 120–6.

8 M. Wine (ed.), *Marston, The Malcontent*, London, Edward Arnold, 1965. Quotations are from this edition.

9 J. B.Brooks (ed.), *The Phoenix by Thomas Middleton*, New York and London, Garland Publishing, 1980, pp. 22–4. Quotations are from this edition.

10 Brooks, ed. cit., pp. 11–12.

11 For an account of the book's popularity see Bennett, op. cit., pp. 82–5.

12 McIlwain, ed. cit., pp. 39, 40.

13 C. Bingham, *James I of England*, London, Weidenfeld & Nicolson, 1981, p. 68.

14 J. W. Lever (ed.), *Measure for Measure* (Arden edition), London, Methuen, 1965, Introduction, pp. xxxiii–iv. Quotations are from this edition.

15 McIlwain, ed. cit., p. 20.

16 ibid., p. 32.

17 Brooks, ed. cit., p. 19.

18 N. W. Bawcutt, 'Middleton's "The Phoenix" as a royal play', *N & Q*, n.s., III (July 1956), p. 287. Also Brooks, ed. cit., p. 20, n.56.

19 McIlwain, ed. cit., p. 38.
20 Brooks, ed. cit., p. 21.
21 ibid., pp. 120–4.
22 McIlwain, ed. cit., pp. 34, 36.
23 E. Partridge, *Shakespeare's Bawdy*, revised and enlarged, London, Routledge & Kegan Paul, 1968, 'do'. See also Brooks's note.
24 Mathew, op. cit., p. 320.
25 Stevenson, op. cit., pp. 155–6.
26 ibid., pp. 160–1.
27 Brooks, ed. cit., pp. 115–6.
28 McIlwain, ed. cit., pp. 18–19.
29 Brooks, ed. cit., p. 125.
30 ibid., note to I, iv, 202.
31 D. F. Gless, *Measure for Measure, the Law and the Convent*, Princeton, Princeton University Press, 1979, pp. 156ff.
32 McIlwain, ed. cit., p. 12.
33 G. B. Giraldi Cinthio, *De Gli Hecatommithi*, Monte Reale, Leonardo Torrentino, 1565, p.[368a*], Sig.8^{1v}.
34 ibid., p. 431. 'Qui dissero i piu maturi, che alla Reale Giustitia e molto degna compagna la Clemenza, perche ella tempera le pene, e che percio si legge, che a Pricipi ella e molto convenevole. Perche induce una certa temperanza ne gli animi loro, che gli fa essere benigni verso i loro soggetti, et conchiusero, che e nella Giustitia e nella Clemenza si era mostrato veramente degno de imperio Massimiano.'
35 G. Bullough, *Narrative and Dramatic Sources of Shakespeare*, London, Routledge & Kegan Paul, 1958, vol.2, p. 474. Quotations are from this text.
36 McIlwain, ed. cit., p. 16.
37 ibid., p. 16.
38 ibid., p. 17.
39 ibid., p. 37.
40 ibid., p. 16.
41 *Hecatommithi*, p.432. 'la quale, come sapete, e l'ultima cosa delle cose terribili.'
42 Lever, ed. cit., tentatively suggests an emendment, but this is not necessary, note to III, i, 120.
43 McIlwain, ed. cit., p. 12.
44 Mathew, op. cit., p. 126, quotes the King: 'I think, that of all, Geneva is the worst.' The quotation is from *The Geneva Bible*, a facsimile of the 1560 edition, Madison, Milwaukee and London, University of Wisconsin Press, 1969.
45 McIlwain, ed. cit., p. 12.
46 *Oxford English Dictionary*, 'conception' 1, which quotes *Timon of Athens*, I, ii, 115 as a Shakespearean example.
47 McIlwain, ed. cit., p. 16.
48 ibid., p. 16.
49 ibid., p. 12.
50 ibid., p. 17.
51 Gless, op. cit., p. 65.
52 ibid., p. 83.
53 McIlwain, ed. cit., p. 30.
54 ibid., p. 16.
55 J. Calvin, *Institutes of the Christian Religion*, translated H. Beveridge, Edinburgh, Calvin Translation Society, 1843, vol.1, II, 2, 10, p.311, 'he who is most deeply abased and alarmed, by the consciousness of his disgrace, nakedness, want and misery, has made the greatest progress in the knowledge of himself.'
56 G. Wilson Knight, *The Wheel of Fire*, London, Oxford University Press, 1930,

reprinted London, Methuen, 1949, p. 80. 'The duke, like Jesus, is the prophet of a new order.' And see Lever, ed. cit., p. lvii.

57 See, for example, W. W. Lawrence, *Shakespeare's Problem Comedies*, New York, Macmillan, 1931, p. 83.

58 U. M. Ellis-Fermor, *The Jacobean Drama*, London, Methuen, 1936, reprinted 1977, p. 262.

59 A. B. Jameson, *Shakespeare's Heroines, Characteristics of Women*, 1832, new edition, London, G. Bell, 1913, p. 54. For a summary of critical references to Isabella see Stevenson, op. cit., pp. 80–90, also E. Schanzer, op. cit., pp. 96–112.

60 E. M. Pope, 'The Renaissance Background of *Measure for Measure*', *Shakespeare Survey*, II (1949), pp. 77–8.

6: ANGER'S PRIVILEGE: *TIMON OF ATHENS* AND *KING LEAR*

1 J. Munro (ed.), *The Shakespeare Allusion Book: A Collection of Allusions to Shakespeare from 1591–1700*, London, Chatto & Windus, 1909, vol.1, p. 272.

2 K. Muir (ed.), *King Lear* (Arden edition), London, Methuen, 1952, p. xxiv.

3 T. M. Raysor (ed.), *Samuel Taylor Coleridge, Shakespearean Criticism*, London, J. M. Dent, 2nd edn, 1960, vol.1, p. 211.

4 H. J. Oliver (ed.), *Timon of Athens* (Arden edition), London, Methuen, 1963, p. xlii. Quotations are from this edition.

5 M. Bradbrook, 'The Comedy of Timon: A Reveling Play of the Inner Temple', *Renaissance Drama*, 9 (1966), pp. 83–103.

6 J. C. Bulman, 'The date and production of *Timon* reconsidered', *Shakespeare Survey*, 27 (1974), pp. 111–27.

7 J. C. Bulman, 'Shakespeare's use of the Timon comedy', *Shakespeare Survey*, 29 (1976), pp. 103–16.

8 R. H. Goldsmith, 'Did Shakespeare use the old Timon comedy?', *Shakespeare Quarterly*, 9 (1958), pp. 31–8.

9 A. C. Bradley had already stressed the similarities between Shakespeare's two tragedies in *Shakespearean Tragedy*, London, Macmillan, 1905, 2nd edn, reprinted 1926, pp. 245–7 and note S.

10 J. C. Bulman and J. M. Nosworthy (eds), *Timon* (Malone Society Reprints), Oxford, Oxford University Press, 1980. Quotations are from this edition.

11 The relationship of the two principal texts of *King Lear*, Q1 (1608) and F1 (1623) is fraught with difficulties that no modern edition has succeeded in overcoming. The new Oxford Complete Shakespeare (1988) provides both texts, which is probably the best solution because it requires the critic to make a distinct choice between the two very different versions. Because Q1 is probably closer to Shakespeare's original version I have decided to use a facsimile of Q1 reproduced from BM copy C34 K18 prepared by Charles Praetorius, 1885, and all quotations are from this unless otherwise indicated.

12 Bulman, 'Shakespeare's use of the Timon comedy', pp. 111–12.

13 See W. Farnham, *Shakespeare's Tragic Frontiers*, Berkeley and Los Angeles, University of California Press, 1963, pp. 50–67, for a summary of earlier views on Timon.

14 O. J. Campbell, *Shakespeare's Satire*, London, Oxford University Press, 1943, pp. 168–97, argues that *Timon of Athens* is non-comic satire influenced by Jonson.

15 W. Wells, 'Timon of Athens', *N & Q*, 12th series, 6 (1920), pp. 266–9.

16 H. Dugdale Sykes, *Sidelights on Elizabethan Drama*, London, Oxford University Press, 1924, pp. 19–48.

17 D. J. Lake, *The Canon of Thomas Middleton's Plays*, Cambridge, Cambridge University Press, 1975, Appendix V (pp. 279–86).

18 See Chapter 5, pp. 139ff.

19 F. G. Fleay, *Shakespeare Manual*, London, Macmillan, 1876, pp. 195–6.

20 Bulman and Nosworthy, ed. cit., p. xv.

21 Lake, op. cit., Bands 1–4 (between pp.252 and 253) finds only one example of the spelling outside Middleton's plays or plays attributed to him, a late example in Ford.

22 Bulman and Nosworthy, ed. cit., p. ix.

23 C. Hinman (ed.) *The Norton Facsimile, the First Folio of Shakespeare*, New York, W. W. Norton, 1968.

24 Lake, op. cit. Band 1 (g). Lake instances: em, 'em, e'm; has, h'as, ha's; doe[']s, do[']s.

25 I am indebted to the Fellows and Librarian of Trinity College, Cambridge, for a microfilm reproduction of the autograph MS of *Game at Chess*.
Compare the following:
MS *Timon*: d'ost, do'st: II, iii, 755, 758; V, ii, 2206; V, v, 2541, 2542.
G at C: do'st, do's, d'os: I, i, 64; II, ii, 234; I, i, 76; III, i, 234; III, i, 17.
MS *Timon*: ti's : I, i, 10; I, i, 112; V, ii, 2195.
G at C: ti's : II, i, 4.
MS *Timon*: ther'es : II, iii, 773.
G at C: ther'es : I, i, 65.
One strange characteristic of the Trinity MS is for Middleton to place an apostrophe after 'sh', producing forms like sh'ee, sh'al, sh'all. MS *Timon* has sh'alt at V, v, 2476. It should be noted that the scribes of the *Timon* MS have attempted to correct a considerable number of these anomalies.

26 Sykes, op. cit. p. 42.

27 Sykes, op. cit., pp. 22–3, compares this speech with passages in *Phoenix* and *Michaelmas Term* in arguing for Middleton's authorship.

28 See D. L. Farley-Hills, *The Comic in Renaissance Comedy*, London, Macmillan, 1981, p. 101.

29 J. Calvin, *The Institutes of the Christian Religion*, trans. H. Beveridge, Edinburgh, Calvin Translation Society, 1843, vol.1, II, 8. p. 293.

30 K. Muir, *Shakespeare's Tragic Sequence*, London, Hutchinson, 1972, p. 191. 'It is surely appropriate that, in a society in which everything is subordinated to gold, sexual relations should also be bound by the cash-nexus.'

31 F. Bowers (ed.), *The Roaring Girl*, in *Dramatic Works of Thomas Dekker*, Cambridge, Cambridge University Press, 1953, vol.3, V, i, 189, 191.

32 G. Bullough (ed), *Narrative and Dramatic Sources of Shakespeare*, London, Routledge & Kegan Paul, 1966, vol.6, p. 267.

33 D. L. Farley-Hills, *Jacobean Drama*, London, Macmillan, 1988, pp. 183–5.

34 See H. J. Oliver, ed. cit., p. xliv.

35 Sykes, op. cit., pp. 32–5.

36 *A Trick to Catch the Old One, 1608*, (facsimile), Menston, Scolar Press, 1970, sig.B2^v.

37 Gonorill, interestingly, makes a similar judgement of King Leir in the old play 'For he you know is always in extremes'. Bullough, *NDSS*, vol.7 p. 342, line 192.

38 Bullough, *NDSS*, vol.7, pp. 310–11.

39 ibid., vol.7, pp. 270–1.

40 ibid., vol.7, p. 270.

41 *Hecatommithi*, p. 383: 'quanto piu e stretto il legame del sangue, e della Natura, e e maggior l'obligo del Figliuolo verso il Padre, che qualunque altro, che imaginar si possa.'

42 ibid., pp. 395–6: 'quanto sia piu benigna la natura delle donne, che quella de gli huomini. . .fu egli nondimeno minore di quelli, che di alcune Donne si potrebbero raccontare.'

43 ibid., p. 396: 'Egli e vero. . .che le donne sono verso i padri, e le madri loro amorevolissime, si per lo bisogno, che maggiore ne hanno, che i maschi, si anco perche sono di molle, e di benignissima natura. Ma se aviene, che alcune d'esse, alle male opere volgano la mente di tanto avanzano gli huomini scelerati, che si possono

veramente dire furie infernali in corpo humano, e la novella, che io mi apparecchio di raccontarvi, cio vi fara forse piu, che non bisognerebbe palese.'

44 None of the conjectured sources of *Lear* is as precise as this about the King's age – much more exceptional for the Elizabethans than for us.

45 cf. *Lear* V, iii, 272–3: 'Her voice was ever soft/Gentle and low, an excellent thing in woman.'

46 I, i, 44–5 these lines appear only in the folio text.

47 *Hecatommithi*, p. 398 'havendogli spetialmente egli dato tutto il patrimonio, senza ritenersene pure un picciolo, oltre che gli dava tanta auttorita nel Regno.'

48 ibid., p. 399: 'che s'ella havea cosi in dispregio le ragioni del sangue, e le leggi della natura, le quali constringevano anco le fiere ad amare, chi generate le havea.'

49 ibid., p. 400: 'conoscendo in te uno spirito grande, e parendomi per cio, che tu non debba meno desiderare la real grandezza, che la desideri io, mi son risoluta di communicar teco questo mio maschio pensiero.'

50 ibid., p. 401: 'perche il pensare alle cose magnifiche e nulla, s'elle ad effetto non si conducono.'

51 Shakespeare often stores away hints and suggestions for later plays.

52 *Hecatommithi*, p. 403: 'di gran nerbo, piglio a traverso Apesio vecchio, e debole, e a capo in giu lo gitto dalle scale, il quale diede cosi gran percossa, che quasi tutto si ruppe.'

53 ibid., p. 405: 'onde si vede manifestamente, che l'operar male, per havere bene, al fine conduce i malfattori, e gli scelerati, a misero fine.'

54 Bullough, *NDSS*, vol.7, p. 343.

55 A. C. Bradley, *Shakespearean Tragedy*, London, Macmillan, 1905, 2nd edn reprinted 1926, p.281; 'the hypocrisy is patent to us at a glance'.

56 Line 60 is emended from the folio text.

57 R. Sherwood, *The Right, and Prerogative of Kings*, London, N[icholas] O[kes] for William Bladon, 1612, pp. 20–1.

58 The folio reading. There are no grounds for accusing Lear of political irresponsibility in abdicating (as asserted for instance by Bullough, *NDSS*, vol. 7, p. 288). The Emperor Charles V had abdicated to European applause to become a monk in 1555. Stage abdications are not uncommon and generally approved (as in Middleton's *Phoenix* and *Hengist, King of Kent*).See also R. Levin, *New Readings vs Old Plays*, Chicago and London, University of Chicago Press, 1979, pp. 149–51, who quotes James I as accepting the legitimacy of abdication.

59 C. H. McIlwain (ed.), *The Political Works of James I*, Cambridge, Mass., Harvard University Press, 1918, reissued New York, Russell & Russell, 1965, p. 34.

60 See for example, Lawrence Humfrey, *The Nobles: or, of Nobilitie*, London, T. Marshe, 1563, sig.S 3ᵛ: 'But listen Bastards, with whom now each corner swarmeth, who also obtain the highest dignity, what Holy Scripture in the 3rd Chapter of the Book of Wisdom decreeth of them: the Imps shall be banished. . .so shall this sport of Nobles be turned to sorrow, their mirth to mourning.'

61 McIlwain, ed. cit., p. 36.

62 Fulke Greville, *The Life of the Renowned Sir Philip Sidney*, London, Gibbings & Co., n.d., p. 163.

63 Bradley, op. cit., pp. 262, 293–4.

64 F; Q reads 'vertues'. Punctuation is modernized.

65 *Trew Law of Free Monarchies*, in McIlwain, ed. cit., p. 54.

66 *Basilikon Doron*, in McIlwain, ed. cit., p. 41.

67 Greville, op. cit., p. 163.

68 Quoted by Muir, ed. cit., p. lii.

69 S. Freud, 'The theme of the Three Caskets', *Collected Papers*, translated under the supervision of Joan Riviere, London, Hogarth Press, 1925, vol.4, p. 250.

70 Bradley, op. cit., p. 285.

71 McIlwain, ed. cit., p. 37.

72 ibid., p. 34.

73 In *The Mirror for Magistrates*, Gonerell marries the Scottish King Albany; Bullough, *NDSS* vol. 7, pp. 323–32.

74 G. P. Krapp (ed.), 'History of Britain', *The Works of John Milton*, New York, Columbia University Press, 1932, vol.10, p. 18.

75 G. P. V. Akrigg (ed.), *The Letters of James VI and I*, Berkeley, Los Angeles, London, University of California Press, 1984. See especially the introduction, p. 19.

76 Sir Thomas Elyot, *Book Named the Governor*, London, Dent (Everyman), 1962, II, p. 156, writes: 'But hard it is alway to eschew these flatterers, which, like to crows, do pick out men's eyes ere they be dead. And it is to noble men most difficult, whom all men covet to please.' Francis Bacon writes 'Of a King', *Essays Civil and Moral*, ed.E. T. Bettany, London, 1894, p. 93, 14: 'His greatest enemies are his flatterers; for though they ever speak on his side, yet their words still make against him.'

77 G. A.Smith (ed.), *Marston, The Fawn*, London, Edward Arnold, 1964.

78 McIlwain, ed. cit., p. 32.

79 Akrigg, ed. cit., p. 17.

80 Aristotle, 'On the Art of Poetry', *Classical Literary Criticism*, trans. by T. S. Dorsch, Harmondsworth, Penguin Books, 1965, p. 48.

81 *The Censor*, 2 May 1715.

82 M. R. Ridley (ed.), *Antony and Cleopatra* (Arden edition), London, Methuen, 1954, I, i, 14–16.

83 C. H. McIlwain, 'A Speach to the Lords and Commons of the Parliament at White-Hall. . .1609', *The Political Works of James I*, Cambridge, Mass., Harvard University Press, 1918, reprinted, New York, Russell & Russell, 1965, p. 307.

84 ibid., p. 308.

85 McIlwain (ed.), 'Basilikon Doron', ed. cit., p. 41.

86 McIlwain (ed.), 'Trew Law', ed. cit., pp. 55–6.

87 This quotation from Horace (*Epistles*, I, ii, 62) is used in *Timon of Athens*, I, ii, 28.

88 McIlwain, ed. cit., p. 52.

89 H. Granville Barker, 'King Lear', *Prefaces to Shakespeare*, London, Batsford, 1930, reprinted 1963, vol.2, p. 28.

90 L.Stone, *The Crisis of Aristocracy, 1558–1641*, Oxford, Clarendon Press, 1965, p. 212.

91 I. M., *A Health to the Gentlemanly Profession of Serving Men*, (attributed to Gervase Markham), London, B.L., 1598, sig.D4^v.

92 G. B. Harrison, *A Last Elizabethan Journal*, London, Constable, 1933, reprinted Routledge & Kegan Paul, 1974, pp. 56–7 (under 1 December 1599).

93 Muir, ed. cit., note to I, i, 297–8.

94 ibid., note to I, iii, 5.

95 'of kindness' is added from F.

96 Text from Muir, ed. cit. Q1 is more than usually garbled at this point.

97 R. S. Burns (ed.), *John Day's The Ile of Gulls*, New York and London, Garland Publishing, 1980, p. 21, n.34.

98 ibid., p. 24, n.39.

99 F; Q reads 'fellow'.

100 Q1 punctuation modernized.

101 Freud, op. cit., vol.4, pp. 253–6.

102 Some minor emendations; 'ague-proof' is the F reading.

103 F reads 'great' for 'smal'.

104 F.

105 E. A. J. Honigmannin, *Shakespeare's Impact on his Contemporaries*, 1982, p. 35, notes that Shakespeare's affectiveness was particularly noted by his contemporaries.

INDEX

221

148, 152, 166–71, 174, 176, 177, 178,
180, 181, 182–206
King Leir (Anon.) 166, 170, 182, 185–6,
187, 188, 192, 196, 200
King's men (formerly Chamberlain's) 48,
50, 128, 130, 136, 171
Kirkman, F. 14
Kittredge, G. L. 73
Knack to Know a Knave (Anon.) 138, 140
Knack to Know an Honest Man (Anon.) 138,
140
Knight, G. Wilson 163
Knolles, Richard: *General History of the
Turks* 104
Kyd, Thomas 10; ur-*Hamlet* 16, 19, 20, 34;
Spanish Tragedy 4, 11, 12, 16, 18, 19,
27, 34

Lake, David 171, 172
Lever, J. W. (editor of *Measure for Measure*)
164
Levin, R. 214n6, 218n58
London Prodigal (Anon.) 109
Love's Labours Lost (Shakespeare) 97
Lucian (*Timon*) 170, 175
Lust's Dominion (Marston, Dekker *et al.*)
12–15, 16, 25, 27, 30, 36, 119
Lydgate, John: *Troy Book* 53–4, 68

Macbeth (Shakespeare) 32, 35, 137, 152,
166, 167, 184, 190, 197
Mad World My Masters (Middleton) 124,
146, 162, 174
Main Plot 144
Malcontent 2, 51, 138–9, 140, 142
Malone Society 171
Malvolio (*Twelfth Night*) 82
Markham, Gervase 198
Marlowe, Christopher 4; *Dr Faustus* 72; *Jew
of Malta* 4, 11, 16
Marston, John 4, 37, 39, 50, 170, 171,
205; beaten by Jonson 2; Calvinism of
39, 57, 71; conservatism of 54;
dislocatory techniques in 70; formal
satires 54, 56; influence on *Hamlet* 10;
pessimism of 70, 73; pseudonym 'Don
Kinsayder' 56, 62; quarrel with Jonson
51; relations with Shakespeare 49; satiric
manner 47, 179
  Antonio and Mellida 54; *Antonio's
Revenge* 4, 12, 15–25, 27, 34, 37, 54,
59, 139; *Dutch Courtesan* 109; *Eastward

Ho 3; *Fawn* 193; *Histriomastix* 56; *Jack
Drum's Entertainment* 54; *Lust's Dominion*
12–15, 16, 25, 27, 30, 36, 119;
Malcontent 2, 51, 138–9, 140, 142; *What
You Will* 54–7, 58–62, 68, 70
Marz, Louis 22
Mathew, David 144
May Day (Chapman) 72
Measure for Measure (Shakespeare) 5, 78, 91,
96, 104, 105, 137, 138, 139–41, 145,
148–65, 166, 167, 170, 171, 182, 191,
205
Merchant of Venice (Shakespeare) 4, 11, 32,
60, 75, 194
Mermaid Tavern 1, 4
Merlin 197
Merry Wives of Windsor (Shakespeare)
208n27
Metamorphoses (Ovid) 80–1
Michaelmas Term (Middleton) 145
Middleton, Thomas 2, 4, 5, 49, 137, 165,
170; hand in *Timon of Athens* 171–6
  Changeling 174; *Chaste Maid in
Cheapside* 173; *Family of Love* 137, 143,
211n18; *Game at Chess* 172; *Honest Whore*
174; *Mad World My Masters* 124, 146,
162, 174; *Michaelmas Term* 145; *Phoenix*
5, 109, 138, 139–48, 162, 171;
Revenger's Tragedy 27, 29, 171; *Roaring
Girl* 174, 175; *Trick to Catch the Old One*
174, 180
Milton, John 26, 133; *Areopagitica* 26;
History of Britain 192
Moirae 202
Monsieur D'Olive (Chapman) 73, 75, 76, 79,
82, 83, 96
Muir, Kenneth 164, 175, 199

New Inn (Jonson) 135
North, Sir Thomas 6, 168
Northward Ho (Dekker and Webster) 3

Oedipus 194
Old Joiner of Aldgate (Chapman) 137
Oliver, H. J. 168
Olivier, Lawrence 114
Orbecche (Giraldi) 25, 28
Orwell, George 189
Osborne, Sir Francis 201
Othello (Shakespeare) 5, 75, 104–21, 123,
124, 125, 126, 127, 128, 130, 134,
135, 148, 166, 167, 176, 182, 190, 205